Henry Noble Day

The science of ethics

An elementary system of theoretical and practical morality

Henry Noble Day

The science of ethics
An elementary system of theoretical and practical morality

ISBN/EAN: 9783337276065

Printed in Europe, USA, Canada, Australia, Japan

Cover: Foto ©Lupo / pixelio.de

More available books at **www.hansebooks.com**

THE SCIENCE OF ETHICS:

AN ELEMENTARY SYSTEM

OF

THEORETICAL AND PRACTICAL MORALITY.

BY

HENRY N. DAY,

AUTHOR OF "PSYCHOLOGY," "LOGIC," "ÆSTHETICS," "ART OF DISCOURSE," ETC.

NEW YORK:
G. P. PUTNAM'S SONS,
182 FIFTH AVENUE.
1876.

Copyright,
G. P. PUTNAM'S SONS.
1876.

PREFACE.

It has been the controlling design in the preparation of this work simply to introduce to ethical studies. After a careful analysis of an act of duty by which the essential constituents of duty are ascertained, the science is unfolded in the light of this analysis, with logical exactness, into a full presentation of its principles and truths in their due relations to one another—into a well-grounded, comprehensive, and organic system of theoretical and practical morality. The elementary character of the work has precluded the introduction of the historical and critical discussion, by which ethical literature is so generally characterized. The peculiarities of the treatise are to be found mainly in the analysis of the concrete act of duty which furnishes the fundamental principles of ethical science; in the systematic development and arrangement of these principles; in their application to the particulars of ethical practice; and the more full and detailed presentation of the practical part of ethics. The results attained in the introductory analysis of duty are supposed to be accepted generally without question. The recognition throughout of the essential constituents of duty attained in the analysis as co-ordinate and complementary, and, therefore, characterizing all duty, has seemed to the writer to give to the treatise a solid and unquestionable basis, together with thoroughly logical harmony and completeness—the characters, in other words, of a truly scientific treatment. As was requisite, however, in an elementary work, the presentation has been didactic rather than argumentative;—the principles and truths being left for the most part to appear in their own light.

NEW-HAVEN, April, 1876.

CONTENTS.

INTRODUCTION.—§ 1. ETHICS DEFINED. § 2. FOUNDED ON PSYCHOLOGY. § 3. ONE OF THE THREE GREAT DEPARTMENTS OF MENTAL SCIENCE. § 4. METHOD.

BOOK I.

THEORETICAL MORALITY—THE NATURE OF DUTY.

CHAPTER I.—ANALYSIS OF AN ACT OF DUTY.—§ 5. The Duty of Regulus to return to Carthage.

CHAPTER II.—SUBJECT OF DUTY—A MORAL PERSON.—§ 6. Moral Person Defined. §§ 7, 8. An Essentially Active Being. § 9. Endowed with Sensibility. § 10. With Intelligence. § 11. With Free Will. § 12. The Moral Faculty—Practical Reason, Moral Sense, Conscience. § 13. Threefold Function of Conscience—Discriminative of Right and Wrong. Obliging to Action, Approving or Disapproving. § 14. Conscience as Source of Pleasure or Pain.

CHAPTER III.— OBJECT OF DUTY.—§ 15. Object of Duty Defined. § 16. A Person. § 17. Rights Correlative to Duties. § 18. Good Essential Attribute in a Duty and a Right. § 19. Duties Classified—(1) to Self; (2) to Fellow-men; (3) to God.

CHAPTER IV.—MORAL ACTION.—§ 20. Moral Action Defined; implies Love in Subject of Duty, Good in Object of Duty, and Rectitude in its Essence. § 21. Systems of Morality on Each of these Elements.

CHAPTER V.—LOVE AS PRINCIPLE OF DUTY.—§ 22. Love Necessary in all Duty. § 23. Fulfils the Whole Law of Duty. § 24. More Exactly Defined. § 25. Its Three Stages. § 26. The Opposite of Love, or Hate. § 27. Unsympathetic Spirit Opposed to Duty.

CHAPTER VI.—GOODNESS OR BENEFICENCE.—§ 28. Good the One Result of all Perfect Moral Action. § 29. Different Senses of the Term *Good;* Good in itself as Happiness, the Primary and Ultimate Good; Good as means, the Secondary and Mediate Good. § 30. Good in itself the Gift of God alone; Secondary Good the only Possible Immediate Effect of Human Effort; Secondary Good either Good of Character or of Condition. § 31. The Highest and Largest Good Required by Duty. § 32. Summary of Doctrines Respecting Good. § 33. Relation of Moral Action to its End § 34. Evil, the Opposite of Good, either Physical or Moral

CHAPTER VII.—RECTITUDE.—§ 35. All Perfect Moral Action must be Right. § 36. Rectitude Respects an Action. § 37. Particularly the Relation in an Action between its Source and its End. § 38. Implies a Natural Fitness or Conformity in this Relation. § 39. An Unswerving Directnesss in its Movement. § 40. And a Parallelism with all Specific Right Acts. § 41. Wrong the opposite of Right.

CHAPTER VIII.—MOTIVES.—§ 42. Motive Defined as Object of the Will. § 43. Two Classes of Motives—Those of Character and those of Condition. § 44. The Three Subordinate Species of the First Class. § 45. Three Species of the Second Class. § 46 Motives as Ultimate or Proximate. § 47. Motives not Morally Right or Wrong. § 48. Selection Among Motives—In What Way Wrong.

CHAPTER IX.—MORAL OBLIGATION.—§ 49. Moral Obligation Defined. § 50. Its Ground.

CHAPTER X.—MORAL LAW.—§ 51. Moral Law Defined. § 52. Divided into Physical and Moral. § 53. Harmonious in its

Requirements. § 54. Commanding. § 55. Excites Sense of Personal Responsibility. § 56. Its Sanctions. § 57. Merit, Demerit, Praise, Blame.

CHAPTER XI.—AUTHORITY.—§ 58. Authority Defined. § 59. Its Seat. § 60. How Expressed. § 61. Natural Law. § 62. Positive Law. § 63. The Bible.

CHAPTER XII.—CASUISTRY.—§ 64. Casuistry Defined. § 65. Its Leading Principles.

BOOK II.

PRACTICAL MORALITY—DUTIES AND RIGHTS.

INTRODUCTION.—§ 66. DIVISION OF DUTIES. § 67. GENERAL RECAPITULATION.

DIVISION FIRST—DUTIES TO SELF.

CHAPTER I.—NATURE AND DIVISION.—§ 68. Personal Duties Explained. § 69. The Ground of Obligation in Them. § 70. Self-Love. § 71. Defined. § 72. Two Classes of Personal Duties—in Respect to Condition and to Character.

CHAPTER II.—PERSONAL DUTIES IN RESPECT TO THE BODY.—§ 73. Ground of Obligation in Personal Duties. § 74. Duties Enumerated :—I. Of Guarding the Body. § 75. II. Of Nourishing it—(1) By Food. § 76. (2) By Exercise. § 77. (3) By Rest. § 78. III. Of Ruling It. § 79. (1) By Overcoming Sloth. § 80. (2) By Regulating Appetite. § 81. (3) By Training to Habits of Ministry. § 82. (4) By Subordinating Bodily Wants.

CHAPTER III.—PERSONAL DUTIES IN RESPECT TO EXTERNAL CONDITION.—§ 83. Nature and Divisions of Personal Duties in Respect to Condition. § 84. I. In Respect to External Nature. § 85. II. In Respect to Property. § 86. Institution of Property Beneficent. § 87. Right to Property Relative. § 88. Relations of

Duty to Property. § 89. Modes of Acquisition. § 90. Personal Duties in Respect to Property. § 91. III. In Respect to Station. § 92. IV. In Respect to Friendship.

CHAPTER IV.—Personal Duties in Respect to Character.—§ 93. Character Defined. § 94. Formation of Character Involves an Ideal, Persistent Endeavor, Principle of Habit, and Use of Outward Occasions. § 95. Maxims. § 96. Culture of the Sensibility. § 97. Of the Imagination. § 98. Of the Intelligence—As Activity. § 99. In Observing. § 100. In Reflecting. § 101. Of the Regulative Faculty. § 102. Of the Free Will—As a Power. § 103. As Dominant. § 104. As Free. § 105. As Finite.

DIVISION SECOND—DUTIES TO OUR FELLOW-MEN.

PART I.

DUTIES TO PERSONS.

INTRODUCTION.—§ 106. General Division of Social Duties.

CHAPTER I.—Definition.—§ 107. Classification Grounded on Constituents of Duty—Love, Good, Right.

CHAPTER II.—Duties to Persons Determined from the Subject of Duty or from Love. § 108. Division. § 109. Sympathy. § 110. Kindness. § 111. Loving Endeavor. § 112. Resentment. § 113. Fortitude. § 114. Anger. § 115. Forgiveness.

CHAPTER III.—Duties of Persons Determined from the Object of Duty or from Good.—§ 116. Divisions. § 117. Courtesy. § 118. Truthfulness. § 119. Its Two Forms. § 120. Truth of the Heart. § 121. Veracity—Its Objects. § 122. Its Sphere. § 123. Trustfulness. § 124. Justice and Beneficence—How Related and How Distinguished. § 125. Beneficence, as Related to Benevolence. § 126. The Crowning Virtue. § 127. Its Specific Forms. § 128. Modes. § 129. Measure. § 130. Its One Object or End. § 131. Justice Defined. § 132. Its Sphere.

CHAPTER IV.—Duties to Persons Determined from the Act of Duty.—§ 133. Two Species of Duties thus Determined.

§ 134. Aim in Duty. § 135. To be Governing. § 136. And True to Its End. § 137. Straightforwardness in Performance. § 138. Harmony with Things and Events.

PART II.—DUTIES IN THE FAMILY.

CHAPTER I.—THE FAMILY INSTITUTION.—§ 139. Family Defined. § 140. Rise of Obligation. § 141. A Moral Community. § 142. Seat of Authority. § 143. Classes of Duties.

CHAPTER II.—MARITAL RIGHTS AND DUTIES.—§ 144. Origin in the Marriage Covenant. § 145. Polygamy. § 146. The Parties to this Covenant Intelligent and Free. § 147. Sanctity of the Marriage Union. § 148. How Solemnized. § 149. Rights and Duties of Husband and Wife Equal and Reciprocal. § 150. Authority Joint and Indivisible. § 151. Rights and Duties Complementary.

CHAPTER III.—PARENTAL AND FILIAL RIGHTS AND DUTIES.—§ 152. Origin and Limitation of these Duties in the Family Relation. § 153. Rights and Duties Correlative. § 154. Duties of Parents. § 155. Duties of Children. § 156. Finiteness of the Obligation.

CHAPTER IV.—FRATERNAL RIGHTS AND DUTIES.—§ 157. Origin and Limit in the Family. § 158. Equal, Reciprocal, and Complementary. § 159. Special Duties.

PART III.—DUTIES IN THE STATE.

CHAPTER I.—END AND MORAL NATURE OF THE STATE.—§ 160. State Defined. § 161. Its Origin. § 162. Organized. § 163. Sphere. § 164. A Power. § 165. Seated in the Free-Will. § 166. Working Through Organs. § 167. The End of the State Life. § 168. Its Moral Attributes. § 169. Not a Mere Jural Society § 170. Comprehensive Duties of the State as Moral.

CHAPTER II.—THE RIGHTS AND DUTIES OF A STATE IN

Relation to Itself.—1. Existence.—§ 171. Enumeration. § 172. Right of Existence. § 173. Origin of States. §§ 174, 175. Threefold Duty in Self-Preservation. § 176. Support. § 177. Right to Property and Service of Citizens. § 178. Taxes. § 179. Direct Taxes. § 180. Capitation Taxes. § 181. Excise Duties. § 182. Imposts. § 183. Stamps. § 184. Income Taxes. § 185. National Self-Defense. § 186. Maintenance of Authority. § 187. Sanctions of Law. § 188. Rewards. § 189. Penalties and their Primary End, Prevention of Disobedience. § 190. A Second End of Penalty, —Moral Teaching of the Community. § 191. A Third End—Reformation of the Offender. § 192. Modes of Punishment. § 193. Degrees of Penalty Vary with the Nature of the Offence. § 194. With Facility of Detection. § 195. With Number and Strength of Offenders. § 196. With the Moral Sentiment of the Community.

CHAPTER III.—Political Autonomy.—§ 197. Autonomy Defined. § 198. Ground of Right. § 199. Duty. § 200. Spheres. § 201. Organic Laws. § 202. The Legislature. § 203. The Judiciary. § 204. Legal Rights and Equities. § 205. The Executive.

CHAPTER IV.—Political Growth.—§ 206. Right and Duty of Growth. § 207. Spheres. § 208. Maxims. § 209. Rights and Modes of Territorial Extension. § 210. Increase of Population. § 211. Internal Strength. § 212. Public Improvements. § 213. Weights and Measures. § 214. Money Defined. § 215. Standard and Unit of Value; Material. § 216. Elements of a Sound Monetary System. § 217. Postal Facilities. § 218. Development of Resources. § 219. Classes of Industries. § 220. Relation of the State to its Productive Industries;—Limitation of its Duty. § 221. Modes of Fostering Private Productive Industry. § 222. Free Trade and its Limitations. § 223. Public Health. § 224. Public Education. § 225. Degree of Public Education. § 226. Modes. § 227. Public Morals—The Duty of the State to Promote Morality. § 228. Modes.

CHAPTER V.—The State and the Citizen.—§ 229. Citizen Defined. § 230. Rights of Individuals in the State—to Pursue the End of their Being. § 231. Freedom of Thought and Action. § 232. Protection. § 233. Special Help. § 234. Duties of Individuals to the State—Loyalty. § 235. Obedience. § 236. Support. § 237. Self-Expatriation.

CHAPTER VI.—INTERNATIONAL MORALITY.—§ 238. International Law—its Divisions. § 239. Sources. § 240. Peculiarities of International Obligations. § 241. Specific Duties—Sympathetic Good Will. § 242. *Lex Talionis.* § 243. Political Retaliation Vindictive or Amicable. § 244. Comity of Nations. § 245. Rules of Comity. § 246. Truthfulness. § 247. Justice. § 248. Beneficence. § 249. International Integrity. § 250. Rights of War. § 251. Recognizable War Must be Public. § 252. Prosecuted by Armed Force. § 253. Have Ostensible Ground of Justice. § 254. Parties Affected by War—Non-Combatants. § 255. Neutrals.

DIVISION THIRD—DUTIES TO GOD.

CHAPTER I.—§ 256. Nature and Ground. § 257. Will of God—How Revealed. § 258. Classification of Religious Duties.

CHAPTER II.—PERSONAL RELIGION—PIETY TOWARDS GOD. —§ 259. Piety Defined. § 260. Religious Gratitude.

CHAPTER III.—PERSONAL RELIGION—REVERENCE, PRAYER. —§ 261. Reverence. § 262. Prayer—its Constituents. § 263. Its Characteristics. § 264. Obligations to Prayer. § 265. Objections to Prayer. § 266. Irreverence.

CHAPTER IV.—PERSONAL RELIGION—GODLY SINCERITY.— § 267. Defined. § 268. True Thought of God. § 269. True Expression to Him. § 270. Idolatry. § 271. Superstition. § 272. Hypocrisy. § 273. Formality.

CHAPTER V.—PERSONAL RELIGION—RELIGIOUS TRUST— OBEDIENCE AND SERVICE.—§ 274. Religious Trust. § 275. Qualities. § 276. Obedience. § 277. Qualities. § 278. Service. § 279. Qualities. § 280. Vows.

CHAPTER VI.—PERSONAL RELIGION—RELIGIOUS INTEGRITY. —§ 281. Singleheartedness. § 282. Unswerving Directness. § 283 In Parallelism with all Lines of Duty. § 284. In Moderation.

CHAPTER VII.—SOCIAL RELIGION—FAMILY RELIGION.—
§ 285. Spheres of Social Religion. § 286. Obligations to Family Religion. § 287. Religious Solemnization of Marriage. § 288. Religious Ordering of the Household. § 289. Special Duties. § 290. Worship.

CHAPTER VIII.—SOCIAL RELIGION—STATE RELIGION.—
§ 291. Relations of Religion to the Political Community. § 292. Special Religious Duties in the State—(1.) Must not Act Irreligiously. § 293. (2.) Must Protect Citizens in their Religion. § 294. (3.) May Enlist Religion in Marriage. § 295. (4.) Recognize Religious Seasons. § 296. (5.) Appoint Special Religious Observances. § 297. (6.) Enlist Religious Sanctions—Oaths. § 298. Four Kinds of Oaths. § 299. Interpretation of Oaths.

CHAPTER IX.—SOCIAL RELIGION—THE CHURCH.—§ 300. Religious Association Natural. § 301. Divers Forms and Relations to the State. § 302. Religious Officials. § 303. Sacred Seasons. § 304. The Sabbath. § 305. Obligations to Observe the Sabbath. § 306. Sacred Places. § 307. Worship.

INTRODUCTION.

Ethics defined. § 1. ETHICS is well defined to be *the Science of Human Duty.*

The science has otherwise been named *Moral Science, Moral Philosophy;* also, *Deontology,* from the Greek, signifying *science of duty.*

Methods. In analogy with other sciences which relate to life and conduct, a system of ethical science may look more to the principles of duty; or to the application of these principles to practice; or, still further, to the result of this application of principles to practice in forming character. The definitions have varied accordingly; and the respective systems founded on these definitions become, characteristically, either sciences of the Laws of Duty, or sciences of the Duties of Man, or sciences of Human Character.

While the method of unfolding the science varies somewhat with these various modes of regarding the science, the substance of the exposition is not, or certainly need not be, materially varied. Ethics never becomes, like Arithmetic or Rhetoric, a proper art; it does not, by apposite examples and exercises, put the learner at the time of the study upon the practice of one after another of the particular duties which it enjoins, nor upon the specific applications of its principles to the conduct. It remains a proper science, whether its more immediate aim be to unfold the principles of duty, or the application of these principles to conduct, or the character which the principles if applied would form.

Moreover, the exposition of the science must cover substantially the same ground whether it founds its method more in the principles of duty, or in their application in specific duties, or in the results in character.

§ 2. Ethical science is founded directly on psychology, or the science of mind.

Founded on psychology.

It accepts thus the enumeration and the classification of mental phenomena, together with their origin and relations, which psychology teaches. It goes beyond that science, inasmuch as taking up one of the three great departments of mental phenomena, or, in other words, one of these departments of mental activity as defined and explained in psychology, it presents that in respect to its laws and its general forms.

Ethics, accordingly, accepts from psychology its doctrine in regard to the human will as one of the three great functions of the mind; its exposition of what its precise function is; how it is modified in its action; how it is related to the other functions of the mind—the sensibility and the intelligence. With this doctrine of the nature and relations of the will furnished to it by psychology, Ethics proceeds to unfold the laws which must govern in a pure and perfect act of will, and the forms in which the will exerts itself under these laws.

In the same way, Logical Science takes from psychology the doctrine of the intelligence—what it is in its essential nature and relations—and then proceeds to derive its necessary laws and its valid forms. As thought is the proper product of the intelligence, Logic is defined as the science of thought; or inasmuch as the perfect in thought is truth, logic is the science of truth.

Æsthetical science, also, accepts the psychological doctrine of the sensibility—its nature and modifications— and then proceeds from this doctrine to unfold its laws and its general modes or states under these laws. As it is *form* which is the sole object of the sensibility, æsthetics is defined as the science of form. Or inasmuch as the perfect in form is known as the beautiful, æsthetics is the science of beauty.

Inasmuch as a perfect act of will in man is duty, Ethics is the science of duty.

Co-ordinate with Logic and Æsthetics. § 3. Ethics, accordingly, with Logic and Æsthetics, makes up the group of sciences founded on the three great departments of mental phenomena which are presented in psychology. The three sciences have a common parentage and are related to one another as strictly co-ordinate sciences.

Sir William Hamilton calls them the three nomological sciences, which respectively present *the laws* of the three great forms of mental activity, all in like manner derived from psychology which presents simply *the facts* of mental activity.

§ 4. The proper method in ethical science will be, first, by a careful analysis of an act of duty to ascertain precisely what elements necessarily enter into duty and make it what it is, and thus ascertain the essential principles of duty ; and then to enumerate and classify the general forms in which acts of duty appear, under the manifold modifications of human experience.

<small>Method.</small>

When we have ascertained precisely what it is that makes an act one of duty—a moral act—then we know what must characterize all duty ; what characters it must have in order to be duty ; in other words, we know the laws of duty or the principles of right action. And when we have ascertained the general forms in which the free-will exerts itself in acts of duty, by a careful exploration of the field of human experience so far as it is characterized as moral, we are enabled to apply to all these forms the laws of duty which we have ascertained. We are enabled, in other words, to determine in regard to all human action what is truly moral in it, and also, on the other hand, to determine what must enter into every form of human action in order to make it truly moral.

This treatise will therefore present in the first book—Theoretical Morality—a full analysis of an act of duty, in order to determine its essential nature; and in the second—Practical Morality—the specific duties pertaining to human life.

BOOK I.

THEORETICAL MORALITY—THE NATURE OF DUTY.

CHAPTER I.

ANALYSIS OF AN ACT OF DUTY.

Instance of duty. § 5. It was a received tradition among the Romans that some two centuries and a half before our era, a certain general of theirs, of the name of Regulus, having been made a prisoner by the Carthaginians, was sent back to Rome to effect an exchange of prisoners under an oath that he would return to Carthage in case of failure; that Regulus failed in this errand, but resolutely and against the protestations of friends, kept his oath, and returned to Carthage to certain torture and death. Cicero tells us that such was the sentiment of the age in regard to the inviolable sanctity of an oath, that Regulus would not have been allowed to do otherwise.

The tradition may have been authentic or not. However this may be, the story exemplifies what will be recognized by all as an act of duty. It was the duty of Regulus to return to Carthage in fulfilment of his oath; he at least recognized it as such; his return was an act of duty. He did that which was *due* to the Carthaginians—that which was owed to them; for the term *duty*, derived to our language from the Latin through the French, means simply that which is owed. Or, at least, he owed it to himself—to his self-respect, to his conscience—to keep his oath. By returning, he simply discharged a debt.

It is immaterial how the debt was contracted; how the obligation was created. It is enough that, in a proper sense of the word, Regulus owed his return to Carthage, and his act of returning was, consequently, an act of duty.

Its three elements. If now we scrutinize this act of Regulus, we discover three elements in it which are very prominent, and which imply one another, so that the supposed removal of either one would essentially change the character of the act and would also involve the removal of the other elements. They are (1) a person owing—Regulus; (2) a person or persons—the Carthaginians—or at least himself—to whom there is something due; and (3) the act discharging what is owed—the return to Carthage. It is plain, moreover, that these three elements are the exhaustive elements of this order or class in the act. There is no other. They are complementary elements.

We have thus given us on the bare inspection of this act of Regulus, the three essential elements

—a personal agent owing duty, a person or persons to whom this duty is owed, and an act discharging this duty. We use language correctly in denominating these elements respectively a *moral person* or *agent ; a moral end or object ;* and *a moral action.*

We shall proceed to unfold in order, in separate chapters, these several elements and the several constituents of each.

CHAPTER II.

SUBJECT OF DUTY—A MORAL PERSON.

<small>Moral person defined.</small>
§ 6. A MORAL PERSON may be defined to be a being capable of duty.

It is the same thing to say that a moral person is a being capable of obligation,—that is, a being capable of owing and of fulfilling obligation—as to say that he is a being capable of duty—that is, a being capable of owing and fulfilling duty.

In the present treatise we confine our view to human duty; and thus we speak of moral persons so far as subjects of duty only as men. In this restricted view, the term *duty* is synonymous with *virtue*, which is a term from the Latin signifying *manhood*; an act of duty being in the case of men simply an act of true or perfect manhood, or an act which a true and perfect man would do.

<small>Mental requisites.</small>
§ 7. Indispensable to a moral person thus defined as a being capable of duty, is the essential attribute of a human mind or soul, viz.:—An active nature endowed with the threefold function of sensibility, intelligence, and free-will.

§ 8. A moral person is an essentially active being.

1. Active nature.

In this statement are involved these two particulars :—

1. That a person is moral only in so far as he is active ; and·
2. That his very nature impels him to act.

The ·proof of the first of these two particular propositions is found in the very notion of duty, as already indicated. A duty is an act. So far as it is owed it is an act to be done: and when it is fulfilled, it is fulfilled only by an act.

All morality, hence, respects an active nature. Every moral person must be one capable of acting or one who is acting or who has acted. If we speak of a moral state, or a moral condition, of a moral habit or a moral disposition, of moral character, or moral responsibility, there is necessarily implied in the expression, a nature capable of action, or acting, or that has acted. Simple and clear as this is, ethical theories and ethical discussions have run into pernicious error by dropping out of view this essential element of activity which must exist in everything that is moral.

Secondly, every moral person is by his very nature impelled to act. It is as natural for him to act, and of course, to act morally, as it is for a stone, when unsupported, to fall to the ground, or for a plant to put forth stalk and leaf, or for an animal to take food. He may within certain limits act in this way ̇or in that, but he cannot refrain from acting in some way. He may act feebly or he may act with energy;—he may, to some extent, control the degree of activity which he will put forth; but he must act in some degree. Indolence is never absolute inaction.

2. Sensibility. § 9. One of the three general and essential functions of a moral nature is *Sensibility.*

Regulus *felt* himself bound by his oath to return to Carthage. Without this feeling, his return could not possibly have been a moral act: so far as any personal morality on his part is concerned, he might as well have been returned a corpse or in a state of utter unconsciousness. Duty to be fulfilled must be felt to be owed.

The analysis of this feeling of duty, as psychology teaches us, gives as its constituent elements, (1) the impression made upon the sensibility of Regulus by the memory of his oath; and (2) the impulse or instinctive tendency occasioned by this impression to fulfil the oath, by returning to Carthage. His memory kept pressing on his sensibility the idea of his oath and this kept alive the impulse to fulfil it. The complex feeling, consisting of the impression and this kind of impulse, is known as *desire.*

In the case of Regulus, as in common instances of duty, desire to fulfil duty is mingled with desires or tendencies in an opposite direction. Regulus, doubtless, felt a strong desire to avoid the ignominy, the torture, and the cruel death which threatened his return to his enemies who would be infuriated by his failure to bring the prisoners; a strong desire also to gratify the earnest wishes of his countrymen, of his friends, of his family, to remain in Rome. But with these desires, there was also the desire of fulfilling duty. It was this desire that prevailed over the others; at least, it was this desire which was the occasion of his determining to return. Without that, such a determination is inconceivable as a moral action.

3. Intelligence. § 10. The second general function essential in a moral nature, is *Intelligence*.

Regulus knew his duty as well as felt it. Nor could there be duty or fulfilment of it without such intelligence. He must have known his oath. As his memory recalled it, he recognized it as real, as binding, as involving certain acts which he understood very well. Had he been without any knowledge of any such oath ever having been made, or of its having any binding force upon him, or of the acts which it required of him, there could have been no fulfilment of duty, no morality, even if he had in some way been taken back to Carthage.

Intelligence or knowledge of duty, thus, is essential in all morality. This knowledge respects the three general attributes of duty:—

First, That it is real—that it exists;

Secondly, That it is in its essential character binding or obligatory; and

Thirdly, That it involves action, which action, also, is intelligible as to its particular attributes.

Among these attributes of the particular action which must be recognized in all duty or morality are:—

First, The end or object of the action;

Secondly, The particular activity to be exerted in accomplishing this end ; and

Thirdly, The mode of exerting this activity.

It is plain that a person is incapable of duty unless he is capable of knowing it in respect to all these attributes.

4. Free-will. § 11. The third general function essential to a moral nature is *Free-will*.

Regulus determined to return to Carthage ; and determination in such a case is known as volition or act of will. His determination was a true act of will before he left Rome ; before he took leave of family and friends and Senators ;— before he had taken a step in his journey. These were but the so-called executive volitions by which his determination was carried out. Had he been suddenly struck down with mortal disease before he had left the Senate Chamber in which he had uttered his inflexible purpose to return to Carthage and in this way or in any other way had been prevented from returning, this unexecuted determination would, nevertheless, have been moral,—would have been a fulfilment, so far, of duty. Even if he had afterwards changed his mind and refused to return, the first determination, if sincere, would have been moral. It might have been too weak ; it might not have drawn into it the strength from feeling, from intelligence, from vigor of soul, that it should ; it was yet a true, if imperfect, act of duty. His falterings, for any cause, in putting forth any of the subsequent executive volitions, in taking any of the steps involved in his return, may have been each immoral in themselves; they could not have altered the moral character of the previous sincere determination to return.

This determination was free; it was an act of free-will. Freedom, as psychology teaches, is an essential attribute of the human will. It is equally essential in all duty—in all morality. Regulus might have been prevented from taking a single step towards carrying out his determination to return; this did not reach back to the determination itself. No irresistible force hindered that. None, indeed, compelled him to determine to return;—he could have yielded to the importunate entreaties of his friends and determined not to return. He was free in this respect—that, while the alternative of determining to go or not to go was before him as an active being, one of whose essential functions is that of free-will, and one or the other determination he was compelled to make, he was as truly capable of the one determination as of the other. In all probability the determination not to return was the easier in a certain sense: the predominance in strength of inducement may have been, in a certain sense, in that direction; but he proved himself to be free in his determining, notwithstanding, to return to Carthage.

Free-will thus is an essential element in all morality. An act of duty, a moral act, is inconceivable if this element be wanting. Free-will implies, first, the general capability of choice—of determination; and, secondly, the inherence in the moral person himself of this capability beyond the compulsory constraint of any external force.

§ 12. This activity, which in its three-fold function is concerned in all duty, is known as the *Moral Faculty*.

<small>Moral faculty defined.</small>

The MORAL FACULTY may accordingly be defined to be that endowment in man which makes him capable of duty. It embraces the three-fold function of sense, intelligence, and free-will.

The Moral Faculty differs from the intellectual faculty in this: that in its exercise, duty is prominently concerned, while in the exercise of the intellectual faculty, knowledge is prominently concerned. The same act may be a moral act and a knowing act. In truth every act of man, so far as it is rational, is both a moral act and a knowing act—is both moral and intellectual. It is denominated the one or the other simply because the one or the other is more prominent, or because the one or the other is selected at the time for consideration to the temporary suppression of the other from view. The moral faculty differs from moral feeling only as a faculty differs from a capacity. The one is active; the other is characteristically passive. But every rational act of man has its active side and its passive side, and is denominated an act or a feeling only because the one or the other is made more prominent to view either in fact or for contemplation.

The expression, *Moral Faculty*, has been in a narrower sense used as synonymous with Practical Reason, Moral Sense, Conscience. In this narrower use it embraces only

<small>Synonyms.</small>

the feelings and the intellectual states concerned with duty or with acts of free-will, and does not include the free-will itself. An act of duty may be so analyzed as to give these two parts: (1) The free-will itself; (2) the combined feeling and intelligence which ever accompany this act of free-will. To this second constituent, the term *Moral Faculty* has sometimes been applied, as also the other denominations—the Practical Reason, Moral Sense, Conscience.

The first of these designations, Moral Faculty, is founded on the general nature of the mind as an activity. It denotes that part of the mind's activity which is concerned with duty—in knowing it, in feeling it, in doing it.

The designation, *Practical Reason*, is founded in the characteristic of man as rational, distinguishing him from the brute creation. It denotes that department of rational activity which is concerned in duty. It includes all moral feeling, however, as well as all moral intelligence.

The designation, *Moral Sense*, is founded in the nature of man as feeling, as impressible by the idea of duty, and as capable of impressing it on the free-will. It denotes simply sensibility so far as concerned in duty. It includes, however, the intelligence associated with it in an act of free-will.

The term, *Conscience*, is but the consciousness limited to the moral sphere. It denotes all that intelligence and feeling of which a man is conscious in an act of duty.

§ 13. Conscience, as an act or state of a moral person, includes three principal functions, all present in it, either one of which, however, may be contemplated separately from the others. The first function of conscience is *to recognize and feel duty*.

<small>Threefold function of conscience.</small>

When a moral action is brought before us, whether it be our own or another's, or whether it be already done or only proposed to be done, we immediately and, if our view be turned towards this attribute of it, necessarily feel it to be right, to be a duty, an action that ought to be done, or the contrary. Every act of duty, every moral act, has this attribute, which accordingly can always be recognized and felt. Conscience always includes this recognition and feeling whenever it contemplates an act of duty.

<small>1. Sense of duty.</small>

A second function of conscience contemplating a proposed act of duty, is to impel or oblige to the performance of it.

<small>2. Obliging force.</small>

Conscience has a peremptory, commanding, constraining character. We attribute to it an authority. Its purpose may be overborne by other influences, its authority may be resisted; but so far as it has existence it presses to duty.

This impelling or constraining force of conscience, is of the nature of an instinct. It is, like the impulsive or constraining force of appetite, seated in our very being. It is, however, the strongest and most commanding instinct of our nature, for it is seated in the highest department of our being. It is, unlike the appetite, authoritative, because its constraining force bears immediately on the free-will, which by reason of its freedom becomes capable of obedience or disobedience, and accordingly subject to authority.

Conscience, thus, is properly denominated the sovereign of the soul. It is the sole function of the mind by which authority can be recognized, or felt, or imposed. Every command, as every obligation, coming from whatever source—from our own being, from our fellow men, or from our creator,—reaches us only through the conscience. To it belongs the rightful supremacy in the soul over all other faculties and capacities. It is the lawgiver, either through its original nature and by its working as left to itself, or as organ and medium of all external authority;—it is either sovereign by right of natural constitution, or is vicegerent of all external sovereignty.

But conscience is law-giver, not doer of the law; its function is legislative, not executive. It prescribes law; it is the free-will that obeys or disobeys.

This function of conscience has a passive as well as an active side. It feels as well as acts. When viewed on this side it is often called *sense of obligation*.

The psychological analysis is obvious and is exactly analogous to that which is applicable to most concrete mental states. An action is proposed to the free-will. Every such action possesses the attribute of right or wrong, which is discernible just as the attribute of bright or round is discernible in the sun. The soul is impressed by this attribute, that is, *feels* it. But the impression or bare feeling continues in the form of an idea of right or wrong, which is kept before the intelligence as before the free-will. The intelligence recognizes the attribute of right or wrong as real, as belonging to the action, and the like. In this feeling from the sensibility and this light from the intelligence, the free-will by the very force of its nature is constrained to act by choosing or refusing. But the legitimate tendency of this activity is to the doing of the action if felt and recognized to be right, or refusing to do it, if felt and seen to be wrong. This tendency is felt also, and in this feeling of the force pressing to duty consists the sense of obligation.

3. Praise and blame. The third function of conscience is to praise or blame; to approve or condemn.

We cannot contemplate a moral action in its full light and character without recognizing and feeling that it is to be praised or blamed. We praise Regulus for observing his oath; while we should have severely blamed him if he had, when under no obligation and without any occasion, freely exposed himself to torture and death by returning to Carthage.

Such is the threefold function of conscience: (1) to recognize and feel duty; (2) to oblige to the performance of it; and (3) to praise or blame.

Source of joy or pain. § 14. To this threefold function of conscience must be added a fourth, if conscience be extended to include the pleasure or pain that naturally attends all right or wrong action. Good usage sanctions this extension. But it is to be remarked that this function of conscience immediately and properly respects only one's own acts, never those of others. It differs therefore in this respect from the three other functions named. There is a propriety, therefore, in maintaining the threefoldness of the functions of conscience. This fourth function deserves, however, a distinct and marked consideration in Ethics.

The fulfilment of duty brings along with it by the law of a moral nature a certain satisfaction, a pleasure. We say conscience is satisfied with it, is pleased with it. If the act is only proposed to be done, this pleasure or satisfaction is expected as certain to be felt in the doing of it or when it is done. If the act be that of another person, we unhesitatingly believe that it brings to him the same pleasure or satisfaction.

This pleasure is precisely analogous to that which attends the legitimate exercise of the intellect or of the sensibility. It is only higher, more intense, because the moral nature is the higher, more predominating nature in man.

On the other hand, the violation of duty brings in, by the very constitution of our moral being, dissatisfaction, pain, which, to distinguish it from the pain from other causes, is called *remorse*.

This pleasure of a good, that is of an approving, conscience, and this pain of a disapproving conscience, regarded in relation to the law which imposes duty, constitute in part the *sanctions* of the law; the *rewards* of right or wrong action.

The doer of the action, moreover, is said to be *deserving* of the reward or penalty. His action places him in a certain relation to the pleasure or pain naturally attending it, which we call *desert* or *merit*. This relation to wrong action is called *ill-desert* or *demerit*.

It will have been observed that conscience includes an exercise both of the intelligence and of the sensibility. It involves perception or intuition and judgment on the one hand, and feeling on the other, both as impression and also as natural pleasure or pain. Much confusion and disagreement have arisen in ethical discussions from the exclusion of one or the other of the two elements. Those writers who have regarded conscience as the same as the Practical Reason have inclined to shut out of view the element of feeling; and the advocates of a Moral Sense, on the other hand, have depressed from view the intelligence side of conscience.

CHAPTER III.

OBJECT OF DUTY.

Object of duty defined.
§ 15. By the object of duty is meant the person to whom duty is owing.

Our analysis gave the three essential elements in an act of duty as a subject of duty, or a person owing and fulfilling the duty; a person to whom this duty is owed and fulfilled; and the action itself of fulfilling the duty. Regulus owed the duty of return to the Carthaginians, who were accordingly the object of this duty.

Ever a person.
§ 16. Only persons can be objects of duty.

Regulus was bound in duty not to the city walls of Carthage; not to the prison from which he was taken; not to any law or principle; but to the Carthaginians, and certainly to himself as a man. The duty of returning was owed to them, or at least to himself.

Duty cannot properly be said to be owed to a stone. It is certainly a duty not wantonly to break or otherwise destroy a precious gem. In a loose sense we may speak of its being due to the gem as a thing of great value that it be kept from injury. But the duty here is properly due to the maker of the gem, that his creative design be not frustrated; to the owner of the gem from whom so much value would be taken by its destruction; to one's self whose moral nature would be harmed by an act of reckless waste. The stone can know no duty to itself. It can put up no claim. It can receive no redress from a withholding of its due.

Nor, any more, can duty properly be said to be owed to a plant. It would undoubtedly be wrong needlessly to trample under foot a beautiful flower, or to withhold the care which may be necessary for its preservation or for perfecting its growth. But this duty is not properly due to the plant, but only to Him who made it, to those who can enjoy its beauty, to one's self to whom it is due that his own nature be not marred by an act of wanton destruction or of inexcusable neglect.

Nor, still further, can duty properly be said to be owed to mere animal nature. We say in loose language that the horse is a noble animal and care and kindness are due to it. But these duties are not properly owed to the animal, but to the Creator, to them who can be benefited by it, or to one's self, to whom wanton cruelty is forbidden. The animal cannot be sensible of any duty owed to itself; cannot exact or be sensible of proper redress. The animal, as such, has no rights.

§ 17. The correlative of duty in a moral subject is, in an object of duty, a right.

A right.

What was his duty in Regulus, viz.: his return, as owed and fulfilled to the Carthaginians, was to them their right. Rights are the correlates of duties. The one implies the other. There can be no duty where there is no right; to every right there must be a corresponding duty. Every creature has a right to reach the end for which i was made; and so we say with reverence, it is due from its Creator that he enable it to reach this end of its being. The creation shows its own perfectness in this that the means are furnished to the creature of fulfilling the ends of its being. This at least is the general truth; the modifications of the statement are to be found only in the case of creatures made subservient to the ends of other beings.

Creatures, moreover, so far as parts of a universe affecting one another, owe mutual duties to one another, and accordingly have respectively rights to which such duties correspond. The same act is a duty in respect to the subject of duty, which is a right in respect to the object of duty. The return of Regulus to the Carthaginians, as stated, is his duty, and their right.

§ 18. The essential character in everything which can be conceived of as duty or as a right is, that it is GOOD.

Good in duty and right.

By *good* here is meant good that lies in experience; good that is felt. In other words, by *good* is meant happiness—blessedness—or that which occasions it.

The good which is thus to be rendered in the fulfilment of duty and which is claimed in the exaction of every right, may be only good in estimation, not necessarily a real good. The return of Regulus might have proved a real evil to the Carthaginians; but it was to them a good, fitted in their estimation, perhaps erroneous, to occasion to them happiness. His return doubtless was a satisfaction to them.

The good in duty and in a right may be indirect or remote. The only good expected by the Carthaginians might have been that it would deprive

Rome of her ablest general, and save them from their most formidable enemy, or it might be the good there might have been in the revenge which they would be quick to execute on their victim when he should return into their power.

A good, real or supposed, immediate or remote, thus enters essentially into duty and into its correlative right. A duty that, fulfilled, should work no conceivable good in any way, and a right that satisfied brings no good, are alike inconceivable.

§ 19. Human duties are most conveniently classified in reference to the object of duty. Inasmuch as human duty from its nature as pertaining to an act, can exist only where human action can reach, the only objects of duty to man are those beings which this action can affect.

<small>Classification of duties.</small>

A man's acts affect himself most nearly and directly. By the law of his being every legitimate exercise of his powers brings a kind of pleasure—is a good. His acts, directly and also indirectly, affect his fellow-men. They also, in a certain way, reach to God. They may reach, moreover, other beings, as the world of angelic and of disembodied spirits ; but this relation of human duty is sufficiently illustrated in the light of the other relations and, therefore, requires no distinct treatment. The three great classes of human duties, accordingly, which the object of duty gives us, are :—

    I. DUTIES TO SELF ;
    II. DUTIES TO FELLOW-MEN ; and
    III. DUTY TO GOD.

CHAPTER IV.

MORAL ACTION.

Moral action defined.
§ 20. A MORAL ACTION is a performance or fulfilment of duty.

More particularly, a moral action is the action of a subject of duty by which he fulfils or discharges what is owed to the object of duty.

A moral action implies an agent and an object, as also the movement of the agent to or towards the object. It implies, moreover, a certain kind of agent, a certain kind of object, and a certain kind of movement, each of which may properly be denominated moral. It follows from this that a moral action may properly be characterized in reference to the agent, or in reference to the object, or more exclusively in reference to the essential nature of the act itself.

We may thus characterize a moral action in reference to the agent; and if, in seeking to do this, we inquire what it is in a subject of duty which makes his action moral, we find the answer to be *love*. Every perfect moral act must be a loving act.

We may in like manner characterize a moral action in reference to the object of duty; and we find that, as good in the object is that which a moral action aims at, so every perfect moral action must be a good action. It must be good in the sense of being beneficent.

Characterizing a moral action simply in reference to its own intrinsic nature, in a similar way, we say it is *right*. Every perfect moral action is a right action.

If we analyze a perfect moral action thus we find it includes the three elements of love, goodness or beneficence, rectitude, essentially related to one another. It must, proceeding from a moral subject, be a movement from love. As resulting in a moral object it must be a movement that is beneficent, bringing good as its proper result. As an action from such a subject towards such an object, it must be direct in its movement from starting-point to goal, and so be characterized as right.

§ 21. It follows from this exposition that *Diversely denominated.* with a certain correctness a perfect moral action may be denominated as an act of perfect love; or as an act of perfect goodness or beneficence; or as an act of perfect rectitude.

It also follows that love as fulfilment of *The three elements essential.* duty cannot be except as both beneficent in its proper result and right in its movement. Nor, any more, can any moral goodness or beneficence be conceived of apart from love as its source and rectitude as its procedure. Nor still further is any right action possible or conceivable without love or without goodness or beneficence.

It follows, still further, that in the discussion of moral questions, while the principles of human thought and human speech allow the designation of a perfect moral act, either as an act of love, or as an act of goodness or beneficence, or as an act of rectitude; if yet either element be excluded from view, error must be the inevitable result.

Threefold system of morality. Hence a perfect system of morals may be founded either on love, on goodness or beneficence, or on right, as its principle, provided always due regard be had to its relation to the other co-ordinate principles.

1. As founded on love. There may thus be a system founded on love which shall have full validity, and also completeness. It may plant itself on a moral action and turn its view to the subject of duty concerned in it. As morality cannot reach beyond the endowments of the agent whom it respects, a system of morality which reaches to the entire nature of a moral subject must be complete. It may be valid and authoritative, inasmuch as it is founded in the very attributes of a moral subject. Love is obligatory on man because his is a loving nature. He is endowed with the faculties of love and is made to love. It is hence the law of his being that he love.

Again, a system of morality may be founded on the principle of goodness or beneficence—on the good that the subject of duty may effect in the object of duty. Such a system may take its stand in a moral action and direct its look to the object or end of the action. This principle, unfolded in the full light of the co-ordinate principles of love and rectitude, may give a system of morality at once valid and complete. It must be valid, for as all moral action respects good as its end and object, and as man as a creature of God is made for this end—to work good—this end or object must contain in it the law of life, just as the destined end of a journey prescribes the progress to be made and the way by which it is to be made. It will, also, in a certain sense, be complete if it embrace the entire good in the object of duty which can be effected by the subject of duty in the way in which he must work to this end.

Once more, a moral system may be founded on the principle of right and be both valid and complete. It may take its stand-point in a moral action and turn its view in the direction of the essential nature of such an action. It may be valid, because its foundation is in the essential nature of an act of duty—a movement of love to good as its end. It may be, in a certain sense, complete, because it may comprehend the entire movement of a moral subject in reference to the end of all his action.

Systems of morality have accordingly been constructed on each of these principles respectively. There are systems founded on love which unfold the law of love in its nature and its applications to human conduct. There are systems founded on good—on happiness or blessedness—which unfoid the law of benevolence in its nature and application to the life and conduct. There are, moreover, systems founded on rectitude, which unfold the law or the rule of right in its nature and applications. None of these systems fail in their validity and completeness because founded on a wrong or unreal principle; but only as they fail severally to recognize the co-ordinate validity of the other systems, and to develope their respective laws or supreme rules in due regard to the others. In other words, their failure, so far as it exists, is to be found in the omission to recognize the principle on which they have been founded, as but one of those principles which are essentially concerned in all morality. The reason is plain. As there can be no morality where there is not a moral agent, a moral end, and a moral action proceeding from this agent to this end, so no system of morality can be in the fullest sense perfect and entire, which does not recognize the relationship between these elements of duty as co-ordinate and co-essential in all morality.

CHAPTER V.

LOVE AS PRINCIPLE OF DUTY.

Love implied in subject of Duty. § 22. We have found that we may, in an act of duty, view it as an act proceeding from a moral subject; and that, so regarded, it must be an act of love. In other words duty, regarded in the light of the subject performing it, appears as love. Duty, moreover, inasmuch as it necessarily implies a doer, that is, a subject of duty, must ever be pervaded through and through with love—with the loving disposition and soul of the doer penetrating it.

Fulfils obligation. § 23. Love is not only necessary in all duty, but it is the fulfilling of the law of duty so far as it respects the subject of duty.

All that the subject of duty can put into the acts of duty is love; for this is all that appears of the doer in such an act. This love, which fills out the measure of duty, so far as the subject is concerned, must have, it is true, the characteristics of a perfect love. It must be intelligent, else it could not be the love of a rational being. It must be sincere, and, in this sense, disinterested, having for its end the good of its object, and not looking beyond that. It must be in due measure and degree. It must be simple and direct, moving unswervingly to its end. With these characteristics of a true and perfect love in a being like man, it fulfils all duty; all that can be morally required of man.

<small>Love defined.</small> § 24. Love, as a principle of duty, may accordingly be defined to consist in a sympathetic endeavor, put forth directly for the good of the object of duty.

In order to love, therefore, that in the object of duty which alone can be regarded in a moral act, his good, must first be brought before the instinctive sympathies of the soul, and then the action be put forth which the securing of that good shall require. Love must be in sympathy throughout, and must be active in obedience to that sympathy. It must be borne in mind that in an act of duty, either one of the three elements, love, good, right, may so predominate as to throw the others relatively into the shade. We speak of duty thus as often truly done, when there is no consciousness of love—when there seems to be absence of all affection, while yet the act relieves a want, as bread thrown to a beggar; or discharges an obligation as in the payment of money to an exacting creditor. The act in such case may be so far morally imperfect; or the love may be actually present, but is not consciously noticed. It still remains that there can be no morally right act without a loving intention.

2*

§ 25. The term love is applied to each of several stages of experience. Of these, three are particularly to be distinguished, respectively characterized as a mere natural affection, a grace, or a virtue.

Stages.

The first and lowest of these stages is mere instinctive sympathy, or *natural affection*. The sensibility of man is sympathetic, inasmuch as he is not only impressible by the condition of his fellow beings, but is instinctively disposed either to the same feeling which that condition awakens in them, as in proper sympathy; or to some responsive feeling, as in gratitude answering to kindness. This sympathy may exist independently of any immediate control of the will. So far, accordingly, it is not moral. It is mere natural affection. If the affection give pleasure, it takes the name of *complacency*; if pain or dissatisfaction, of *displacency* or *dislike*.

1. Natural affection.

The second stage is that in which the affection is the predominant characteristic, but yet the free-will enters as a directing or controlling element. Just so far as the natural affection is thus reached by the will, either in simply allowing it, or by selecting its object, or regulating itself, it becomes moral. But inasmuch as the feeling predominates over the free-will in giving it character, this stage of love is called a *grace* in distinction from a *virtue*, in which the will predominates.

2. As a grace.

The third stage is that in which the free-will gives the character to the

3. As act of will.

exercise, not only awakening and directing the sympathy, but leading it forth in appropriate action towards its object. This is love in its fullest sense. This is the love which fulfils duty.

Its opposite, hate.
§ 26. The opposite of love is *hate*. Hate is, like love, marked by three distinguishable stages—simple *dislike* or *displacency; misanthropic* or *unloving spirit* allowed or cherished by the free-will; and positive *malevolence* appearing in acts of evil to others.

§ 27. Inasmuch as man's nature is essentially active, and therefore must go out in positive action, duty admits no neutrality and therefore disallows all disposition or action which does not seek positive good. Not to sympathize is therefore wrong. An unsympathetic spirit, so far as sustained or cherished by the free-will, if not so heinous, is as truly opposed to duty as positive hate and ill will.

CHAPTER VI.

GOODNESS OR BENEFICENCE.

Good the end of all duty. § 28. All action, in so far as it is moral, aims at good in the experience of the object of duty as its one comprehensive result.

Every act of an infinite and perfect being, as of God, must not only aim at, but actually effect, good and good only. Perfect love can seek only good: and as God is perfect love and can accomplish all he seeks, all his actions must result in good. Perfect goodness or beneficence accordingly characterizes all he does.

The action of a finite and dependent being cannot in itself always assure the result which it seeks. But his endeavor must seek that result and that result only. This is implied in good, as the only end or result of love as an act, and as thus its correlative. Love and good imply each other—one being the source of action, the other its result. In more general terms the only end or aim of the human will is good, as truth is the only object of the intelligence. All volition, whatsoever object it may respect, whether act or pursuit, or plan, or thing, chooses its object only so far as it is, or at least appears to be, good. It is in strictness of thought, the good in it with which alone the will is concerned. Even a wrong will, a sinful choice, seeks a good; and the wrong and the sin lie in the choice not of pure unmixed evil, but of an inferior good or of the wrong kind of good. Even malignity itself moves to the good there is in gratifying its hate; and, but for that, could not move at all.

§ 29. The term *good* is used in a primary and also a secondary sense;— to denote (1) good in itself, that is, happiness, blessedness, or enjoyment; and (2) what works or occasions good, that is, the agent, means, instrument, or condition of this good in itself. In the latter sense it is applied to an agent or means; as *God is good*, that is, works good; *water is good*, that is, is a means of health and so of enjoyment. In the former sense it is applied to a state of experience, as *he is reaping the good of his virtuous conduct*, that is, is experiencing the happiness that attends his virtuous conduct.

<small>Twofold sense of good.</small>

Moralists have thus distinguished three kinds of good;—the good of pleasure, the good of interest, and the good of virtue. The first named, the good of pleasure, is good in itself—happiness. The last two are means or occasions of happiness; the good of interest being that which is instrumental of happiness, and the good of virtue or character being that which is naturally attended by happiness.

§ 30. It will be evident on a little reflection that man cannot be said in strict use of language to work or produce good in itself or happiness immediately and directly, that is, otherwise than instrumentally and mediately, either in himself or in others.

Happiness not immediate end in duty.

He can bestow a favor—can give bread to a hungry man, and the reception of that favor may relieve a want and awaken gratitude. The relief of the want, the taking of the bread, may give its appropriate happiness, and the exercise of the grateful spirit may give its peculiar joy. But the giver of the bounty has only furnished the means or the occasion of the happiness. In the same way, a man cannot directly create happiness for himself; he can at best only secure the occasions or means of happiness. He can acquire treasures in health, reputation, character, outward possessions; from these, the happiness comes which his creator has connected with them. He can contemplate his blessings, and the contemplation may bring joy; still it is not the joy, but the contemplation which is the immediate object and effect of his endeavor. He can form a perfect character; he may give himself to virtuous pursuits; he may do noble deeds; this character, these pursuits, these deeds, are through the laws of his nature attended by happiness, by the pleasures, the joys of an approving conscience, by the happiness immediately waiting on all lawful exertion. Character, virtue, is a means only of happiness. But it obviously stands in a closer relation to happiness than property, friends, and other outward good. This outward good is means or occasion of virtue; and this virtue is the immediate occasion of the happiness.

There is no other good conceivable besides these —good in itself or happiness, and good as means or occasion of happiness. This latter species, however, is distinguished into the two varieties, (1) outward good, as property and the like; and (2) internal good, as character, virtue, action in accordance with the laws of man's being. Of these varieties, it is to be remarked that the first or outward good can effect happiness only through the second or internal good.

§ 31. The inquiry, what is the chief good—the *summum bonum*—has greatly engaged the attention of philosophers, who have been far from harmonious in their answers. It is apparent that much at least of the difficulty has arisen from the ambiguity of the term good, and from overlooking the fact that while on the one hand it is not within the province of man to produce happiness immediately, but only mediately and instrumentally, still the secondary or instrumental good which he may produce is good only by reason of the happiness which it brings. If the meaning of the inquiry be, what is the chief good in man's nature, then certainly the answer must be, the highest happiness of which that nature is capable. Accordingly when it is asked what is the chief end in the creation of man by his maker, it must be replied, the fullest and highest happiness of man. For to suppose that it is the perfecting of

Summum bonum.

that nature—a perfect character—is to exclude from the act of God in creating man all love, and to reduce man to the rank of a mere machine or a plant. We can indeed conceive of a creature endowed with sensibility, with intelligence, with free power, who should be insensible of all happiness; and such a creature might be conceived to advance from comparative weakness to a perfect maturity of capabilities. But we should be constrained in reason to rank such a being infinitely below man, and deny to it any proper moral nature. The chief good then in man's nature is his capability of the highest and completest happiness, and the chief good in man's experience is such happiness.

If it be asked what is the chief good for man to desire, the answer must be the same. He was made not ultimately and chiefly to be a perfect machine, but to be supremely blessed; and it is the instinct of his nature to desire this end of his being as his chief good.

But if it be asked what is the chief good which man is to seek to effect as the immediate product of his endeavor, the answer is, first, to perfect his character as a man, and, secondly, in connection with this, to perfect his condition. For this is all he can do directly, perfect his own capabilities and place them in the right relation to all those things which can minister to his welfare. Character—the most perfect virtue—is indeed the most important, perhaps, in a certain sense, the highest of the two. But condition is as needful of his pursuit. In order to happiness, he must have not only character, but also right position to the objects which the virtues of that character respect. And this right position, this needful relation to those outer objects, is as truly, if not as fully, within the reach of his determination as character. Property, friends, and the like, are a good to man; indeed are a good in such sense that character cannot be without them.

The truth remains, however, that good in itself or happiness is not within the power of man directly to produce. The best, and indeed all he can do, is to produce that which under the appointments of his creator will bring in this good in itself or happiness. Man's effort ends ever with secondary or instrumental good.

The highest good—*summum bonum*—is thus, either a good of *experience*, which consists of blessedness and is the sole gift of God as creator and ruler, or a good of *attainment* in character or condition, which is the result of effort and is the occasion of that blessedness which is the direct gift of God. Between this right character and condition as possible to be attained by man, and this blessedness as possible to be experienced by man, the creator has established a necessary relation—a relation designated sometimes as *worthiness* to be blessed. This worthiness expresses, however, it will be observed, no essential attribute of perfect goodness or rectitude, but only a mere relative attribute—a mere relation between character and blessedness.

We are enabled in the light of this general survey of the subject to advance the distinctions and propositions that follow.

§ 32. Good as the end in all duty is of two kinds: 1, good in itself, or happiness; 2, good as means of happiness.

Two kinds.

Good in itself—happiness—is the primary and ultimate good. It is the immediate product of the creator alone.

1. Good in itself.

Good as means is secondary and mediate or instrumental. It is good only as the means or instrument or condition of good in itself.

Secondary good is the only good which the effort of man should aim to effect; which nevertheless he should aim to effect only because of the ultimate good in itself which it may bring under the ordinance of heaven.

2. Good as means.

Secondary good is of two varieties, which are distinguished from each other by their being more or less immediately productive of happiness. They may be denominated *the good of condition* and *the good of character*.

The good of condition embraces all the objects, occasions, means, or helps of any legitimate energy in man—everything which can occasion or facilitate or enhance any exercise of any of the faculties or capacities of man's nature.

Good of condition.

The good of character embraces all the good which springs from the energies of man's nature, whether habitual and so forming character, or only specific in single acts or states, so far as they are naturally and immediately followed by happiness.

Good of character.

Exemplifications of this last variety are such as a virtuous habit. Beneficence, or the habitual exercise of a loving spirit, is a source of joy and happiness. Even when it is not in special exercise, but only cherished as a fixed governing principle of the soul—the beneficent spirit itself when not working out special deeds of charity—sheds a light and a cheer over a man's experience. In contemplation, or in directing a particular act of kindness, this light and cheer often brighten and warm into a joy and delight that is as rapturous as it is pure. It is the inheritance of virtue that cannot be taken away. Another exemplification is such a special act of kindness itself. The consciousness of the act gives a legitimate pleasure, and, it may be, a more intense delight ; but a virtuous act by the very constitution of our nature brings happiness, even if it be not taken up into distinct consciousness. Even acts that in themselves have no special moral character, as the exertions of power or skill, physical or mental, the exercises of any of our faculties or capacities, are followed by pleasure. The active man is a happier man than the idler or the sluggard.

§ 33. We may now set forth more exactly and definitely the relation of moral action to its end or result.

The ultimate end and object of all moral action is happiness. No action can be regarded as moral the last end of which is not to be found in happiness.

As happiness is the immediate gift of God alone, the more immediate end of all human action, so far as moral, must be found in some secondary or mediate good either of character or of condition.

To aim to produce happiness, accordingly, directly and not through character or condition, is for man ever vain and futile. To attempt it is to usurp the prerogative of heaven. Man can only produce happiness mediately and instrumentally. His action to be moral must ever seek this ultimate result of happiness only by securing that in which this happiness rests as its necessary condition.

Perfect moral action must aim at the highest good in the object of duty which is practicable in the case;—must aim at that highest perfection of character or condition to which the Creator has attached the highest blessedness.

For the same reason that all free action should seek to work good in its object, it is bound to seek all the good, the highest and largest good, that is practicable.

Inasmuch as happiness is of divers grades or ranks, the highest grade of happiness is to be sought in preference to any lower kind. And inasmuch as an act may by the doer be determined or shaped to work a larger or smaller amount of good, duty requires that the largest amount should be intended, rather than a lower amount. The rule of duty is: the highest and largest good must be the designed effect of all moral action.

§ 34. EVIL is the opposite of good.

Evil.   Like good, evil is either *natural* or *moral*.

NATURAL EVIL is evil in experience, as pain, suffering, unhappiness.

MORAL EVIL is wrong moral action.

To work natural evil, that is, to produce unhappiness as the ultimate end of the action, is ever wrong.

It is a perversion of the proper design and tendency of the natural faculties of man, which are designed to work good only. It is directly opposed to the character and will of God, who works good only, and constituted all his creatures to work good only. It is, in the object of an action, the correlative of malevolence or hate in the subject or doer, and possesses consequently the same moral character.

To produce unhappiness as the designed means and condition of a higher and larger happiness is not necessarily contrary to duty. On the other hand it may be, for the time, the most imperative duty.

The amputation of a limb by which life may be saved and pain relieved, although itself for the time causing immediate and severe pain, may be an act of love, and often is an imperative duty. No happiness arising from condition, as from wealth, fame, friendship, is unmingled with evil. Even under the rule of perfect love armed with infinite wisdom and power, evil exists. We may be unable to conjecture why it was not excluded, or why it is not prevented; but we must recognize the fact that it exists under this perfect rule. We may reasonably presume that its existence may be justified in consistency with perfect love and infinite wisdom and power. We must at the same time believe that the permission of evil is a necessary condition of the highest and largest good.

CHAPTER VII.

RECTITUDE.

Right as element of duty. § 35. All moral action, so far as perfect, must be right in its procedure.

All action has a direction as well as a source and an end. All perfect moral action, as we have seen, proceeds from love as its source to good as its end. This procedure in a perfect moral action has the attribute of rightness or rectitude. The term *rectitude*, accordingly, as applied to moral action, respects immediately this procedure—the action itself—so as relatively to repress from view for the time the doer and also the object of duty.

The idea of right is so extremely simple that it baffles effort to explain it. The best that can be done is to set forth the leading attributes that belong to it as it is applied in morals.

1. Implies action. § 36. First, moral rectitude always respects an action.

To conceive of an absolute right as independent of all action is impossible. It is an attribute, and an attribute of action.

2. Relation of action. § 37. Secondly, moral rectitude always respects the relation of an action—the interior relation of its source to its end.

As has been already stated, moral rectitude respects the relation of love to its end in good. It has this feature of relativeness always attaching to it. It includes, of course, as involved in this relation, the proper proportion between the love in the subject and the good effected in the object of duty.

§ 38. Thirdly, moral rectitude implies that there is a natural, a fitting movement in the action from its source to its end; and it denotes properly and strictly this naturalness or fitness in the relation of an action between its origin or seat and its end or result.

3. Fitness.

The moral nature of the soul is its loving nature, and the end for which it is designed and fashioned to act is good. Its action is right so far as fitting this nature and end. Rectitude is thus so far correctly conceived as consisting in fitness.

Rectitude is also correctly conceived as consisting in conformity to rule or law; for conformity to rule can mean nothing else than conformity to the nature of the soul, and to that of the end for which it was designed by its maker.

The objection to such definitions of rectitude is that they are interpreted and applied to rectitude as if it were an absolute or independent entity, subsisting of itself separate from action and from an agent. But we can as easily conceive of an absolute love without an object in good to be effected by the love, as of an absolute rectitude. It cannot be too frequently declared that love, good, right, are inconceivable as independent separable entities; they necessarily imply one another in all cases.

Right is absolute, accordingly, only in this sense: that, given the action and the conditions in which it is to be exerted, there is a mode of action which is universally and necessarily to be recognized as right. It is the same when the same subject, object, and circumstances are given, always, and every where. It will be pronounced right in the same way by every mind equally informed of all the elements in the case. It is in this sense a necessary idea. The mind is necessitated to recognize the right when the action with its subject, object, and circumstances are given.

The idea of right is absolute, universal, and necessary, in the same sense as the idea of the angularity of the triangle. The triangle cannot be without angles. The angularity does not exist before the lines are constructed into the triangle; but it attaches necessarily to the triangle as it is formed. The sides as mere lines have no angularity; but constructed or put together in a certain way the angularity exists. No construction can exclude it.

§ 39. Fourthly, rectitude implies an unswerving procedure in the action from its source to its end.

4. Directness.

We may conceive of a perfect love and a perfect good intended and effected by its expression, while its movement is irregular, circuitous, indirect. So far moral action is imperfect.

When, as is often the case, we limit our consideration to the movement of love towards its end, leaving out of our view for the time the source and the result, this direction of the action, whether direct or circuitous, whether, in other words, the fitting direction for love to take in the case, is the feature that determines to our judgment whether the action is right or wrong. In a similar way, we pronounce the solution of a mathematical problem to be imperfect, if it does not proceed in the directest way to the result, even although the principles on which the solution starts and the result itself are correct.

5. Parallelism with all other duty. § 40. Fifthly, all specific right action is parallel with all other specific right action.

This characteristic of right is founded in the assumption that the universe is a perfect creation, so that all beings in it are exactly fitted to their own ends, and also each is in harmonious relation to every other. All rectitude consequently is harmonious; right can never cross, or trip, or oppose right. In the eternity of consequences of perfect moral acts, no clashing can ever occur. All their movements in the flow of eternal consequence are in parallel lines.

Wrong. § 41. WRONG is the opposite of right. It respects an action and the relation between its source and its end. It implies a fitness or conformity in this relation which is not regarded in the action, and consequently an indirectness in the procedure which necessarily crosses and disturbs the lines of rectitude.

It should be observed that the term *right* is frequently used in the sense of perfect, and the term *wrong* in the sense of imperfect, in whichever of the three elements in all morality—subject, object, and action of subject in relation to object—the imperfection may exist. Action is equally pronounced wrong if the love is imperfect; if it be too feeble or too strong, or if the object be an improper one, or if in effecting it, a devious way be pursued. Sometimes, moreover, only the incidental manner of the action is regarded and the act is recognized as right or wrong, according as that is perfect or otherwise. Thus good counsel may be imparted in blunt words; there may be true love prompting the counsel, a real good aimed at, but the manner of carrying the love into its effect may be imperfect by reason of previous defective culture, and the act may be judged so far to be wrong. Strictly, however, the act should be recognized as right; only the manner wrong. The morality of the manner attaches only to the culture which has failed to furnish a proper body of words in which loving action is to be embodied.

CHAPTER VIII.

MOTIVES.

§ 42. By MOTIVE is to be understood *Motive defined.* the good which, as apprehended by the mind, is the object of the free-will or the end to which the action of the will tends.

The term *motive*, properly signifying that which moves, is employed in ethical discussions, in a modified sense. It denotes not the physical cause, but rather the occasion of the mind's action. It denotes the occasion of such acting, however, in the peculiar sense of an object or end so related to the mind as to invite and call forth its endeavors. It is thus not merely the necessary negative condition of a moral action, as a weight is necessary condition to the act of lifting a weight, but is so related to the mind as positively to attract or provoke its action. It is of course in moral discussions used only as it can be viewed in relation to the action of the free-will.

The only possible object of will, the only end to which the will can be moved, as we have already recognized, is good. As essentially active the free-will must act; and as made for good only, it can act only in reference to good as the object or end of its action.

This good, however, in order to be an end to the free-will, must be apprehended by the mind. It is only as so apprehended that it can be chosen. It must be brought to the mind through the mind's capacity of receiving external objects; it must be felt; it must not only be felt, but felt as good. In other words, there must be sympathy with it; there must be instinctive tendency towards it; there must be desire for it. It must also be apprehended by the intelligence; it must with this feeling be perceived, be known as real, as attainable by the will. Only as so apprehended by the mind through its sensibility and intelligence can any good be a motive.

It should be observed, moreover, that the good which is proper object or end to the will, may be only a supposed or believed good. It must be apprehended as good by the mind; but this apprehension may be a mistaken one. The object addressed to the sensibility may be a phantom; it may be erroneously perceived or known in its character and also in its practicability. The imperfect mind of man often pursues unreal objects, unattainable ends. But it fancies its objects and its ends are good and also attainable. So far as mere motive is concerned, it is what is apprehended as good only, whether that apprehension be well grounded or not, which gives it its effect on the will.

Still further, as we have found, the primary good

—good in itself, happiness—is immediately of God alone. The only good that man can effect is the secondary good, the means of good, which lies either in character — that is, in perfecting the faculties and capacities of his nature, or in condition —that is, in securing the objects or occasions for the exercise of these faculties and capacities.

§ 43. Motives, accordingly, are of two classes :—1. those which have their end *in character;* 2. those which have their end *in condition.*

<small>Two classes.</small>

As character is to man more than condition, as the energy, the capability of acting is more in itself than the object on which the energy is to act or the occasion of its acting, the motives of the first class are generally of a higher nature than those of the second class. The highest duty to man is accordingly to perfect his nature ; to train and mature his faculties and capacities to their highest and largest perfection, so as to bring in by their exercise the fullest good in itself, the completest happiness for which he was destined and fashioned by his creator. In this good of perfecting character, is to be found the highest motive by which human action is to be determined.

§ 44. Each of these classes of motives is subdivided into lower classes.

<small>1. Motives in character.</small>

Those of the first class—those which respect character—may be distributed into the three species of 1. those which lie in the training and developing the moral nature ; 2. those which lie in the culture of the intelligence and the sensibility ; and 3. those which lie in the regulation of the animal nature.

These three species stand in rank relatively to one another in the order in which they are stated. Those motives, that is, those ends or objects to be pursued by the free-will which lie in the moral nature, are of the highest rank and should be taken in preference to determine the action and the life. They should be kept nearest and most constantly before the will. He that thus ever sets before him as the end which he will pursue in preference to all things else, this perfecting of character, will secure the highest good possible to him to secure ; he will, in other words, put the object of duty whether himself or his fellow men, in the state or condition to which his creator has attached the highest welfare, the fullest blessedness.

The ends which lie in the perfecting of the other departments of the spiritual nature of man —his intelligence and his sensibility both as feeling and as imagination—are subordinate to the first named and are properly conditioned to them. To place these first is to degrade man's nature and so far to hinder the attainment of the highest good. The predominant culture of the intellect and the taste, is therefore an immorality. To make it the chief and commanding motive in action, whether for one's self or for others, is wrong, because exalting to supremacy what should be subordinate.

The ends which lie in the perfecting of the animal nature of man are lowest in rank. To pursue them otherwise than in subordination to the other species is contrary to morality—is sinful. It is most effectually to hinder the attainment of the highest good.

<small>2. Motives in condition.</small> § 45. The motives which have their ends in perfecting the condition of man so as to make it most serviceable to his faculties and capacities, are of three species, as they are found in persons, or in things, or in relations.

It should be a motive or end in life to place ourselves in such relation to other persons as that they may, as objects of duty, both invite right action in reference to them and also facilitate it.

Hence arises the duty of friendship, of companionship, of society generally. Only as a man is within reach of others can he exercise towards them the faculties and capacities on the exercise of which his highest good depends. He cannot otherwise be beneficent; he cannot be in sympathy; he cannot receive good. To provide objects of duty is a leading end, a prominent motive in a well ordered life.

Things are helpful and sometimes indispensable conditions of acting. All those objects accordingly which can minister to right action, are within the scope of man's lawful pursuit. They furnish legitimate motives or ends to pursue. Hence the duty of industry, of care and economy in acquiring and preserving; for possessions are needful conditions of acting.

Not only persons and things in themselves thus furnish motives or ends of pursuit, but certain relations to them are to be sought as furnishing worthy motives.

Rank, thus, and station are often conditions of beneficence; and remotely of respect and gratitude and trust. Positions of control and direction in the administration of authority and of power in any way, are legitimate objects to be sought. In them men are placed in relations favorable to that activity on which their highest good depends.

§ 46. Motives are classed, moreover, in reference to one another, as *ultimate* and *proximate*, according as their ends are final, or only subservient to other ends.

Ultimate and Proximate.

The ultimate motive relatively to all others, or that to which all others should be subservient, is for man the highest and fullest development and exercise of his faculties; in other words, the perfection of his character.

There can be no higher end to a creature of perfect wisdom and goodness, than to fulfil the end for which it was made. The nature of man as a spirit is essentially an active and, at the same time, a growing nature. As an activity capable of growth, the ultimate end for which he was made must be found in the fullest development of his powers for the action to which they are designed. His creator can design or expect nothing beyond this. In this man most perfectly "glorifies" his creator, by realizing the end of his creation. The joy or happiness which comes from this perfecting of his character, it is his creator's to bestow, not man's to create, except by furnishing the condition on which it is bestowed in this perfect character. We may accordingly make this distinction: God's ultimate end in the creation of man is man's blessedness; man's ultimate end under this creation is to become and do what his creator designed. The absolutely ultimate motive for man is therefore the perfecting of his character, implying not only the full development of all his capacities, but also the full exercise of these capacities under the law of their nature.

But there are relatively ultimate motives. They are all subordinate to the one absolutely ultimate end—perfecting of character, but to them other ends may be subservient.

Wealth, thus, may be a proximate motive as subservient to health, to usefulness, to the best character. But it may be ultimate, in reference to other subservient motives, as, among many others, punctuality, order, temperance.

§ 47. Motives in themselves are not, strictly speaking, morally right or wrong.

In themselves not moral.

Right and wrong belong only to actions; but motives are only prompting occasions of actions. But the free-will can, by virtue of its very freedom, adopt and pursue any one of divers ends presented to it. Regulus had before him two ends or objects to be pursued; both true motives, being each a good, and each being a worthy good to be pursued, each being, therefore, a proper motive;—the good in home and country on the one hand, and the good in fidelity to his promise on the other. His free-

3*

will fastened on the latter good. It is consequently in the selection among divers motives of action, that we are to find the proper morality or the right or wrong in the case. A motive can only be regarded as right or wrong, in so far as it is the proper motive to be selected or otherwise, and so implies that the action of the will in the selection was morally right or wrong. To adopt and pursue a lower end in preference to a higher is against morality.

<small>Wrong selection.</small> § 48. There are three ways in which the selection among divers motives may be wrong.

<small>1. As ends and acts or means.</small> 1. The end may be sought immediately which should be sought only through other ends.

To seek good in itself or happiness directly and not through character primarily, and condition secondarily, is wrong, because only God gives happiness itself, and man can obtain it only by placing himself in the state to which his creator accords it. In the same way to seek intelligence without the labor of study, or wealth without industry, is against morality.

<small>2. Of subordinate ends.</small> 2. A subordinate end may be adopted as the chief and governing end.

To make condition thus predominate, as to seek wealth without subordination to the higher end of character or ability to use it aright, to amass for the sake of having, with no reference to a better doing, is a sin against a pure morality. It debases the higher nature of acting, and thus hinders the higher good.

3. Excess.

3. The end, rightly selected and subordinated, may be pursued to excess.

The wrong here is really but an incomplete subordination. Food, thus, is a condition of a healthy body, which is itself a condition of the highest spiritual character. But food taken in excess is wrong, because although taken for the sustenance of the body, yet its limitations being transcended, the very object in taking it is defeated or impaired.

CHAPTER IX.

MORAL OBLIGATION.

Moral Obligation defined. § 49. By MORAL OBLIGATION is meant that attribute of duty by which it holds and draws to its fulfilment.

We have recognized the fact that when certain actions are presented to us, we feel ourselves bound to perform them; such actions are duties. All duty has thus an obliging force; it holds the soul and draws to the performance of it. The soul feels itself bound, as both held to it and also impelled to perform it.

Of this obligation it may be said, first, that it is inherent in the very nature of duty and inseparable from it. As well may the sun be conceived without figure or brightness as duty without obligation.

1. Attribute of duty. Duty and obligation are accordingly used interchangeably to a certain extent, just as the sun and the luminary. To fulfil or discharge duty is the same as to fulfil or discharge obligation. They are, however, distinguishable in meaning. Obligation is best conceived of as being an essential attribute of duty regarded as a concrete—as an essential attribute of a right action.

2. Inexorable. In the next place, obligation is inexorable in its demand.

It holds till the duty is discharged by performance, or till it is abrogated by the authority which imposes it.

3. Impelling power. In the third place, obligation has a certain power drawing to its fulfilment.

This has been included in the definition; obligation draws to duty. No one who has a sense of duty or feels obligation fails to experience a certain impulse from within to do it.

4. Resistible. In the fourth place, obligation is resistible.

This follows from the very nature of duty which ever respects freedom of will in the agent. As free, by very virtue of this essential attribute of freedom in the will, the soul is superior to all outward force. So soon as an irresistible necessity arises which destroys the possibility of performing an act, or which constrains performance without the free consent of the will, duty disappears, obligation ceases.

Its ground. § 50. The ground of obligation is to be found ultimately in the nature of man and his relations to other beings and things.

Several perplexing questions have been raised in regard to the ground of obligation which are easily resolved when the obscurity and ambiguity involved in the use of words are removed. It is asked thus:

why am I bound to do right; to be virtuous; to love other beings; to do good to them? These questions are generally to be interpreted as equivalent to the question—why am I bound to duty. If to be understood in any other sense, they are to be answered each according to its own special sense in the application which is made of the language, and may be answered in terms showing their relation to this one common element—that of duty—involved in them. Thus: I am bound to do right, because duty obliges me to do good in hearty love *in the direct way of nature*—to express my love in beneficence to others *in the way proper to my nature and theirs.* I am bound to be virtuous because duty obliges me to be what I was made to be, namely—*a true man.* I am bound to love other beings, because duty obliges me *to act out my loving nature to them.* I am bound to do good to others, because duty obliges me *to work good* in all my free action. If these questions are equivalent to the question,—why am I bound to duty, and respect merely the ground of obligation the one answer is: such is my nature in relation to other beings and things; this is what I was made for. Duty is loving beneficence to others in the way in which it can most directly be done. I have a nature which is essentially loving, which, therefore, seeks the good of others; and a way is opened to me by which this love can go out and effect this good; therefore am I bound to duty. Or, in other words: I was purposely created lovingly to do good to others and was placed in a condition in which by following a certain course I might act thus. Or, still again : I am bound to duty because all duty is essentially grounded in the nature of the subject of duty in relation to other beings and things. The objective ground of duty, and, consequently, of obligation, for, as we have seen, duty has obligation for its essential attribute, is to be found thus in the nature of man and his relations.

The doctrine that duty is ultimately grounded in the fitness of things, differs from this view only in its being less comprehensive ; as it seems to look only at the one phase or element in a perfect moral action, its rectitude or the relation between the loving subject and the benefited object of duty.

The doctrine that all duty is grounded in love equally founds duty in the nature of man, inasmuch as to love is what he was made to do. It only so emphasizes that element of duty which is given in the subject of duty as to overshadow the other two elements given in the object of duty and the relation between love and good.

That doctrine, once more, which grounds obligation in good, grounds itself in the nature of man as made for good, and is faulty only as depressing from view the other essential constituents of duty—love and rectitude.

The objective ground of human duty, then, is ultimately to be found in the nature and relations of man. The question ; why am I bound to duty, receives the only answer of which it is capable in any proper meaning of the words, in this statement. The subjective ground of duty in the narrower sense of the phrase, as presented in the question : how do I come to have a sense of duty, or why do I feel myself under obligation, demands a slightly modified answer. The subjective ground of obligation in this sense is in the rational nature of man, as capable of apprehending duty. I come to have a sense of duty, by my natural capacity of feeling duty when it is properly brought before me, just as I come to have a sense of warmth when a heated object is brought properly to me : it is my nature to feel in both cases and therefore I feel.

There is a twofold function in man's rational nature carefully to be recognized. First, there is the sensibility or capacity of being impressed, and then, there is the intelligence or faculty of perceiving and judging. This twofold function of feeling and knowing can be called into exercise only on condition of its proper object being furnished to it. Duty must then first be presented ; that is, a moral action, either done or to be done. When thus presented, there is first the impression or the feeling ; then the perceiving with a discrimination of attributes ; and finally recognition followed by the feelings that such recognition produces. Necessarily in this way when an act of duty is presented, there is, through the impression which it makes, a recognition of the attribute of obligation as essentially belonging to it. Just as the presentation of the sun through the outward sense to the mind is followed by the recognition of the attribute of brightness ---that it shines---so is the presentation of an act of duty necessarily followed by the attribute of obligation belonging to it—that it obliges and so that the subject of duty is bound to it. The discernment of obligation thus is intuitive. We recognize obligation when an act of duty is brought before us simply by contemplation—by intuition, not at all by any reasoning from antecedent truths. The obligation belonging to all duty may, indeed, be proved by a form of reasoning, because all truth is consistent with itself and one lower truth implies other lower truths. Thus, a basis of argument may be found in other truths; just as I can prove that the sun is bright from many facts, as for instance, from the fact that plants modify their growth under the effect of its light. But just as I know that the sun is bright primarily because I see the sun, so I know duty is obligatory because my reason immediately discerns it.

This intuitive recognition of obligation is followed by appropriate feelings, among which is prominent that of an impulse to fulfil it. This is the obliging function of conscience, as we have recognized it.

CHAPTER X.

MORAL LAW.

Law defined. § 51. Law is well defined to be a rule of action.

Such is the definition of law in its widest sense and largest application. In this sense, law applies to all things that are made. "All things in heaven and earth do her homage; the very least as feeling her care, and the greatest as not exempted from her power."

The law of everything that exists is written in its very nature and its relations to the universe of being around. We read this law in the respective attributes that belong to existing things. The stone falls to the ground, the tree grows, the bird flies, because gravitation, growth, flying, are the respective attributes of these objects.

These are all attributes of action. Law is read in these attributes rather than in the so-called attributes of quality belonging to simple being. Law more immediately respects action. The comprehensive law of every being is nothing else in its content than the sum of the attributes which constitute it regarded as an acting thing. Quality is regarded in law only indirectly and impliedly. We say the law of the crystal of common salt is that it be cubical, by which we only mean that in the action by which it comes to exist, it must, according to its nature, assume this form. The law of this action—the law of crystallization in the case of this salt—is that it be cubiform. This attribute, although one strictly of quality, yet implicitly looks back to the action that forms it. Law thus properly respects action.

Farther, law respects a mode of action and prescribes that it be in this rather than in that particular way. The stone falls to the earth—does not of itself move along the surface: falls, if left to itself, directly not in zigzag lines to the earth; falls with a certain accelerated velocity. The tree grows upward, not downward; it grows by an inward force, not by mere accumulation or by adding on part to part from without. The bird flies by the action of its wings, not by leaping; forward not backward. When it is said it is the law of the stone, of the tree, of the bird, that they respectively fall, grow, fly, it is meant that these are the prescribed or established modes of their action.

Once more, law implies a lawgiver. The very term signifies that which is laid down or established; and thus imports a being that lays down or establishes.

§ 52. Law is conveniently distributed into *physical law* and *moral law*. The former respects physical action; the latter, moral action.

Physical law. PHYSICAL LAW comprehends and is read in the attributes that belong to all things in nature, that is, to all things outside of the properly moral world. Its essential character is what is denominated necessity. As a thing cannot be other than its attributes, it is necessary that the law which is read in these attributes remain an unchanging rule. Otherwise, the attributes, more or less, cease to be and the being to which they belong likewise so far ceases to be.

The whole natural world, the universe without and all of men within, save only his freedom or moral nature, conceived of as a creation, is thus under the law of the Creator which is established and prescribed in the respective attributes with which he has endowed whatever he has made. The law of the physical world is, in fact, thus but the expression of the creative will. Accordingly, almost of necessity, against their inclinations, the men of science whose sphere is bounded by the world of mere phenomena, the mere modes and sequences of things, are constrained to speak of the attributes of the several things of which they treat as laws, because things are what they are by reason of the will of their Creator; and hence the essential attributes of these things, which it is the province of science to discover and to disclose, are very laws; being expressions of a will, even of that will which gave them being and made them what they are.

Moral law. MORAL LAW is the law of moral action, that is, of duty.

It ever respects action that is free—free in this sense, that the action which it prescribes may be withheld. The action prescribed is not necessary to the being of the agent, because unlike the physical world, the essential attribute—the law—of the free-will is an alternative of action—doing or refusing.

Everything in man, accordingly, except this freedom of action in doing or refusing, is under physical law. Man gravitates to the ground, grows, moves, breathes, under the law of necessity. The happiness that attends on right action and the unhappiness that attends on wrong action are equally under the law of necessity; they are not alterable at his pleasure, except through the action which is free to him. This happiness that waits on the legitimate use of his endowments is beyond his control otherwise than thus mediately. It is as wrong, therefore, as it is idle for him to attempt to control it except thus mediately.

The Creator has invested man with the attribute of freedom—the alternative of doing or refusing. The action of the free-will is necessary in so far as that it must act, and must act by choosing or refusing; but it is free in this respect that it may choose or it may refuse. The law, however, reaches to this alternative so far as to prescribe one as well as the other. The law of man's nature is, as we have seen, the law of loving beneficence in the way of rectitude, rather than of malignant ill-doing in the way of evil. This is his nature: for this he was made and constituted; this is his distinguishing attribute, that he be freely thus beneficent; and in this attribute is read the will of his Creator.

But man is but a part of a universe. As but a part he is constituted to act only as a part—in harmonious relation to the universe of which he is a part. And this attribute of his nature implies two things; first, that his action respect other beings so as to further the end of their creation—that is, their well-being or happiness; and secondly, that this action go out without disturbing the harmonious relations in which all the parts of the creation have been established by the one perfect will. In this light we discover the essential elements of all morality, of all perfect moral action. Man in himself was made to love; but as a part of a universe his loving action must respect the good of others in it; and lastly, this action must be in accordance with the established relationships of the universe. Love, beneficence, rectitude, are the constituent elements of all morality.

An expression of will. We are brought thus both in physical and in moral law, to the recognition of the innermost characteristic of law that it is the expression of a will. No truer doctrine can be found than this grand utterance of Hooker, that " of law there can be no less acknowledged than that her seat is the bosom of God; her voice the harmony of the world."

Physical law expresses the will of the Creator that the things which he has made be what he has made then and so act as he has constituted them to act.

Moral law expresses the will of the Creator that

the beings he has endowed with freedom, in the use of this freedom choose ever the end for which they were made—loving beneficence; that, as active, in this freedom they ever do good; and that as parts of a universe they act in harmony with all the other parts.

§ 53. Inasmuch as the one Creator has one all-comprehensive end in his creative work, making all things in their legitimate action to conspire harmoniously towards this end—the highest good of his creatures—all law, physical and moral, must be consistent and harmonious with itself.

Harmony of law.

All the specific diversities of action which the creative law prescribes must accordingly flow on together in one peaceful current, never hindering nor disturbing the movement one of another, but rather each aiding on every other, just like drops of water in one stream, since all are subject to the one law bearing all to the same sea of love. The loving bosom of God being the one seat and source of all law for every creature he has made, his creative word which is the voice or utterance of this word is the harmony of the world.

§ 54. Law as thus implying and presupposing a personal will as its ultimate seat and source, gives at once to the sense of obligation the character and force of command.

Its obliging power.

The feeling of obligation ever carries with it the feeling of an imperative. Conscience, which is the organ through which God makes known his will, not only holds to duty and draws to it, but commands duty. It speaks with the voice of authority. It utters a will back of the action, back even of the obligation ; or, rather, it utters a will penetrating the obligation and the action so as to make it imperative duty.

§ 55. Law, as presupposing a personal will as its seat and source, gives to the sense of obligation the character of responsibility.

<small>Imports responsibility.</small>

The fact that this feeling of responsibility naturally accompanies the feeling of obligation, is undeniable. It is witnessed by universal experience. The recognition of duty gives not only a sense of an imperative obligation, but carries with it, or rather bears in it, the feeling that there is a power back of duty that in prescribing it will enforce it; and that to this power, the subject of duty must in some way be accountable. This character of responsibility comes into duty and obligation and law, from the presence of the personal will that makes law what it is. A will pressing on in resistless might to its purposed end must sweep along every obstacle with it. The drop in the mighty current that should refuse to flow on or should seek to move up the stream or across and away from its prescribed direction, must inevitably be crossed and borne down.

In the necessity of things, therefore, the law of the universe, bearing the personal will of its creator, moving to its end in good, must bring every creature into its current. Man, created with freedom, while created to gravitate in the same current to good as his end, yet, as free, capable of withholding this gravitating movement or opposing or crossing it, cannot but experience the consequences of such opposition or resistance. He is made capable of discerning these consequences as appointed by the creator and necessitated in the divinely instituted order of things. He cannot, therefore, when he freely contemplates duty, but recognize and feel himself subject to these prescribed consequences; in other words, feel himself responsible to a personal will to the creator and disposer of the universe of which he is a part; who will certainly, as he is true to himself, enforce his will in some suitable way.

§ 56. That element of law by which it enforces itself upon the subject of duty, is called its *sanction*.

Sanction of law.

Law not only prescribes, not only commands; it also enforces. The sanction of the creative law is discovered legitimately and primitively in the consequences experienced by the subject of duty who, in his freedom, disobeys its command. These consequences consist primarily in the defeat of the end for which he was made. As he was made for good, to do and to enjoy good, the inevitable consequence of disobedience to the fundamental law of his being is that he fails so far of the end of his being—fails of good. He fails of good both in doing and in enjoying it. The consequences are not, however, merely negative, consisting merely in the loss of the good which his fulfilment of duty would have brought. But the whole tendency of his active

4

nature, being under the beneficent law of his creation to perfect happiness as the immediate and necessary result of his obedience, is by this disobedience crossed and opposed by the entire flow of the universe. Positive unhappiness or misery is thus experienced.

This result is the effect of the creator's will. It is what he purposes, what thus he effects. It is the fulfilment of what he implicitly declared in the very creative law which made things as they are. The fundamental law of the universe contains thus both precept and sanction.

It is, however, a very low, a very unworthy and erroneous conception of the relations of the creator to his creatures, that he creates them with certain attributes and relations and then dismisses them to experience the sunshine or the storm, the favoring breezes or the desolating gales, which may befall them on their voyage towards the haven for which he made and destined them. Reason forbids any other notion than this, that he as truly concerns himself personally with the action of his creatures as he did with their creation; that he superintends that as truly as he effected this; that he brings by his own direction the happiness that attends every act of obedience, as well as the unhappiness that waits on disobedience.

The truest notion, therefore, and the only one which reason sanctions, is that the consequences of fulfilling or resisting duty express the feelings of the creator himself, and that these feelings are those of satisfaction and approval in the one case, and of

MORAL LAW. 75

displeasure and disapproval in the other. We are to remember here that man is utterly impotent to produce directly any happiness; that the most he can do is to effect that action on which his creator has made happiness to depend. We are to remember, also, that approval of another's acts is naturally expressed and can be appropriately expressed only by return of good, of happiness. There is, moreover, no conceivable way in which any action or line of conduct can be enforced on a free being, save through the governing appetences of his nature, which in man at least are comprehensive for good— save through his desire for good and his corresponding aversion to misery. The inevitable conclusion is that the sanction of moral law is the happiness or unhappiness declared by the lawgiver to wait on obedience or disobedience, as the expression of his approval or disapproval, and for the sake of enforcing compliance with his law.

The sanctions of moral law are the good attending on obedience and the evil waiting on disobedience. They are also called the *rewards* of moral action.

The sanctions of law enforce obedience through the hope of the good that follows right action and the fear of the evil that follows wrong action.

§ 57. The relation of the subject of duty to the sanctions of law is that of *merit* or *demerit*.

<small>Merit and demerit.</small>

MERIT, otherwise named *desert*, is that relation in which the obedient subject of duty stands to the good promised to obedience.

DEMERIT, otherwise named *ill-desert*, is that relation in which the disobedient subject stands to the evil threatened to disobedience.

<small>Praise and Blame.</small> PRAISE and BLAME are the expressions of the lawgiver through the sanctions of the law—the expressions of his approval of obedience and disapproval of disobedience.

Under the perfect administration of God merit and demerit are unalterably connected with praise and blame. The full expression of approval or disapproval may not be immediate; but conscience, the faithful oracle of God, expresses ever his approval or his displeasure, in some degree, thus declaring the merit or desert on the one hand or the demerit or ill-desert on the other hand, which attaches to every moral act.

The third function of conscience, as before stated, is but this recognition of merit and demerit—of the relation between obedience or disobedience and good or evil. A right moral action reveals to the eye of conscience this relation established in the very nature of man—the relation between right and good on the one hand and between wrong and evil on the other. Its voice in praising or condemning is the utterance of its creator through it, affirming ever the constancy of this relation.

CHAPTER XI.

AUTHORITY.

Authority defined.
§ 58. By AUTHORITY is properly meant the essential attribute of a lawgiver— that which makes him what he is.

It includes both the power and the right to make and enforce law.

It consequently gives all its peculiar character and force to law.

It is the immediate ground of obligation.

It is, moreover, that personal element in law which addresses its imperative to the conscience and lends to it its commanding power.

Its seat.
§ 59. The ultimate seat and source of authority is in the creator.

The power and right to create implies the power and right to determine the special end for which the creature is made and the faculties and endowments by which that end is to be attained.

The moral perfection of the creator involves a like perfection in the creature, to the extent of his endowments in so far as there is likeness in natural attributes; so that man, in so far as he is rational and free, must be made to be like his creator—sympathizingly and intelligently loving, beneficent, and righteous. Man was in fact thus made in the image of his creator; and hence in this creative will, determining the end for which he should be created and the endowments by which he should fulfil this end, is to be found the law of his being. The seat of law is in the bosom of God; in his sympathizing, intelligent, loving, beneficent, righteous, creative will.

There is nothing below or beyond this creative will of a self-existent creator. Only as we can conceive of a creator of the creator of all things, can we conceive of a law in the created universe back of the will of God. If, as language sometimes seems to imply, there be a standard by which the action of God can be judged, such a standard can only respect the relation which we think between love as source of all his action and good as end of all his action. This relation, lying in the action itself, which we can characterize only in respect of its continuousness, its directness, and parallelism with all other right actions, we can conceive to be right or wrong in these respects. But as a relation, it can not exist in either term of the relation, either in the law as source, or in the good as end, and is, therefore, in a sense independent of either, just as in the equation $2 \times 4 = 8$, the equality is not in either term—either 2×4 or 8—and is therefore in a sense independent of each taken separately. But as it would be absurd to conceive of an equality existing antecedent to all quantities, so it is equally absurd to conceive of a rectitude which is antecedent to all action. God is absolutely his own law. The outgoings of his own perfect nature, which is love towards the one end of all his activity, even the good of his creatures, are the precedent ground in fact of all rectitude, before which all attempted conception of a pre-existing rectitude is absurd and self-contradictory.

Twofold expression. § 60. The authority of God is expressed in a twofold way: first, in the nature of the beings that he creates and the condition in which he places them; secondly, in some expressed command.

The former expression of divine authority is called *natural law;* the latter, *positive law.*

1. Natural law. § 61. The NATURAL LAW is to be interpreted out of the nature and condition of the subject of law.

Man, as endowed with sense and reason, is qualified to read this law of his action. This is an essential function of his conscience. It were no more necessary to speak forth specific commands or rules for all the particular acts of his life than to tell him in audible voice every time that he opens his eye to the sunlight, "this light is from the sun."

The facility to read this natural law, as we should presume on every ground it would, grows with the readiness to obey it. "He that will do his will shall know of his doctrine." The reading of the law, the knowing of duty, is conditioned, to a great extent, as in reason it should be, as from the necessity of things it must be, on the will to do it.

It should be borne in mind that the whole fashioning of man's nature by his creator is for duty, and of course furthering to duty. The impelling power of conscience takes into itself to augment its own force this created tendency in the way of duty. This circumstance prompts and helps to the reading of the divine law as it is written in the nature of things. It puts upon the right way to discover and to interpret it. It aids in detecting mistakes and errors. A supposed duty which is hostile to sympathizing love or to good in its result, or to the established relations and harmonies of things, must at once be suspected as an erroneous reading of the divine will. The promptings of a loving nature point to the line of duty. The good resulting from an action raises a presumption that it was right—a presumption, indeed, too often allowed excessive weight, yet a valid presumption and worthy of trust when lawfully applied.

§ 62. The POSITIVE LAW of God consists in those special revelations of his will which on particular occasions he has made to men.

2. Positive Law.

That the creator would communicate, as occasion might require, with his rational creatures in a rational way, that is, by means of language, is a most natural presumption. It is a presumption which there is nothing in his known character or works or in their nature or condition to rebut. That there might be occasion in their experience for fresher, fuller, more articulate revelations of his will, than they could well intepret out of the ordinances of nature, is an equally lawful presumption. If morally perfect, their imperfection in knowledge might reasonably be supposed to furnish occasion for some fuller light from him, and their immaturity and consequent weakness in will might furnish like occasion for the encouragement and cheer which comes from expressed sympathy and reiterated expressions of his will. It is unreasonable to suppose that God would withhold all communion with his rational creatures continuing obedient to all his will, and especially unreasonable to suppose that he would withhold all reinforcements of his authority by fresh revelations of his will in the times of their weakness and ignorance. If morally imperfect, men might reasonably be supposed still more to need divine interposition to recover them to obedience, to reclaim them from their wanderings, and guide them back to duty.

With such presumption in favor of special revelations of the divine will, only ordinary evidence is necessary to convince us of the fact that he has made such revelations. Such evidence we have given us in the history of the race in a most ample measure. His actual interpositions to confirm and reinforce the law of nature, and to point out new lines of conduct which the changes in their history might require, have been authenticated as truly his by supernatural signs and works. While it may be safely admitted that the proof of such interpositions without some supposable design or end is impossible, on the other hand, if we can apprehend some worthy rational end or design in such interpositions, the proof of the fact is as simple, and easy, and valid as of any action within the province of man which we may happen to know he had designed or intended.

§ 63. The Bible is such a special revelation of the creator's will.

The Bible.

The Bible is supernatural, inasmuch as while it confirms and reinforces the revelations of the divine will in the ordinances of nature, it also, in addition to this, sets forth other commands which could not easily be interpreted out of nature by man in his mental and moral weakness, certainly not in their fulness and completeness and authoritative distinctness. These special supernatural revelations, indeed, are all in perfect harmony with all that appears in the constitution and on-goings of nature; but these last are only as the enwrapped germs to the expanded flowers and the matured fruit.

The Bible discloses an end and object to be accomplished by its revelations, that is altogether worthy of God, and that commends itself to human reason. Its revelations are attested by those marks and signs which should be expected to accompany divine interpositions that they may be identified as coming from him and be fully accredited. It is supported, moreover, by testimony which, when it is admitted that there was a worthy reason for divine interposition, should at once command belief that he has thus interposed.

The Bible contains all the special revelations of God to man that have been sufficiently accredited for man's acceptance.

The revelations of the divine will in the Bible are in the form of express positive precepts or commands, and also in the form of inspired examples.

There are manifold precepts given in the Bible, to individuals—as to Abraham, to Moses, to the prophets—and to communities, as especially to the Jewish people through Moses. The life of Christ, as the divine incarnate or embodied in the human, is an exemplification of the will of God in all the specific acts of his which are imitable by men. These imitable acts of condescending, self-denying, sympathizing, righteous beneficence, are so many expressions of the divine will, and thus are laws or commands of his, binding the consciences of men.

CHAPTER XII.

CASUISTRY.

§ 64. By CASUISTRY is to be understood the application of the principles of morality to particular instances of duty.

Casuistry defined.

The term *casuistry* has been extensively used in a bad sense, to denote a sophistical or perverted application of moral principles to action. But it has a good sense, and it is in this sense that the term is here employed.

It not frequently occurs that rules of duty seem to conflict. In a loose and popular way of speaking, we say duties conflict. But the line of duty, strictly speaking, is ever single and direct. No one is ever bound in duty in opposite or diverging directions at the same time. A weak conscience need never be disturbed by the thought that two conflicting calls of duty cannot be followed. Regulus could not listen to the calls of country and of family, and to the calls of his oath to the Carthaginians, at the same time. When the decision was fairly arrived at that the obligations of his oath were paramount, his conscience could not reasonably be disturbed because his country and his friends were given up, however much his natural affection may have been pained. The field of casuistry is as extended as the conflicts of authority, or of rule. The law of self preservation seems, sometimes, to be in collision with the calls of patriotism bidding the soldier to expose his life for his country. The command of a parent, or of a superior, sometimes comes into conflict with the laws of the land; or either may be opposed to the law of God. It is the province of casuistry to resolve such conflicting claims, and to determine in which direction the single duty leads. It fulfils its function by a comparison of the rules that seem to come into conflict, and a selection of the rule which is of paramount obligation in the particular case.

If it be borne in mind that the life of man on earth is ever meeting these conflicts of authority; that, too, a man's character depends greatly on the promptness and correctness with which he resolves them, as a weak spirit hesitates and falters from irresoluteness, while one of low morality mistakes or prefers the lower claim instead of the higher; that thus, a great part of the discipline of life consists in the treatment of these conflicting calls to duty; and, moreover, that there are principles which may greatly help to the settlement of those conflicts, and which must indeed be recognized and acted upon in any right settlement of them, it will be understood, how casuistry comes to claim a distinct recognition in a system of morality.

It will at once be perceived that it is the simple province of casuistry to resolve the doubts as to duty when different specific rules call to different lines of action.

§ 65. The leading principles of casuistry, which help to the solution of doubts in regard to duty arising from conflicts of authority or of rule, are the following:—

Its principles.

First, the subordinate authority should, all other things being equal, yield to the higher.

1. Prefer higher authority.

The rule of parental duty thus is paramount to that of neighborly duty; consequently, all other things being equal, the relief of the wants of one's own child is binding in duty in preference to such relief of the wants of a neighbor. The claims of the bodily nature again are to be subordinated to those of the spiritual nature.

Secondly, the higher the source of authority, other things being equal, the more obligatory the claim.

2. Higher source.

The will of an elder brother, thus, is to be subordinated to that of a parent; of the parent to the law of the state; the law of the state to the law of God.

Thirdly, a clear and definite rule of obligation is to be preferred before one that is obscure and doubtful.

3. Clear rule.

Fourthly, the rule which favors law is safer to follow than that which favors freedom, a restrictive than a permissive rule.

4. Law rather than freedom.

If, for instance, the doubt in conscience arises whether a certain amusement should be forborne because of evil influence on others, or be allowed on the ground of personal freedom and independence, it is safer for conscience to follow the prohibitory principle, because, by reason of the general bias of our nature towards indulgence, we are most likely to err in this direction.

Fifthly, that line of conduct which improves character and strengthens virtuous principle, should be taken in preference to that which degrades or enervates.

<small>5. Favor character.</small>

Sixthly, the more beneficent act or course is to be preferred.

<small>6. Prefer the more beneficent.</small>

Seventhly, the line of conduct which is direct to the end of all virtue or goodness or beneficence, is to be preferred to that which is indirect or circuitous; that which is parallel with the general current of rectitude to that which crosses or is counter to it.

<small>7. The direct to the indirect.</small>

It should be observed that these very principles of casuistry will often come into collision as applied to a given case of doubt. It becomes necessary then to weigh their respective claims and determine which has the preponderance.

BOOK II.

PRACTICAL MORALITY—DUTIES AND RIGHTS.

INTRODUCTION.

§ 66. Having, in the preceding book, explained the nature of duty, we proceed in this second book to enumerate the particular acts of men which come under the law of duty. As has been intimated, § 19, we shall classify them in reference to the respective objects of human duty. This classification gives us at once the three general divisions of :

Classification.

I. Duties to self ;
II. Duties to fellow men ; and
III. Duties to God.

§ 67. Before entering upon the study of this second part of our treatise, it will be of use to recall the several steps we have taken in unfolding the nature of duty.

Recapitulation.

INTRODUCTION.

Ethics defined. We defined Ethics or Moral Science to be *the Science of Human Duty*.

Duty exemplified. The nature of duty was exemplified in the fulfilment by Regulus of his promise to return to Carthage. An analysis of this act as a duty gave us at once three elements of all duty: First, subject of duty; secondly, object of duty; thirdly, act of duty.

Subject of duty. A subject of duty, or a moral person, must be a being essentially active, having the three endowments of sensibility, intelligence, and free-will.

Conscience. Conscience includes the first two of these three elements—sensibility and intelligence. It has a threefold function: first, to recognize and feel duty; secondly, to impel or oblige to the performance of duty; thirdly, to praise or blame. In conscience, moreover, is seated the peculiar feeling of pleasure or pain consequent on the performance or the violation of duty.

Object of duty. The object of duty is the person to whom duty is owing and is ever a person—that is, a being, having sensibility, intelligence, and free-will.

Rights. Rights are the correlative of duties. Rights belong to the object of duty; duties, to the subject of duty. The Carthaginians had a right to what was due to them from Regulus.

Good in duty. The essential quality of a duty or a right, in the experience of the object of duty, is good — happiness or blessedness. A moral action, as the performance of duty, includes three necessary elements: love in the subject of duty; good in the object of duty; and rectitude in the act or doing of duty. In other words, all moral action must be loving, good or beneficent, and right. It cannot be loving without aiming at good in the object of duty, or without proceeding directly towards this result. It cannot be good, except as it proceeds from love and moves in rectitude. It cannot be right, without being also loving and beneficent.

<small>Moral action.</small>

Love consists in a sympathetic endeavor directly for the good of the object of duty.

<small>Love.</small>

The opposite of love is hate.

Good as the end in all duty is of two kinds: 1. Good in itself, or happiness, which is the gift of the Creator; 2. Good as means of happiness. This secondary good is either the good of condition, as wealth, friends, health, etc., or the good of character.

<small>Good.</small>

The opposite of good is evil.

Rectitude respects the procedure in a moral action, as love regards its source, and good its end or result. It accordingly respects the relation in an action between its source and its end. This relation is that of an unswerving procedure from love, its source, to good, its end. This procedure must be parallel with all right moral action.

<small>Right.</small>

The opposite of right is wrong.

Motives. All right moral action proceeds from a motive which is defined to be the apprehended end or result at which the action aims. This end must always be some good.

Motives are of two classes: 1. Those which have their ends in character; 2. Those which have their ends in condition.

Moral obligation. By moral obligation is meant that attribute of duty by which it holds and draws to its fulfilment. It is inherent in all duty; it is inexorable in its demand; it impels to the performance of duty, but may be resisted by the free-will.

Its ground. The ground of obligation is ultimately in the nature of man and his relations to other beings and things.

Law. Law is a rule of action. Moral law is the law of duty. It implies a law-giver; it is the expression of his will. It gives to the sense of obligation the character of responsibility. It enforces itself upon the subject of duty by its sanctions, which are the good attending on obedience to law and the evil waiting on disobedience.

Authority. Authority is the essential attribute of a law-giver. It includes both the right and the power to make and enforce law. It is the immediate ground of obligation. Its ultimate seat and source is in the Creator.

Casuistry. Casuistry is that department of moral science which applies the principles of morality to particular instances of duty.

DIVISION I.

DUTIES TO SELF.

CHAPTER I.

NATURE AND CLASSES.

Personal duty. § 68. The first named of the three great classes of human duties is that of *duties to one's self,* or, as they have been termed, *personal duties.*

Explained. In this class of duties, the object of the duty is self—the duty is owing to one's self. The propriety of such language, importing that I am under obligation to myself, will be recognized at once if we consider that some of our free actions terminate on ourselves. A large share, indeed, of our active life has immediate respect to ourselves, not to our fellow beings, nor to God. Our nature is complex, constituted of manifold elements, to any one of which, separately from the others, we may direct our care and our endeavors. The act of duty finds its end in such case in that part or element of our nature. Care is due thus to our body that it be kept in health, and to the mind that it be instructed and exercised. The aggregate of these acts of duty, terminating in specific parts of our being or condition, makes up the sum of personal duty.

§ 69. The ground of obligation in the case of personal duty is found in this complex nature of man capable of receiving care and effort in its several parts or elements and of his free active nature capable of expending this care and effort.

<small>Ground of obligation.</small>

While the ultimate ground may be traced to the Creator's will in forming man with this two-fold receptive and active nature, or still more remotely to the character of the Creator himself as the ever loving worker of good in the line of perfect rectitude, the more immediate ground of obligation must be laid in this nature of man himself as constituted by his maker.

§ 70. This department of moral activity has been denominated *self-love*. The field of self-love is thus the same as that of personal duty, the exercise of proper self-love being nothing else than performance of personal duty or of duty to one's self.

<small>Self-love.</small>

Self-love should be carefully distinguished from selfishness. Self-love is a proper regard to self, to one's own condition and character; selfishness is an inordinate regard to self. Selfishness is thus an abuse of the principle of self-love.

<small>Selfishness.</small>

This principle of self-love is as necessary to the best interests of the universe and as fundamental in the nature of man as the principle of love to other beings. There is in every one, on the one hand, a strong instinct to the exercise of this self-love, and on the other, an urgent demand for it. It is, accordingly, a law of man's being, ordained by his maker in constituting him what he is. In the form of self-preservation, this principle of self-love is one of the highest and most sacred principles by which we are governed. As a creature of God, and as subject to wants and having rights, a man is at least as worthy to receive the offices of a kind and watchful care from himself as from his fellow men.

Self-love defined. SELF-LOVE may be defined to be sympathizing beneficence to one's self.

Like love generally, it is sympathizing. In self-love the soul considers one's personal needs and demands; it suffers itself to be duly impressed by those needs; it cherishes these impressions; and finally it yields itself to be moved by them.

The action to which in self-love the soul is prompted is beneficence—doing good to one's self, as one's needs require or his nature admits. The good, which self-love seeks, is various, according to the variety of a man's needs; it varies in degree and in quality. It is, however, always a secondary good; not happiness itself, but the condition and means of happiness. A proper self-love can only seek to secure for one's self that character and that condition on which the Creator has made happiness to depend, and with which he has indissolubly connected it.

As love generally, so self-love must ever be in

rectitude; it must move directly to its object—good in one's self, and in a line parallel with all perfect moral action. Self-love is right in so far as its movement is thus direct to its lawful end and just in degree, entrenching on no other duty.

§ 71. All personal duty is thus under the threefold law of morality: 1. It must proceed from a sympathizing and kindly impulse — from true love to one's self; 2. It must seek this single end, the truest and highest good of one's self; and 3. It must move unswervingly towards this end and thus infringe on no other line of duty or of right. It must be loving, beneficent, right.

<small>Its threefold law.</small>

§ 72. Self-love is of a twofold nature, according as its immediate end is condition or character. The several classes of personal duties may be conveniently considered under this twofold division:

<small>Classes of personal duty.</small>

I. Personal duties in respect to condition.
II. Personal duties in respect to character.

The first class embraces the two divisions of duties pertaining to the body and duties pertaining to outward possessions.

CHAPTER II.

PERSONAL DUTIES IN RESPECT TO THE BODY.

§ 73. The moral relationship of the body
<small>Ground of duty.</small> to the rational spirit, which so far determines the duties to the body, lies in the fact that the body is the medium between the soul and all outer things.

The body is the condition both of all outgoing activity of the spirit and also of all receptive capacity of impression or influence from without. Even in the most private personal thought, the brain is moved; it may be that the nerves also quiver; and sometimes, as in remorse or in sense of wrong, the heart beats and the blood rushes with strong vehemence. The soul is bound to the body in fastest bonds of dependence. In this is seen the force of the great Latin satirist's maxim: Pray for a sound mind in a sound body—*Orandum est ut sit mens sana in corpore sano.* The guardianship of the body is, to a large degree, entrusted to the mind. Duty to itself requires that, to the full extent of the guardianship thus entrusted to it by its Creator, the mind secure this soundness of body.

It is a well established fact that instinct decreases as intelligence rises. Life in the lowest order of animals goes on through the force of mere natural laws without the need of the guidance and help of intelligence. In the higher order, there is required intelligent selection of food and of shelter. In man, while mere natural constitution does much, reason is required to direct, control, and supplement the merely automatic functions of the body. In childhood and youth, more may be left to instinct and impulse; in advancing age, the appetites and the instinctive tendencies need more the supervision and direction and active control of the reason and intelligence.

The degree of care and thoughtfulness due to the body is measured by its relation to the soul as being simply subservient. The function of the body is, as stated, that of medium and condition; the soul lives in it and through it, but not for it. On the contrary, the body is for the soul. Hence the rule, that the body receive such care only as best to fit it for the soul's uses. To guard and nourish the body for its own sake, in order to perfect it as a mere animal organism, is as truly wrong as to be indifferent to its wants. As an animal organism it has no rights (§ 16); to treat it as having rights is contrary to morality. For the greater good of the soul it may even for the time be thrust out from consideration; it may be left to exposure; it may be allowed to suffer; even its dissolution may be welcomed rather than the soul itself perish.

§ 74. The duties which the soul thus owes to

<small>Threefold duty to the body.</small> the body are those of *guarding* it, *nourishing* it, and *ruling* it.

<small>1. To guard it.</small> I. It is the duty of every one to guard his own body from all harm.

<small>Suicide.</small> This law of duty prohibits *suicide*. Certainly never until it can be shown beyond all reasonable doubt that the death of the body is necessary to the higher interest of the spirit, can suicide be thought of as justifiable. But this, it is safe here to hold, can never be done. Man is too ignorant of the condition of a disembodied spirit to assume that death by one's own hands can be for the spirit's good. The presumption is all against it. No pressure of outward evils can warrant the destruction of the body; for the rational relief from such evils is through the virtues of fortitude and of trust in the wise and beneficent ordering of all events. No evils of spirit, as remorse or vicious habit, can warrant it; for the proper relief here is in repentance and trust in the forgiving and gracious ordering of all human interests.

<small>Mutilation.</small> The law also prohibits all *maiming* and *mutilation* of the body, by which it shall suffer in its own integrity or in its fitness as the outer organ of the soul. The amputation of an injured or diseased limb is justified when needful to save the whole body. That maiming for any moral interest can ever be necessary, is not susceptible of proof; and all presumption is against it.

The law prohibits such ascetic practices as are

Asceticism. hurtful to the body, whether of positive infliction of pain or of abstinence from needful food or protection, except under the limitations stated. The improvement of the bodily or the spiritual condition must be made to appear before there can be ground and warrant for such violations of the natural laws of physical health and soundness. Fasting or other "mortifications of the body" can be justified only as remedial of other ills of body or soul.

Positive care. This law of duty, further, requires a positive care for the body by a sympathetic attention to its exposures; by vigilance in discerning and timely effort in avoiding dangers that may threaten it; by vigorous resistance to violence that assails it. Needless exposure to cold or heat or wet, to contagious disease, to danger of any kind, is a sin, as real if not as flagrant as suicide, or falsehood, or theft. Excessive strains on the bodily powers in violent or prolonged labor, when no higher law of duty prescribes, are equally wrong, whether for curiosity, in idle competition or strife, or for heedless sport. Prohibiting indifference, negligence, and recklessness, the law enjoins a reasonable care and prudence in regard to all bodily needs.

Shelter and dress. More specifically, the law requires such provision of shelter and dress as shall secure the highest degree of bodily comfort and well-being compatible with higher interests. The provision for these wants must of course be measured by one's resources, and be shaped by his surroundings in life. Moreover, it must be made in a certain subordination to the demands of the aesthetic and moral nature. But both in respect to the dwelling and also in respect to dress, the highest moral refinement and the truest taste may be regarded while the physical wants are best consulted.

§ 75. II. It is the duty of every one to *nourish* his body.

2. To nourish it.

This is more positive in its character than the preceding rule. The particular acts which it enjoins include to some extent those that have been specified, as the duty of nourishing involves that of guarding.

Food.

This rule requires, in the first place, that every one provide and use such *food* as the body needs, in kind and in quantity. The grand dietetic rule is: choose what is healthful, not what is palatable. The natural appetite is a trustworthy guide to a certain extent; it resents too close watching. Its suggestions are worthy of heed; but they must ever be kept subject to reason. It is often vitiated, often morbid; and even when sound it is insufficient of itself and is liable to mislead. It is subject to change; artificial appetites are common among all peoples. As the general rule, the most healthful diet will, in time, prove to be the most palatable. On the other hand, one of the soundest maxims for the promotion of health is: forbear all unnecessary anxiety in selecting, taking, and digesting food. The function of digestion, like those of respiration and circulation, is best left to itself; nature takes the care of that into her own hands and resents all needless interference.

The general hygienic rules of food require, 1, in respect to quality or kind, the provision of such as will furnish all the elements that enter into the constitution of the body to form its bones, its muscles, its brains and nerves, and supply its motive force; 2, in respect to quantity, so much as will satisfy the cravings of a sound appetite; 3, in respect to time, that it be taken at regular intervals and at leisure; and 4, in respect to place and condition, that it be in retirement, in relaxation from care and thought, in society and with entertaining conversation.

Exercise. § 76. This rule requires, in the second place, a certain amount of well-regulated *exercise* for the healthy maintenance and development of the body. The vitality and restlessness of childhood are nature's provisions for that activity which is necessary at that period of life for the sound and vigorous condition of bodily organs. As intelligence advances, this duty of securing needful physical exercise is left more and more to the control of the reason, till old age comes on with its infirmities and its indisposition to bodily movement, when healthy activity of body is left to be sustained almost wholly by the spirit's activity. The involuntary functions, indeed, such as those of respiration and circulation continue; and there is, besides, the strong force of fixed habit which, if right and sound, will go far in maintaining soundness and vigor of body. Still the bodily organism, which in childhood was redundant with life and vigor and had no need of spur or goad, but rather of check and bridle, becomes in age inert and indisposed to effort and needs nursing and animation from the spirit which inhabits it. The case is now reversed in the relations of body and spirit; in childhood the instinctive activity of the bodily organism kept the spirit awake and earnest; in old age the great source of activity and life to the body is in the spirit itself.

The relation of muscular exercise to health consists in this: that sound health depends on the constancy and amount of the change effected in the body by the processes of waste and repair; and it is the action of the muscles in alternate contraction and relaxation, which acting immediately on the circulating organs, starts and sustains these processes, supplying thus the force which carries forward the whole machinery of life. By this muscular action the blood is propelled in more rapid currents, forcing more rapid changes in all the minute cells to which it is carried, and thus stimulating the digestive, the respiratory, excretive, and formative functions of the living body. It is a force called in by the will, supplementing the proper instinctive movements of the bodily system. Most evidently the body was not designed to be left to its own instincts so as to take exclusive care of itself; it is dependent on the care of the rational spirit. This care, being voluntary, comes under the control of morality which prescribes the duty, on the part of the rational spirit, to render this ministry freely and faithfully. Exercise is thus brought under rational control.

It should be intelligently adapted to the wants and conditions of the body in respect of time and of degree. It should be systematic and habitual, while at the same time it should be held to be simply subservient to the higher interests of the spirit in so far as these interests are involved in the sound condition of the body.

§ 77. Together with food and exercise, this general duty of nourishing the body involves a due provision for *rest*. There is a tidal character to the bodily life; it has its ebbs and flows. While it demands exercise, it demands also responsive rest. Nature has thus ordained sleep, in which voluntary action and communication with things without are suspended. The needful amount of sleep to the soundest health varies with individual natures and conditions. To determine this amount for one's self is the task assigned to his rational nature. There may be such a thing here as excess or there may be deficiency. The rule of duty requires that it be intelligently determined in amount; that it be regular; and that it be brought under the control of the laws of sound habit.

There are other modes of rest needful for the best condition of the body. They are, for the most part at least, for wakeful life, comprehended under the general denomination of *recreation*. If by this term in its most generic application only change of employment be understood, it must be borne in mind that for the most part the labor to be interchanged with rest is imposed by some law or principle, or necessity from without, and that the most effective and most salutary change must be a change from such activity to activity that is free and spontaneous. The highest and best recreation, simply as recreation, is thus proper play. And as competitive play calls forth the highest and freest exertion, games of skill or agility furnish the best kind of recreation, particularly for youth who are yet comparatively strangers to the satisfaction that comes, through habit or through interest awakened by experience, from chosen employments. With the well-trained man of mature age, simple change of pursuit wisely directed, may constitute the best recreation. But the need of this rest by means of recreation or change of activity, in order to the soundest physical condition, remains the unquestioned fact; and the law of duty requires that it be wisely and of set purpose provided in character and amount to meet those wants of the body.

§ 78. III. It is the duty of every one to *rule* his own body.

<small>3. To rule it.</small>

The union in one being of two such opposites as body and spirit makes it necessary that one or the other should have the mastery. There cannot be two masters here. A divided sovereignty is the worst of anarchies. The higher nature of the spirit determines that it should wield the scepter. The wretchedness of a bondage to bodily appetite evinces that the body was never designed by its Creator to rule the spirit. Its function and station is that of organ and minister. It is the duty of the spirit to maintain this relation and keep the body ever in subjection. It is practicable to meet the legitimate demands of the body in accordance with the true interests of the spirit. The apostolic injunction to eat and drink to the glory of the Creator presupposes this practicability of gratifying the wants of the body in subserviency to the higher interests of morality and religion which concern the spirit only. The body is adapted in perfect wisdom to be the organ of the spirit and its best condition is that in which it can serve the spirit best as such organ.

§ 79 The particulars of this rule by the spirit over the body are the following :—

1. By resisting its inertia.

1. It is the part of the spirit to resist the bodily tendency to inertness—to ease, inaction, sloth.

This is the perpetual bent of the body as material, which requires perpetual watchfulness and resistance.

§ 80. 2. It is the part of the spirit to direct and regulate the appetites of the body.

2. By regulating its appetites.

Being planted in our natures, they have a lawful position and existence there. They are not to be extirpated ; they are to be trained and regulated in respect to the degree and manner in which they are to be indulged. They easily become inordinate in their cravings, and through unbridled allowance come to be beyond easy control. They are to be indulged also, in entire subordination to the interests of the spirit. Hunger, however intense, may not satiate itself on anything and everything on which it can seize. It must respect the rights of others, as well as the decencies and proprieties of personal life. They need to be kept in subjection to the respective end and design which they were created to subserve. The very indulgence of them should be not only intelligent, decent, and rightful; it should in addition be made habitually serviceable to the interests of the spirit.

§ 81. 3. The body should be trained to habits of direct ministry to the spirit.

3. By training it to right habits.

The senses, the limbs, the body generally should be used and controlled for this service. In manifold ways and applications may this ministry of the body to the spirit be enforced. The questions that press in common upon all men: "What shall we eat, what shall we drink, and wherewithal shall we be clothed," are not to be held as paramount, but as subordinate to those higher questions which pertain to the nourishment, and protection, and gratification of the spirit.

§ 82. 4. The spirit should, in a certain sense, live above bodily infirmities and distresses.

4. By being superior to its infirmities.

There is such a thing as tranquillity and joy even in sickness and anguish of body. These conditions may be made to work for the spirit's good; even in them, therefore, the spirit may rejoice. Not infrequently Christian submission and Christian hope lift the soul to higher peace and enjoyment by means of bodily weakness and pain. In such cases we recognize the true relation of the soul as one of mastery and supremacy to the body.

CHAPTER III.

PERSONAL DUTIES IN RESPECT TO EXTERNAL CONDITION.

Nature and kinds.
§ 83. Every man exists in a moral relationship to other things around him. He is a part of a great whole, and must recognize himself as such in determining his duties. From this relationship, looking only on his side of the relation, there are seen to spring obligations which may properly be ranked as personal; while, at the same time, in perfect harmony with these and in part exactly corresponding to them, there are seen, as we look on the things around him, to arise on their part claims on his care and effort, which take the proper character of social duties.

Simply because man exists as one member of this relation, from a regard to his own being and destiny, and irrespectively of all claim of other objects on him, there are duties of this personal class :—duties owing to himself, arising out of his own nature as formed in relationship to other things around him.

These personal duties which respect the external

condition may be classed under those which respect external nature; property; station; and friends.

§ 84. PERSONAL DUTIES IN RESPECT TO NATURE.

Man is a part of a system of things with which, for his own good, he is bound to keep himself in sympathetic and harmonious relation. This system embraces objects existing in space and events occurring in time. Amid these objects and these events his life is cast. He must come in contact with them every moment. He is dependent on them as well as able to influence them. As all are ordered and disposed by the same loving intelligence, his course among them may, if he order it aright, be peaceable, prosperous, happy; whereas if he misdirect his course or his individual actions, collision, difficulty, evil of manifold forms, must certainly arise.

The particular personal duties springing out of this relation are the following:

1. Duty of Sympathy with things and events.

1. It is every man's duty to recognize himself as placed in this relation to the objects around him and the course of events, as a part; to be and to act in them and with them in perfect harmony, in cordial sympathy, and in reciprocal inter-dependence. The fundamental maxim of reason here is: maintain yourself ever in kindly sympathy with the order of nature and of providence.

2. Of recognizing their beneficent mission.

2. It is every man's duty to view and treat the order of nature and of providence, as wisely designed to be in

perpetual ministry of good to him. The evils that come along to be borne in this system of things are in consequence of a thwarting of this design directly or indirectly by himself or by others; and what there are may be turned to profit, if not otherwise, at least through the better furtherance of higher spiritual interests. In the ordering of affairs the wise and beneficent power that created, ever holds the sceptre, and is ever out of seeming evil educing a higher good. It is man's own fault if all things do not work together for his good.

3. *Of furthering their end or design.* 3. It is every man's duty to uphold, so far as he may, and to improve and perfect the disposition and condition of things in nature and the general course of events. This disposition of things and course of events have a good end and design. Every thing exists or occurs for some good. Every plant that grows has a nature and an end of its own. It is every man's duty, not to destroy, not to waste, not to prevent, but rather, as in the case of his body, to nourish and protect. Crystalline symmetry, vegetable beauty, animal grace, are to be admired, enjoyed, improved, not maimed or marred.

4. *Of profiting by their ministry.* 4. It is every man's duty to make the order of things and events subservient to his own highest uses, and not be servilely ruled by it. He may not be able in manifold respects to change or break up this order; but he can direct and control its influence upon himself so as that he shall, after all and in the whole, be the master and not the slave.

§ 85. Personal Duties in respect to Property.

Ground of right to property.

While there are some things existing about us which cannot be appropriated, as for the most part air and light, there are others which may be held as property—as one's own, and not another's. Corresponding to this is the instinct, the desire of property, founded in man's nature. This is the ultimate ground for the rights and duties in regard to property—the constitution of things in which on the one hand are objects to be appropriated or held as one's own, and on the other hand the instinct to possess such objects. This is the foundation for the general right of property only, however, and is not the foundation for the right to hold any specific object or property. That I have a right to hold property is proved from the nature of things around me and of my own person; that I have a right to hold this house or this book, or any specific property, depends on something besides this general, absolute right of property founded in my nature.

§ 86.
Uses of property.

The institution of property is one of the wisest beneficence. This proposition remains true although it should be conceded that the history of property, of the working of the greed for gain in self-torture and degradation, and in wrongs and distresses to others, in frauds and thefts and robberies, and quarrels, and wars, makes up a great part of the history of evil among men. These evils are but the abuses of the native instinct for property in man. The great evil in the abuse proves the great good lying in the right use. The beneficent working of this institution of property is seen in the immediate effect on the individual, keeping him awake and vigilant, careful and prudent, earnest and enterprising, frugal and industrious, keeping him thus from vicious sloth and recklessness; and on the general welfare in increasing the supply of necessaries and of comforts for the good of the race, as well as of those things which minister to the elevation and refinement of mankind. In the expressive language of Chancellor Kent: "The sense of property is graciously bestowed upon mankind for the purpose of raising them from sloth and stimulating them to action. It leads to the cultivation of the earth, the institution of government, the establishment of justice, the acquisition of the comforts of life, the growth of the useful arts, the spirit of commerce, the productions of taste, the exertions of charity, and the display of the benevolent affections."

§ 87. The right to property in any specific thing is ever only relative. My right to my house may be perfect as against my neighbor; but my ownership is not absolute, for the state may rightfully take it from me on occasions of its necessity. The house, which is mine to the fullest extent as against all other individuals, may be destroyed to stop a general conflagration without any consent on my part; it may be removed if standing in the way of a great public improvement; it may be appropriated for the government's uses in pestilence or in war. So if I

The right to property relative.

have found money in the highway, it is mine as against any other person, except the owner or his representative, or the public officer; no other one has a right to take it from me or to interfere with my treatment of it, except in the simple interest of the loser or of the public. Farther than this, all rights of property in man are but the rights of stewards, holding all subject to the higher and all embracing ownership of God. The right of property thus is ever relative, not absolute.

§ 88. There are three relations of right and duty in which man stands to property:—of acquisition, holding, and disposal. *Threefold relationship.* Man brought nothing into the world; he carries nothing out. He must acquire whatever he comes to hold; he holds only for a time; he must sooner or later dispose of all he ever holds.

§ 89. Property is acquired in the several ways of: 1. *Appropriation* of what is common or unappropriated, as of new-discovered land; 2. *Labor*, as by imparting new value to material or extracting new values from the earth by mining or by culture; 3. *Exchange* of one commodity for another; 4. *Gift*, or inheritance from others. *Modes of acquisition.*

§ 90. The personal duties in respect to property are the following: *1. Duty of acquiring property.*

1. It is man's duty to acquire property. The law of instinct as to property he should obey for his own good—for the cultivation of all those manifold and most important virtues which are fostered in the right acquisition and use of

property and the avoidance of all those vices which spring from a disregard of this instinct. He should obey this law of his nature for the good of others, that he may be more capable of ministering to their welfare. This is the general rule of duty, that he seek to increase the general stock of goods that may be held as property by men, avoiding all unnecessary waste and destruction of property.

2. Of holding it in subordination. 2. It is man's duty to acquire, hold, and use property only in strict subordination to higher principles.

Property, wealth, is to be considered and treated only as a means, not as an end. Not for itself, but for what it may occasion or effect, is it to be sought or held. It is to be acquired and held, moreover, in conformity with principles of equity, and in deference to the higher claims to it of the state and of God. It is to be sought and managed so as to promote the virtues in character with which it is so clearly associated, such as those of wakefulness, enterprise, industry, prudence, economy, beneficence. It is to be pursued in moderation, subject ever to the duties of personal health and capacity, to other interests of the body and spirit, as well as to the interests and rights of others. It is to be disposed of wisely and usefully, as a most important trust, so as on the one hand to nurture the spirit of self-denial and of beneficence, and on the other hand, particularly in the final parting with it, so as to save from waste and misappropriation.

§ 91. Personal Duties in respect to Station.

Under the comprehensive term *station*, is here included all that in a man's condition which gives him power and influence over others. It includes the distinctions of family, of personal worth and ability, of social position, and of civil rank and office.

Distinctions in respect to station.

There is in human nature this instinct of ambition—of desire of power and influence over others, and men are so constituted as to be susceptible to this influence. The very notion of a social nature in beings, like men, involves this relation of influence and dependence. The proper culture and regulation of this instinct is thus imposed on man by his very nature and his relations to his fellow men.

Desire of power instinctive.

The desire of power, like the desire of wealth, is an instinct of man's nature, giving rise thus to a peculiar species of personal duty. It differs widely from that desire in respect to the character of its object: the desire of property fastens on things that have no rights; the desire of power is directed towards men endowed with rights. We do not hold men as we hold property. We can manage property with no regard to any claim inherent in itself to be respected; we can manage men rightfully, only as free beings, only as having rights equally with ourselves. We may lawfully desire the power to influence their condition, to mould their opinions, to draw their affections, to determine their actions; but only in the way in which free, intelligent, and loving beings are to be influenced and in accordance with all the principles of social duty. Emphatically no true or lawful ambition can ever seek power over others by lowering or crippling them in any way. In its lawful workings, ambition can only aim at the advancement and elevation of the condition of others.

The evils rightly attributable to wrong or false ambition, are to be paralleled in extent and severity with those that have flowed from the evil thirst for gain. Such evils are to be regarded as the results of the abuse of this principle. On the other hand, the blessings to mankind, which are traceable to this instinct, may well be set over against the evils from its abuse. The elevation of the individual, the advancement of society, the promotion of all industrial and elegant arts, the extension of science and learning, the furtherance of freedom, the accumulation of the blessings generally which make up our idea of a true civilization, could hardly be conceived of as attainable, except through the labor and sufferings of men actuated by a worthy ambition.

To be without any aspiration for the esteem, the confidence, the gratitude, the respect of others, on which a lawful ambition must ever rely as the condition of its proper power to bless them, and, moreover, to be without any aspiration to be able to influence favorably their welfare, is to be without one of the noblest endowments of man. His own perfection, irrespectively of the effects on others, demands the recognition and the careful culture of this instinctive desire of power. It is to be cultivated, however, only in moderation, that is, in due subordination to other principles of our own nature and to the rights and needs of others. It is to be exercised, moreover, as well as cultivated, in strict regard to all those principles which regulate our actions towards our fellow men.

§ 92. Personal Duties in respect to Friendship.

Friendship.

In conjunction with the desires for property and for power, we find in man's nature the desire for friendship. This instinct finds its fitting objects in society.

We discover at once a line of personal duty leading from this natural relationship. Its significance to human life is well likened by Cicero to that of the sun to the external world.

Its specific duties.

Like property and power, friends are to be acquired, and held, and treated, under certain clear and familiar moral principles. The particulars of personal duty here may be thus summarily enounced:

1. The spirit of friendship is to be considerately nourished and developed.

2. The acquisition of friends is to be effected by a right regard to the conditions of friendship. Friendship is a reciprocity; it cannot exist except as what is required shall be freely given, of confidence, esteem, forbearance, good-will. We win friends only by being friendly: we gain the confidence and esteem of others by trusting and esteeming them. The selection is to be governed

by considerations of fitness, congeniality, moral worthiness, and helpfulness.

3. The maintenance of friendship is to be sought through the faithful discharge of the friendly offices, not with self-seeking, but in disinterested affection. True love, here as everywhere, is so far a setting aside of self as object. Charitable constructions of fault, and forbearance towards imperfections, are eminent duties in the maintenance of friendship.

4. The particular rights and duties of friendship are to be determined in intelligent consideration of the general principles of morality. Friendly feeling and acting are to be held in due moderation. They should never be allowed to transgress the fundamental laws of truth and justice, of patriotism and piety.

CHAPTER IV.

PERSONAL DUTIES IN RESPECT TO CHARACTER.

Character defined.
§ 93. By CHARACTER, as the term is applied to a moral being, is meant a form of spirit, and by a perfect character is meant a perfect form of spirit.

The moral relation of a man to his character lies in the fact that as a free being he is charged with the shaping of his own character under the conditions in which he is placed. He has a certain instinct of character—an innate desire to be perfect. This instinct, unrepressed and unperverted, prompts towards an ideal of excellence both in regard to character generally, and also in respect to particular actions, the aggregate of which constitutes character. It is thus a law of man's nature that he prefers perfection in everything that he does or is. His sense of freedom causes him to feel that the formation of his own character is, under certain conditions, in his own hands. He feels, consequently, that he is responsible for what he is and may become, so far as his moral nature is concerned. He is free to choose his ideal of character ; he is free to bring his actions under this ideal ; he is free to observe the conditions by which his particular activity may go to nourish up and shape a perfect character.

Personal duties in respect to character fill out a great part of the whole field of personal duty. The duties of condition are, in fact, subordinate and subservient to the duties of character. And all relative duty is harmonious with duty here, and also, in fact, subservient. Every right act goes to form a perfect character ; as every wrong act mars or enfeebles it. The consciousness of perfect character, in connection with the divine favor, which is indeed the life of such a consciousness, is the condition of the highest possible blessedness.

Character implies ;

§ 94. There are several things involved in the formation of character which may advantageously be separately presented. First, the formation of character implies

1. An ideal. an ideal—a model—to which the spirit is to be developed and shaped.

Secondly, it implies also a well-directed

2. Endeavor. and persistent endeavor to mould the spirit into this ideal.

Thirdly, it presupposes the principle of

3. Habit. habit as the condition of spiritual growth and shaping, and involves compliance with the laws of habit.

The nature of habit and its necessary laws may be exhibited very summarily thus The most essential attribute of the human spirit is activity. We accordingly most perfectly represent it to ourselves under the ideas of motion. The activity of the spirit moves toward an end; and of this motion, as of all motion, the two comprehensive views are those which respect its direction or tendency and its momentum or intensity. We seek, accordingly, as the first things in a perfect character, first, a right tendency or disposition, meaning by this a right direction in the general activity of the spirit; and secondly, the putting forth the full energy of the spirit in this activity.

The two great principles of habit are, accordingly, first, that the spirit moves in the direction and with the energy given it by any and every impulse on its activity; and secondly, that it holds on in this given direction and with this imparted energy till impressed by a new force.

4. Providential aid.
Fourthly, it presupposes such a wise ordering of things and of events in the world around it as to further the formation of a perfect character.

This outer world presents the chief objects and occasions which call forth the activity of the spirit. On a priori grounds we must suppose that the infinite wisdom and goodness of the Creator and Ruler of the world would frame and govern it so as to work harmoniously and helpfully in respect to the spirit's growth and perfection. Actual scrutiny reveals to us the truth that the influences from without ourselves either are positive helps or they are hindrances which, with the divine help, may be overcome, and so, through the very struggle which they occasion, be made helpful. The actual experience of men demonstrates the practicability of perfecting character in the gracious conditions which are thus furnished to them.

§ 95. The general maxims by which we are to be governed in the formation of character may be derived from this summary view of what it implies:

Maxims of character.

First, keep ever before the forming spirit the highest and most perfect ideal of character.

1. Ideal.

This ideal is to be formed by contemplation of examples or models of excellence; by study of the divine will as revealed in his acts and ways, but especially in his word; and by reflection on our own capabilities. This ideal, it is to be borne in mind, will in the progress of experience be ever rising, enlarging, perfecting itself. To it as it is formed, are to be conformed all the free movements of the spirit, so that its whole activity shall be shaping it into the proposed ideal.

It is the proper function of the imagination to shape this ideal, and also to keep it before the spirit. Its province here will be more fully presented under the culture of that faculty.

Secondly, yield freely to every right impulse from within or from without, and vigorously resist and overpower every impulse in a wrong direction.

2. Impulse.

The nature of habit instructs us that every impression on the mind and heart, as well as every exertion we put forth in thought, or in feeling, or in purpose, sets the spirit further on its way, or turns it back or aside. Not an impression, not a thought or feeling, is without its effect on the spirit's condition and character. A wrong influence, an evil yielding, may be afterwards thrown off or repented of; but the spirit remains different from what it would have been had the resistance been effectual at the beginning. All received truths or errors, all pure or corrupt affections and desires, all good or evil purposes, enter into character and leave ineffaceable traces in it. All the indiscretions, the vices, the sins of earlier life, unite to make up and disfigure the character of mature age, as does every just thought and pure desire and kind endeavor leave its impress on the permanent state of the spirit. The omniscient eye reads in the actual condition and character of the soul's moral nature its whole past moral history. And this history, recorded in the very condition of the spirit, makes practicable a just retribution for every past thought and deed.

3. Trust.   Thirdly, maintain a cheerful faith in the general helpfulness of all influences from without—from the world of objects and events around, from fellow men, from God himself.

The positive aids are abundant and ample. The seeming hindrances turn to helps when rightly met and trusted. All true virtue in man presupposes struggle. Temptations to evil resisted and overcome are the chiefest conditions of advancing virtue. The power for good is greater than all the forces of evil, and controls them all.

Fourthly, Cultivate with special and separate care the three great departments of spiritual activity—the sensibility, the intelligence, and the free will.

<small>4. Culture of spirit.</small>

§ 96. The particulars of duty in the culture of the sensibility are, first, in respect to the passive sensibility, that the soul be kept in wakeful, responsive sympathy with the world around—with the objects and beings, the events and actions, which make up the system of things of which it is a part; that it allow its susceptibilities to be engaged by the fitting objects and scenes, turning itself away from all that is unworthy, and keeping ever right impressions within due measure and degree.

<small>Of the passive sensibility.</small>

§ 97. Secondly, the duty in regard to the active sensibility or the proper imagination, embraces that of keeping it active and that of regulating its direction and degree. In this department of the mind's activity we find the chief instrument of self-culture. It is the function of the imagination to put into form all the material of character that comes to the mind through sense and reflection, and all conscious experience. The impression which the outer world makes upon the mind, it takes and re-presents, more or less modified, to re-impress the soul and furnish thus material for ever new forms by which to reproduce the impression on itself. Thus the feeling of anger which an insult or an injury produces, the imagination takes up and re-impresses, but now in deeper characters, and so goes on repeat-

<small>Of the imagination.</small>

ing the impression, or more truly perhaps, branding it deeper and deeper, till the angry feeling becomes a passion. All truth, all emotion, all endeavor, the imagination thus puts and keeps in form before and upon the soul so as to impress it, and ever in its continued exercises to make the impression deeper and deeper. It is in this way character forms itself and grows and strengthens. The spirit takes shape from these ideals which the ever active imagination is holding up before it and impressing upon it. Its character thus is much according to the imagination. The vigorous imagination, impressing more energetically, develops a vigorous character. An imagination that is bright and sunny, and so ever holds up forms of hope and cheer before the spirit, makes a joyous, hopeful character. An impure imagination is ever busy, shaping to low and base thought and vicious desire and evil practice. A sound imagination, that takes up just and reasonable impressions, and represents them again to the soul in their harmony, and proportion, and exactness, forms the character to reasonableness and fairness and truthfulness.

Thus it is through the whole catalogue of specific virtues and vices; it is the imagination which is the chief instrumentality that determines their growth and so shapes the character which they constitute. It is a power that the will may awaken and direct and regulate to a degree; but it works on spontaneously when it is left to itself, with equal power to benefit or injure, to mend or mar the character of the spirit. A leading maxim, therefore, in self-culture respects the imagination, and enjoins that it be kept alive and active, but that it be furnished with ideals that are true and pure and beneficent, while every impression or thought or act that can debase, or distort, or corrupt, are scrupulously kept from becoming part of the mass out of which it creates its forms and its images with which to impress the soul.

There is a twofold training here imposed. There is the training of the mind in respect of its mere automatic nature, through which it tends to hold on in any activity awakened in it; and there is the training also of the mind through its volitional nature, by which particular forms of its activity are freshly awakened and determined. A familiar illustration of the bearing of this principle of self-culture is in the training of the mind to the ready reproduction of previous thoughts—of objects, facts, truths, words, previously in the mind. This power to reproduce the past on occasion of need, in the form of a reproductive memory, is mainly the result of the observance of two conditions: First, of giving what is thus to be remembered deep and distinct impression, giving the activity of the mind thus a strong, lasting impulse; and secondly, of practicing the mind in formal exercises of recalling what has thus been received. The usefulness of committing to memory, and then of frequently repeating passages in discourse that are rich in sentiment, or beautiful in expression, or animating in effect, exemplifies and enforces this general principle of self-culture.

The obvious maxims accordingly of self-culture here, are: First, in respect to impressions received, keep the soul free only to pure and just and true impressions, and let the best impressions be deepest and strongest. Secondly, keep the highest and best ideals from these impressions of truth and nobleness and energy most before the spirit, and practice much the voluntary reproduction of these ideals.

§ 98. The particulars of duty in the culture of the intelligence respect the several operations of the mind in knowing. There is, however, first of all, and ever to be borne in mind, the fundamental duty here of keeping the intellect or faculty of knowledge awake and active, with due observance of its needs of rest—of absolute rest for a time from all voluntary intellectual exertion or of relative rest, recreation, by change of intellectual activity.

Culture of the intelligence.

§ 99. The primary operation of the intelligence is that of *observation*, or, as it is technically named, of perception and intuition. The duty in self-culture here is to exercise and train the faculty of observing. There are two sides in this operation—the passive side of receiving impressions from objects, and the active side of noticing or perceiving them. The two should be kept in responsive relation to each other, so that the perception or the intuition shall exactly answer to the impression on the sense, whether the outer or the inner. It is needful that, as has been indicated, the soul should train itself to be in wakeful sympathy and impressibility to-

Observation.

wards all that concerns it, and receive true and full impressions from these objects and occurrences, and then that the mind perceive these impressions—that the intelligence actively apprehend them both in respect to kind and degree. The specific maxims here are : Cultivate and train the instinct to know, developing a well directed curiosity—*seek to know.* Conform the perception accurately to the impression, avoiding the confusion of impressions from divers objects and taking in the full impression—*perceive as you feel.* Make quick, accurate observation a habit, that knowledge may be fed up and grow spontaneously and without labor of will, and at all times and in all occupations—*observe habitually.* The intelligence may thus be trained to a constant and perpetual growth, which shall be maintained in the engrossment of active life, as well as also in the lassitude or weakness of fatigue and sickness, and the heaviness of old age, so long as there can be sense to be impressed from without or from within.

Thought.
§ 100. The second stage of intelligence is the *reflective*—the stage of proper thought. Perception is comparatively worthless except it lead to reflection. Animals observe ; it is the attribute of man to reflect. Observation is not thinking ; it is, however, the indispensable condition of thinking, and naturally leads to thinking.

There are three stages in reflection or thought, presenting so many forms of our knowing activity, to be separately and systematically cultivated.

Judging. The first is that of simply *judging*—of recognizing, in what we observe, a subject with its attribute. Every object of our knowledge presents to our thought that of which we think—the subject of our thought—and also that which we think of it—the attribute which we connect with this subject.

Classing. The second stage of thought is the grouping of objects that have the same attribute—the logical *generalization*, or its counterpart, the grouping of attributes belonging to the same subject—logical *determination*.

Reasoning. The third stage of thought is the derivation of one thought from another—logical *reasoning*.

The duty in intellectual self-culture is thus comprehensively that of training to ready, systematic, and accurate habits of judging, of generalizing and determining, and of reasoning. The principles applicable to all training prescribe that in this intellectual self-culture these forms of thinking be separately recognized and practiced and regulated, so that habit shall keep the mind ever active in free, spontaneous, and therefore unwearying thought. In this lies the secret of great intellectual power—the result of wise and careful culture in a habit of ready, free or spontaneous, and accurate thought.

Directive function. § 101. The third stage of intelligence is the *directive* or *regulative*. Man is not only a reflective being; he is also rational. That is, he is made to observe and reflect in reference to some intelligent end or aim. Without this aiming intelligence, observation and reflection lead to no useful results ; they amount to little more than empty dreamings. The two stages in this form of intelligence are the selective and the proper regulative.

Selection. First, in all observation and in all grouping of subjects or attributes—all logical generalization and determination—and all reasoning, the end or aim in respect to which the observation or the grouping or the reasoning is made, is to be consciously determined upon.

Regulation. Secondly, the actual observing, and generalizing, and reasoning, must be intelligently directed in reference to this selected end or aim.

The duty in intellectual self culture here, then, is thus shaped and particularized: 1. Have consciously an end or aim in all observing and thinking; 2. Select the true and proper aim in the case; 3. Govern the whole movement of the intelligence in subordination to this selected aim ; 4. Make this regulative mental action habitual, so that it shall spontaneously take place and properly direct in all intellectual effort.

Culture of the free-will. § 102. The particulars of duty in the culture of the free-will are suggested by the leading attributes of this function of the mind.

1. As a power. First, the free-will is essentially a *power*. It is, accordingly, to be cultivated as a power by supplying to it the suitable occasions for its exertion, and by actually exciting

it in conformity with its nature, and to the highest degree. Human life offers ample occasions for the exercise of choice--determination. These occasions are to be sought, and such as are best fitted to the culture of the spirit selected. One may throw himself into a condition where there is little call for selection or decision, where all is stagnation, or quiet, changeless drift; or he may place himself where there is call for determination and effort. All choice involves responsibility; but to shun occasions for free determination in shrinking from the responsibilities which attend it, is a mark of weakness, and inevitably stunts and dwarfs character. Strength grows by use. That the free-will as a power may increase, it must be judiciously exercised. This is the first injunction of duty in self-culture, so far as it respects the free-will.

§ 103. Secondly, the free-will is the *dominant* element in man. Its proper culture must train it to the maintenance of this sovereignty over the rest of his being. It must rule the body in its appetites and propensities and tendencies, and never suffer itself to be overpowered by them. It must rule the sensibility, keeping it awake to its duty, sympathetic, and impressible by the objects around it, and never suffer it to be swept away in any torrent of temptation or of evil influence. It must rule the intelligence, keeping it active, quick-sighted, reflective, and moving ever in the line of principle or rational aim and purpose, and never suffer itself to be overborne and lost in the accumulations of learning. It must

2. As sovereign.

rule ever the culture of all the other capacities and powers, both enforcing this culture and controlling its direction and its proportionate degree in the several departments of man's nature. It is to rule, and in order to maintain its rule must actually exert its sway, and act out its ruling power. It is to train itself to this habitual sway over the whole being in order to secure its highest perfection. Duty in self-culture enjoins that the free-will be trained to rule as sovereign over the whole man.

§ 104. Thirdly, the will is *free.* Freedom is of the very essence of the will.

3. As free.

Its originative and determining power is to be recognized and put in exercise in order to its proper growth. There is meaning and force in this direction: be determined;—be determined in particular acts of will, in particular choices and determinations; be determined as a habit; seek to make it a settled thing, that determination is determination; that it is one's self that determines and not another, and that each determination shoulders the full responsibility that properly attaches to it; that each determination is sovereign for the whole mind and body. In this recognition and culture of the will as free, it must not be forgotten that, like the whole active nature of man, the will is truly automatic—that is, that once impelled it keeps on its action, as thus impelled in direction and force, till a new determination comes in to change its course or energy. Without this automatic attribute, it could not be subject to any true culture, it could attain no proper character. I determine thus to walk to a certain spot; the determination, by virtue of this automatic characteristic, acts on, moving my steps with no necessary fresh act of consciousness, bending my course along the determined way, bringing me to the purposed destination, with no necessary repetition of the determining act. The path of human experience is ever forking, and so calling for true selecting and determining action. To train one's self to habits of quick and just resolve, in all these experiences, is one of the most important parts of self-culture. A resolute character, while it is the result of judicious and faithful training, is one of man's highest attainments. A weak, hesitating, vacillating, irresolute spirit has none to blame but itself for what it is. The dictate of duty here, is: Train the free-will to be really free in all free action, unconstrained by any force foreign to its nature or its sphere.

§ 105. Fourthly, the human will is *finite*. It begins its action in weakness, and has in its own nature the limits of its particular exertions and of its attainments of power. Its nature is that of dependence. It is dependent for every occasion of its exercise, with the small exception, perhaps, of what is furnished by its own previous acts. It is dependent on the other mental functions—the sensibility and the intelligence. It can act only as it feels and has its object presented before it in suitable form by the imagination; and only as it acts intelligently, in the light of the properties and relations of its ob-

4. As finite.

jects. At least the free-will can never act as it should, except under the lead and prompting of the enlightened sensibility. True freedom is not arbitrariness, nor obstinacy; it is rational,—that is, sympathetic with things around and moving in light and knowledge. When it sinks to doggedness or mulishness, it sinks from rationality to animalism. A finite, rational free-will, such as is that of man, is accordingly believing. It is animated by a true depending faith on objects and powers without itself. It accepts the occasions for its exercise which are offered to it, and makes no quarrel with fate, as assured that in its high prerogative of freedom, under the rule of a gracious Providence, it determines its own destiny, of perfectness or of ruin. The rule of duty here is: Train the free-will to habits of trustful dependence.

We have thus the summary of maxims for the culture of the free-will: 1. Exercise it in sought occasions; 2. Let it rule, and ever be the dominant power of the soul; 3. Be freely determined, and grow to a resolute habit; 4. Depend with a trustful faith on nature, and on Providence.

BOOK II.

DIVISION II.

DUTIES TO OUR FELLOW-MEN.

INTRODUCTION.

Classes. § 106. The general division of duties to our fellow-men embraces those which respect men individually or simply as persons, and those which respect men collectively or as united in society. This latter class includes the two species of duties, which arise under the two great social organizations established among men—the family and the state.

We have thus the several sub-divisions of the duties to our fellow-men, as follows :—

I. DUTIES TO PERSONS;
II. DUTIES IN THE FAMILY; and
III. DUTIES IN THE STATE.

We will consider them in this order.

PART I.

DUTIES TO PERSONS.

CHAPTER I.

CLASSIFICATION OF DUTIES TO PERSONS.

<small>Principle of division.</small> § 107. Classifications of duties to persons may properly be grounded on either one of the three constituents entering into all duty—love in the subject of duty, good in the object of duty, and right in the act of duty. In fact, duties are named in common speech, according as one or the other of these constituents is made prominent. It should be ever borne in mind, however, that there can be no instance of duty in which is not to be found each of these constituents—love, good, right. In the classification of duties, which we shall adopt as seeming to be most in accordance with the requirements of true science, each of these three constituents will be recognized as a principle of enumeration. It is necessary, however, to caution against the possible notion that a duty mentioned in one class does not embrace the constituent, which is the principle in another

class—against supposing, for example, that veracity excludes sympathy, or that benevolence excludes justice. There cannot be, in the possibility of things, moral veracity without a loving subject, nor moral benevolence without rectitude. But, as generally in the case of mental phenomena, the particular act is characterized by the predominant feature in it.

CHAPTER II.

DUTIES TO PERSONS DETERMINED FROM THE SUBJECT OF DUTY.

Threefold division. § 108. Duties to persons founded on the principle of love in the subject of duty are distinguishable into three classes, in respect to the three stages or degrees in which the moral nature of the subject is engaged :—loving sentiment, appearing in the duty of *sympathy;* loving disposition, appearing in the generic duty of *kindliness;* loving act, appearing in the generic duty of *benevolence.*

1. Sympathy. § 109. It is the duty of every man to cherish a sentiment of sympathy with all his fellow men.

They are entitled to this sentiment by virtue of their being men; it is one of their rights. Pagan and christian morality, alike, recognize this duty. The classic sentiment that to man as man nothing of human concern can be foreign to his interest; *Homo sum; humani nihil a me alienum puto,* is embodied in the christian injunction to "rejoice with them that do rejoice, and weep with those that weep." The fundamental duty of man to his fellow man, as determined by his very nature, is that he sympathize and cherish a true and ever growing sympathy with every true interest of his fellow man.

This duty of sympathy is universal. It is owing to man as man.

The degrees and the forms of this sympathy vary with the degrees of relationship, and with the conditions of men as affording occasions for this sympathy.

It is variously modified, also, in respect to the object of sympathy. The English language abounds in works derived from the Greek, the Latin, and the vernacular Anglo-Saxon, signifying the divers degrees or forms of this affection. We have thus condolence in reference to persons in sorrow; compassion, commiseration, pity, in reference to persons in suffering need; mercy, clemency, leniercy, in reference to the ill-deserving. There are also corresponding words, signifying the negative or opposite of these graces of character, such as; hard-hearted, inhuman, rancorous.

§ 110. It is the duty of every man to
2. Kindliness. embody this sympathetic spirit in the active instincts of his nature, thus forming a proper disposition which unites to the fundamental sympathy, desire and tendency to expression. This is the general duty of *kindliness*, of being genial.

This class of duties embraces the divers modifications expressed in such terms as liberality, generosity, charitableness, bounteousness, and the negatives or opposites of the disposition, such as: illiberal, churlish, grudging, jealous, envious, and those denoting the different forms of selfishness, as miserly, niggardly, sordid, mercenary, greedy, and the like.

§ 111. It is the duty of every man, still farther, to carry out this sympathetic disposition into positive act on every occasion that may properly invite—to put his kindly disposition into actual expression, in loving endeavors or benevolence.

3. Benevolence.

The comprehensive maxim in this general division of duties to persons, is: Be habitually loving to all men. The specific maxims, founded on the several distinguishable stages of development of the principle of love, are: *Be sympathetic; be kindly or genial; love all men.*

§ 112. Under this general duty is included a species of duties which are in their nature responsive, and are by this characteristic distinguished from the rest of the class. They are proper *re-sentments*—in the old and more comprehensive meaning of the word, denoting properly, *feelings back* or *in return* for what we have experienced from others. This species includes the several duties arising in response to good and to evil experienced from another.

Resentments.

§ 113. GRATITUDE is the duty responsive to the reception of good. It is an instinctive impulse of man's nature to be thankful for kindness.

Gratitude.

Gratitude is a sentiment, the cherishing and expression of which not only meets a demand of conscience, but gives itself a peculiar joy; the good, the blessedness, for which man is made, is, in large part, to be secured by the exercise of gratitude. The obligation arising from favors can often be discharged only by a grateful spirit. Our great poet well says:

> A grateful mind,
> By owing, owes not, but still pays, at once,
> Indebted and discharged.

But gratitude is not merely a grace—a sentiment cherished in the bosom of the recipient of favors, or merely expressed in words; it is a virtue also—an outward act of good to the benefactor in appropriate ways and measures. The simple law of gratitude is that for every good received, a corresponding good be returned to the benefactor.

As a moral exercise, gratitude is due only to intentional benefactors. It is due only to moral persons; and is due to them only so far as they act morally, that is, intentionally. The good that comes to us through others acting without intention as mere occasions, calls for gratitude only to the beneficent Disposer of all things. For this good, inasmuch as it is unceasing, gratitude as unceasing is due to Him. Hence, one of the most fundamental and comprehensive duties of man is an habitually grateful spirit.

Anger. § 114. The resentment responsive to ill received takes a two-fold form: that of *anger* prompting to retaliation, and that of *forgiveness*.

ANGER is an instinct of man's nature, arising at once and spontaneously, on receiving an injury from another.

So deeply implanted in man is the feeling that evil comes from a person, and that all suffering comes from a wrong-doer, that in children and in uncultivated men anger is freely exercised towards brutes and inanimate objects when occasioning pain or suffering, where there cannot be supposed to be any intention. But anger properly respects only persons intending the evil which awakens it, and is in fact but the natural sentiment of justice in respect to a wrong-doer.

In selfish natures, like man's, the duty in reference to anger is chiefly that of moderating it, so that it shall only be exercised towards real wrong-doers and shall never be allowed to be excessive, either in respect to the evil which arouses it or the character and condition of the sufferer. The retaliation to which anger naturally prompts in man, is not, necessarily, a retaliation to be inflicted by his own hands, but only a retaliation which the rightful Avenger of wrong may administer. The main uses of anger in man are, accordingly, that it prepares for a free recognition and expectation of the divine justice, which redresses all wrong, and for free service as his instrument when bidden to that ministry. A vindictive spirit is inhuman; it is a usurper of divine prerogative: "Vengeance is mine," saith the Lord.

Forgiveness. § 115. Peculiarly fitting for man in his present condition is the other resentment of this species—*forgiveness*, in which the evil received is resented in good returned.

In this form of duty, the instinct of angry resentment is suppressed; the instinct of generosity and good-will becomes sovereign; the suffering is borne in meekness; the injury is forborne; the blessing overmasters the wrong. To forgive does not necessitate entire forgetfulness, but only extends so far as suppression of the spirit of retaliation. We need to remember even to forgive. As consciously needing forgiveness, man should be forgiving, for the just rule is that only as he forgives, can he be forgiven. Penitence and acknowledgment with redress of the wrong are not always to be exacted as conditions of forgiveness with men, however it may be with the divine administration. There is this wide difference between their relations to offenses and His: they need forgiveness themselves, and their wrongs He will amply redress. The rule for men, therefore, is to bear, to forbear, to forgive, even although the wrong-doer persists in his malice—to bless when he curses and despitefully uses them. A tranquil trust in the sufficiency of the divine rule, a proper sense of one's own imperfections, and the growth of the spirit into the divine fulness of mercy and forbearance, all enforce on man the duty of cherishing a forgiving spirit.

CHAPTER III.

DUTIES TO PERSONS DETERMINED FROM THE OBJECT OF DUTY.

§ 116. Duties to persons founded on the principle suggested by the object of duty are distributed into three species, corresponding to the three departments of his personal nature—those of *courtesy*, which more immediately respect the feelings; those of *truthfulness*, which respect the intellectual nature; and those of *trustfulness*, *beneficence*, and *justice*, which are respectively founded in the proper moral nature of man, as interdependent, as made for blessedness, and as having rights.

Three species.

It is true that to all duties there are corresponding rights, and that, accordingly, as it is man's duty to be courteous to his fellow man, so it is each one's right as a man to be treated with courtesy; still the closer scrutiny of these three classes of duties will evince that they severally respect more directly and immediately the several departments of our personal being which have been named.

§ 117. COURTESY respects more directly the out-

1. Courtesy. ward carriage and deportment by which the sensibilities of others are impressed.

The essence of the duty lies in this: that the *form* of our intercourse with our fellow-men should be such as befits man towards man; that this *form* of our behavior by which he is affected be loving, right, benignant.

Obligation. The obligation to courtesy is founded in the social relationship of man to man. On the one hand is the acting spirit made to impress favorably, and, on the other hand, the recipient spirit to be thus favorably impressed, the two made for each other, to act reciprocally on each other. Man is made to be courteous; and also to be blest by courtesy.

Sphere. The sphere of courtesy lies properly within that of good manners. The synonyms by which the duty is denominated point to the condition of social intercourse, and to the highest degree of that condition, as that in which this grace of character is best developed. Such synonyms are courtliness, urbanity, civility, good manners, and the like.

Forms. The forms of courtesy vary with the relative condition of the subject and the object of the duty. Towards superiors, it takes the form of respect, reverence, homage, worship; towards equals it appears as comity; towards inferiors, as gentleness, suavity, affability.

Discourtesy. The vices of character here or the forms of discourtesy are such as those of insolence, irreverence, incivility, rudeness, arrogance, haughtiness, scornfulness.

Although courtesy looks more immediately to the outward form of conduct, yet it necessarily engages the heart—must be loving; since to be insincere or hypocritical, or to endeavor to seem what one is not, is radically immoral; and, moreover, all assumed or pretended courtesy will betray itself, and therefore can never be as true courtesy to the hearts of others. Still, as the acts of courtesy engage less or more the inward feeling and disposition, it is variously characterized in language which sometimes points more to the inner nature or spirit of a man and denominates him as bland, sunny, gracious, friendly, or, on the contrary, as austere, sour, testy, cross; or more to the outward expression, and designates him as polite, refined, urbane, courtly, complaisant, or as rude, unmannerly, rustic, surly.

Courtesy sustains this important relation to other duties to persons that it is generally needful in order to their perfect effect. The manner of doing affects the doing itself in its essential character. Acts of beneficence and kindness lose much of their moral worth if done in violation of those principles which regulate the forms of our intercourse with our fellow men. Good intent acted out in a savage way is well exemplified in the fable of the lion that, in gratitude for the healing of his wound, strikes a heavy blow at the fly that disturbs his benefactor's rest; he kills the fly but crushes his master's face as well.

§ 118. TRUTHFULNESS is a duty which is root-

2. *Truthfulness.* ed in the intellectual nature or the mental faculty of the true, as courtesy is more immediately seated in the sensibility or mental capacity of form. It may be defined as the duty of conforming ourselves to the truth in our thoughts and feelings, and in our expressions of them.

Obligation. The obligation to be truthful both in thought and in expression is founded in the nature of man as related to other men in the harmonious system of things. The truth of things is the harmony of things as parts of one whole. A disturbance of the truth of things works disharmony in the system of things, and so far as it extends, is the frustration of the divine end in creating. The active nature of man must act thus truthfully, or the machinery must so far move disorderly and ill. In being truthful, man only acts out himself just as he is, in respect to other beings or things as they are. His fellow-men depend on this truthful expression of himself as one wheel in a well constructed machine depends on the true play of the other wheels in connection with which it moves and performs its function. The unperverted tendency of man's spirit is to truthfulness in thought and expression on the one hand, and to a trustful dependence on what is expressed as true on the other; it is a perverse will that is at the bottom of all untruthfulness. The very end of man's being must fail if he is not truthful himself, or cannot move in trustful dependence on others as truthful to him. The obligation to truthfulness, as founded in the duty to form a perfect character, is well implied in the apostolic direction to grow up into perfection by the one means of "speaking truth in love," in the general sense of observing and conforming to truth in the spirit of love. And the necessarily fatal result to blessedness—to all good in experience—if truthfulness were disregarded and the lives and actions of men were but phantoms or lies, is but too apparent. The social nature of man would be, but for truth, a cheat and a curse.

Twofold.
§ 119. Truthfulness, as implied in what has been said, is either *internal*, conformity to the truth of things in the shaping of our feelings, our thoughts, and our endeavors—"truth in the inward part"—truth of heart; or *external*, conformity to truth in expression—truth of the lip. This second form of the general duty is more specifically known as *veracity*.

1. Inward truthfulness.
§ 120. The virtue of inward truthfulness involves, first, *candor*, or perfect freedom from all bias, from all distorted or discolored apprehension of the words or acts or condition of our fellow-men; and, secondly, *impartiality*, or the free reception into our view of all the particulars which should affect our judgment in the case, and the fair allowance to each of its own weight and importance.

Not only have our fellow-men a right to the exercise on our part of this candor and impartiality, but, as already intimated, the perfect working of the social system of which they and we are integral parts enjoins these duties. Still further, our own highest perfection and interest require them. It is not well for man to hold a lie.

§ 121. The objects to which veracity is due are actual persons.

2. Veracity—due to persons.

As animals have no proper rights by virtue of their own natures, but only by reason of the persons to whom they are related and by virtue of that relation, (§ 17,) so there can be no obligation of veracity to them. Traps, snares, scare-crows, are designed to deceive; but they are not necessarily forbidden by any principle of morality. So men, who have lost their proper personality, as the insane, are not objects to which veracity is properly due. In so far as their rational nature remains to them, and, it should be noted, seldom if ever is insanity the wreck of all rationality, the obligation may subsist, but no further. To men, moreover, who so act as for the time to forfeit the rights of persons, as robbers and assassins, it is certain that they can set up no claim that others, to whom they have forfeited this right, observe the truth in communications to them. The highwayman clearly cannot enforce the moral obligation of speaking truth in the interest of his wicked purpose. Whether it be morally right to deceive for the purpose of saving life, or generally of preventing wrong, is a question of casuistry that it has been found very difficult to resolve. Generally, if not always, the circumstances in which the question may actually arise will be such as to evince either that the deception is not absolutely necessary in order to prevent the crime or that greater evil might result from the deception than from the perpetration of the crime. Martyrdom is not always the worst evil to be suffered. We cannot suppose that any deception could be regarded as of doubtful morality in a perfect being under a perfect rule. That the Infinite One should be untruthful in any way or degree, it is irreverent to imagine. It must be difficult to show that deviation from a perfect standard is ever right. Man certainly may not seek to prevent evil by doing wrong. If deception be not in every supposable case wrong, still it is impossible for us to say that in any circumstances in which we are placed in the ordering of Divine Providence, it is right. We may safely conclude that, on the one hand, idiocy, insanity, wicked intent, can have no rights, and can originate no obligations; while on the other hand there ever exist the obligations to respect our own natures and also the perfect rule of God over us. Duty to ourselves and to Him may require of us that which would not be required of us by beings devoid of rationality or of morality. In passing judgment in such cases of doubt, it should be borne in mind that the moral intent may be right, may be as perfect as the imperfections of man's nature will permit, while the outward action itself is not that which a perfect being in a perfect condition of things would perform.

§ 122. *The comprehensive duty of veracity respects both the habitual deportment and the specific act.*

Sphere.

Every man owes it to his fellow-men to make his outward life a truthful expression of his inner spirit;

to be ingenuous and frank; to be open and sincere; to be simple-minded and straightforward, and carefully to shun the opposite vices of character. His own highest well-being and the welfare of society demand it of him that his outer life be the fair expression of what he is—of what he feels and thinks and intends inwardly. The very basis of society is mutual trust and confidence, to which disingenuousness, double-facedness, dissimulation, are destructive. If his Creator designed man to be social, He designed him to be veracious.

The specific duties of honest statement, faithful representation, accurate expression in every form, are so obviously comprehended in this generic virtue of veracity that they demand no additional or more specific enforcement.

Modes. The obligations of veracity reach to all the modes by which one man communicates with another—by the general life, by words, by signs, by any expressive acts whatever. Lying, vicious deception, may be practiced by means of signs as fully as in actual speech.

These obligations may be violated, moreover, by exaggeration or by suppression. Veracity implies exactness or accuracy in expression, and forbids both overstatement and excess of coloring, as well as also all garbling, understating, shading.

Veracity forbids, moreover, falsification in any respect of the intention, in representing or expressing—forbids all prevarication and quibbling, as also all deceptive evasion.

It forbids, still further, duplicity and equivocation, all juggling in the use of words, by which the expression, although true in a certain construction, is designed to lead to false opinion.

It forbids, once more, all feigning, as well as all cloaking of the true—simulation as well as dissimulation—setting forth what is not as well as disguising what is.

It is ever to be borne in mind that lying involves the guilty intent to deceive. A man may utter what is untrue, not knowing it to be so; such utterance is not necessarily blameworthy. Even veracity may thus occasion false representation, as the utterance is of what, although false, is supposed to be true. Works of fiction, parables, and romances, are not necessarily in violation of veracity, since there may be no intent to deceive.

Moreover, the obligations of veracity are not necessarily violated by withholding the truth. Reticence is as truly a duty as utterance. Even evasion may not offend against veracity, which requires only that, if we undertake to speak, we utter only truth. We are not always under obligation to tell all we know; but what we tell must be told truly.

§ 123. **Trustfulness** is a duty founded in the interdependence of men as constituent parts of the same moral system.

Trustfulness.

Men are made to be dependent one upon another. They exist towards each other reciprocally as beings to trust and be trusted. The good for which they were made comes to them in large degree through their fellow-men; they must look to them for its supply. They were made also to do good, and their active nature must go out to work this good for others. Men honor themselves in trusting, and are honored in being trusted. The depravity of men has not wholly extirpated these native roots of confidence. Honor is found even among thieves.

As dependence in man is not absolute, is limited by reason of his moral imperfection far beyond what it should be, so the trust which is grounded in it must not be absolute, must be limited. A blind trust may be ruinous, inasmuch as dependence on man is insecure. But a rational trust is yet the duty and the interest of men. Human nature may be relied on to a certain extent; it is safe to trust thus far. To trust, to show confidence, begets a spirit of fidelity in answer to what is expected. The trusting man is less likely to be wronged than he who manifestly expects to be defrauded or misused. To show expectation of evil invites the doing of the evil. Even a knave will honor the confidence that is reposed in him. To trust another naturally awakens in him sense of responsibility that may of itself prevent wrong-doing. The trustful spirit is intrinsically bright and cheerful and joyous; distrust saddens and sours. The small losses from occasional betrayal of trust are counterbalanced by the habitual cheer of a confiding spirit. The collective interests of humanity are furthered just in proportion to the prevalence of a true rational trust and confidence between individuals and between communities.

Beneficence and Justice. § 124. BENEFICENCE respects wants; JUSTICE respects rights in others.

These are duties which, still more characteristically than trustfulness, respect the individual moral nature of man as object of duty. The twofold character of the duty thus determined results from the twofold view we are obliged to take of this moral nature. We recognize man as having wants and having rights. As made for blessedness, the fundamental instinct of his being is towards blessedness. This he craves; it is his deepest, broadest want. Duty is owing to him as such creature of wants. Every man is bound in duty to do good to his fellow man, to be beneficent. But,

Distinguished. again, being made for blessedness as the great end of his being, he must have the right to attain this end. The observance of this right,—in other words, the practical recognition of man as having rights,—is the duty of justice. Beneficence regards wants; justice regards rights as the proper natural outgrowth of those wants. Sometimes the naked want presents itself to our regard, and sometimes the want in the garb of a right. Beneficence and justice are, therefore, distinguishable duties. They are, however, never in proper contradiction, any more than love and goodness, or knowledge and freedom. When they seem to be opposed, or when they lead to opposite effects in the experience of the object of duty, as when justice bids punishment and goodness suggests forgiveness, it is where they are determined by different relations. In the subject of duty, mercy can never conflict with justice, for the right which justice respects can be but an embodiment of some

7*

want which mercy or goodness could relieve. Beneficence and justice come into conflict, therefore, only as they respect different objects or different interests in the same moral person. Thus it may be justice to society to punish while it is mercy to the offender to pardon; and a son may have a right to paternal bounty as a son, while goodness may withhold that which he would use only to his ruin.

Wants crave, rights demand. Beneficence, as a duty, responsive to wants, accordingly obliges through the nature of the subject of duty as loving. Justice, on the other hand, obliges through the nature of the object of duty. The claims of the two come to the conscience by those opposite directions. Beneficence is by its nature, thus, as ever respective of a want, entreating, soliciting, persuasive. Justice, as respecting a right, is exacting, enforcing, imperative. To be perfectly good is a higher virtue of character than to be perfectly just, inasmuch as a self-moved spirit ranks higher than one impelled from without. On the other hand, justice is a more sacred duty in society than goodness; because when rights are disregarded, wants will go unrelieved. To be wanting in justice imports looser morals than to be wanting in goodness.

Correlative of benevolence. § 125. BENEFICENCE is the exact correlative of benevolence. The benevolence seated in the soul as subject of duty appears as beneficence in the object of duty. Love felt in the subject is expressed as good effected in the experience of the object.

The two may be correctly regarded as the opposite sides of the same duty. The consideration of our own moral nature enforces upon us the obligations of benevolence; the consideration of the nature of our fellow-man enforces the obligations of beneficence. The subjective virtuous disposition and endeavor of benevolence must, in order to its own perfection, have its outcome and full maturity in beneficence.

§ 126. Beneficence is, in a true sense, the crowning virtue. To do good is godlike. The ultimate and comprehensive end to be realized in the experience of man is good. In doing good the doer brings to himself his highest happiness. "The way to be happy," says Barrow, "is to do well."

The crowning virtue.

§ 127. In the exercise and culture of beneficence the view is to be turned outward on the object. The specific duties here involved are sympathetic contemplation of human wants; kindly disposition to relieve them; positive acts of bounty.

Species.

§ 128. The modes of beneficence are as various as the ways in which we can affect any of the interests of our fellow-men in their persons, character, or condition, by our habits and modes of life, by our words, by our actions. The disposition and the determination to be beneficent should be so formed and fixed within as to be ready to flow out in any appropriate way which occasion may open.

Modes.

§ 129. The measure of benevolence is given in the golden rule: "Do unto

Measure.

others as you would that they should do unto you." The instinctive craving for good in them is to be ranked with the craving for good in ourselves, equally and alike to be satisfied, with like sympathetic interest and with like earnest and hearty endeavor. The principle of nearness of relationship by nature or occasion must of course come in to determine the measure of the endeavor. Our own well-being is our nearest concern; and the opportunities to do good, which are given us under the divine rule as calls to duty, are more to ourselves than to any other being. But to exalt our own cravings for happiness above those of others around us, and especially to exclude or depress them from their due consideration, is selfishness. Kindred and neighborhood possess lower degrees of demand on our beneficence than our own well-being, but yet higher than those which belong to strangers. We are to do good only as we have opportunity. The principle of opportunity thus, as a rightful measure of beneficence, determines its degree in reference to ourselves, to kindred, to neighbors, to foreigners.

§ 130. The one object in true beneficence, in real goodness, is the relief of want in a fellow being, the satisfying of his craving for good. To confer benefits for the sake of procuring his favor or for any other purpose, or even for the mere purpose of strengthening the principle of beneficence in our own hearts, is not true beneficence. This virtue looks exclusively to the good in the experience of the receiver of the benefit. It does not seek as its motive even grati-

Its one object.

tude in return; although favor may rightly be withheld simply on the ground of a heartless or ungrateful reception of it. It may be wrong to encourage such a disposition, just as it is wrong to encourage profligacy or indolence by beneficence. The type and model of true beneficence is given to man in the example of Him who "is kind unto the unthankful and to the evil."

§ 131. JUSTICE is the satisfaction of rights. It supposes rights in the object of duty and aims at good only as it recognizes a right to claim it. Its immediate motive is a right to be satisfied in the experience of the object of duty.

Justice defined.

The elements of justice as a duty are ready recognition of the rights of others, and ungrudging satisfaction of them. Impliedly, also, justice requires all reasonable protection and upholding of the rights of others. Hardly less atrocious than incendiarism would be the refusal to extinguish a kindling fire that threatens the destruction of another's dwelling; hardly less atrocious than downright murder, a refusal to rescue, when in our power, a human life from peril.

Justice has been regarded by moralists as twofold: (1). *Distributive,* as it awards what is due to merit or demerit: (2). *Commutative,* as it practically recognizes what is equal and right in exchanges and in promises and contracts.

§ 132. Justice has for its sphere all the rights of men, whether they respect personal enjoyments, condition, reputation, or property.

Sphere.

It enjoins a practical recognition of the right to be and to be happy; and forbids all wanton and all inconsiderate harm to any interest of our fellow man.

It recognizes his right to place—in roads and walks, in conveyances and at inns, in the family, in the schools, in the assembly, at work and at play. It recognizes his rights in time also, to labor and to rest, to speak and to be silent, to be in public or in private.

It requires the vindication of his good name; and forbids any direct or indirect, any intentional or thoughtless sullying of his fair reputation. It condemns the idle gossip which plays with a man's good name as if he had no rights, as well as the malignant slander which would banish him from the courtesies of social life.

It enjoins equity in our dealings, equal balances for his and for our interests; and forbids all concealment that would hinder satisfaction of actual rights, all double-dealing, all substitution of the letter for the intention in covenants, all use of superior vantage-ground for enforcing or exacting rights.

Inasmuch as rights often change in their specific form with change of condition or of circumstances, with lapse of time and change of place, the law of justice requires that the literal and specific right acquired in any way be not allowed in any such way to work a higher injury. The exact justice is sometimes the worst wrong:—*Summum jus injuria summa.* Not the letter, but the spirit of the law is to be regarded.

CHAPTER IV.

DUTIES TO PERSONS DETERMINED FROM THE ACT OF DUTY.

Two species. § 133. Duties looking more directly to the act of duty constitute the third class of duties to persons. They may be distributed into species, according as they are viewed in their own nature or in relation to other duties.

1. Straightforwardness. § 134. Of the first species mentioned are the duties of having an aim in our conduct, of keeping our aims ever true to the ends proposed in our actions, and of being straightforward in carrying out our aims in fulfilment to their ends.

These several species are given at once in an analysis of rectitude as distinguished from love and from goodness. Rectitude or rightness in action implies an aim or intention, an end or object, and a direct motion from aim to object.

Governing aim. § 135. It is the duty of every man to have a governing aim or purpose in his living.

The first dictate of man's nature as rational is that he regulate his conduct ever by such a governing aim. An aimless life is so far a wasted life; an aimless act is an irrational act. It should be borne in mind that in the formation of character our great duty is to bring even our automatic or spontaneous life under the rule of a rational aim.

§ 136. It is the duty of every man to keep his aim true to its end.

<small>True to its end.</small>

Inconceivable as it is in physical nature, it is unhappily true in moral history, that a man often aims one way while his action somehow terminates elsewhere than in that purposed way. The aim is feebly held or the end is faintly discerned; and aim and end fail to meet. There is such a thing as to have a sinister end in an action; it is a vice to be shunned. Men often confer benefits not to relieve wants but to procure merit or favor, or to hush conscience, or to win esteem. They have an aim, but it looks to something else than its proper and rightful end.

§ 137. It is the duty of every man to be straightforward in execution of his purpose.

<small>Direct in pursuit.</small>

Uprightness in life we recognize as a virtue in which not so much the loving spirit or the beneficent effect, but the rectitude of the acting, is regarded. The straightforward, upright life is the efficient life for all life's purposes. The devious walk is tardy or fails altogether of its purpose. The habit of directing all our action unswervingly to its designed end not only gives confidence and ministers to energy, but more than almost anything else in ourselves ensures success.

§ 138. Of the second species of duties Harmony with providential rule. to persons indicated by the essential nature of rectitude in action, are the several duties involved in keeping our life and conduct in harmony with the divinely ordered course of nature and of events.

All duties are parallel; they never cross one another. It is good ground of suspicion that we are wrong, when our actions clash with the rightful actions of other, or, with the equal flow of Providence. The man that is ever chafing from his collisions with the progress of events may well question whether his own course is not cross to the will of his master. Guizot well argues that mere duration in society proves the presence and power of order and truth and justice. If, therefore, in settled social life a man finds his way perpetually obstructed or crossed, it is a sign that his course is oblique and tortuous. Virtue, so long as man is imperfect, must, of course, at times antagonize itself with vice. Hence even virtuous acts may be often in conflict with settled customs. Still the truth remains that order and rectitude rule human affairs; and to be ever in accord with the divine will, as it manifests itself in the disposition of things and the course of events, is man's highest privilege and unfailing duty. It is a vice in him to put himself in disharmony with things around him; to distrust the divine order. His duty lies in perfect harmony and parallelism with this outward ordering. The correction of existing abuses in the community is generally best accomplished by imparting greater energy to what is right ; weeds die when overshadowed by the thrifty plants.

Involved in this duty of directing our actions in parallelism and harmony with the divine ordering of things is the duty of regulating them as to degree, so that relatively to the condition and course of outward things our actions be allowed to be neither excessive nor deficient.

The particular maxims of uprightness in duty are then these two :—*Be straightforward*—having an aim, keeping it true and level to its end, and acting unswervingly towards it ; and *Be in harmony with all lines of rectitude without*, maintaining parallelism in direction and moderation in degree.

PART II.

DUTIES IN THE FAMILY.

CHAPTER I.

THE FAMILY INSTITUTION.

The family defined.
§ 139. THE FAMILY is an organized community divinely established for the continuance and training of the race of man.

A divine institution.
That the family constitution is an appointment of the Creator we should believe on the simple ground that families come to be in the natural course of things. The very nature of man, also, in its instincts, its consultations for its comfort, peace, and well-being generally, its necessities and its spontaneous activities, leads him into the family. Reason and revelation agree in teaching that the family is a divine ordinance.

Its twofold end.
The twofold end of the family is the continuance of the race of man and the training of it to its best and highest condition.

Distinctive feature. The distinguishing feature of the family society as compared with other societies existing among men, is that its membership is constituted by community of blood. It is by virtue of this participation in a common origin and line of descent—a participation so far in the same blood—that the peculiar duties arise to kindred and to persons not in the family proper but yet of the family. It is this community of blood in which originates the prohibition of marriages within the near lines of consanguinity. It is hence that inspiration, history, instincts of man, agree in the reprobation of transgressions of such inter-marriages. It is this community of blood from the original singleness of the primitive parentage and the consequent unity of the race, that brings all mankind—men as men—into true relation of brotherhood.

As a permanently established community, the family society needs for its most salutary working to be organized; to be constituted under the relations of higher and lower in moral order. It demands a head and implies subordinates in its membership.

§ 140. *Rise of duties in it.* Inasmuch as the duties incumbent on men follow them into every department of their free activity, duties arise at once on the organization of the family state,—on the simple rise and coming to be of a family.

As morality must exist in the family, as there must be order, and as the family is a community of moral persons, there must be duties and there must be correlative rights. The ground of obligation here is in the nature of man as made for duty, both as subject of duty and object of duty, in connection with the accompanying fact that the family is a divinely instituted sphere of man's free activity.

§ 141. As instituted by God, and as made up of moral persons bound together in a community of life, which embraces the interests, the sympathies, and the endeavors of all the members in a singleness of experience and of destiny, the family life must be accepted as being truly moral.

Moral in its character.

In addition to his personal responsibility, each member of the family participates in a joint responsibility, attaching to the whole membership. Most important moral interests are bound up in the family life. The character of each member is shaped by the influences that rule in the household. Each family has a character of its own by which it is recognized by others, and by which it influences others. The peace, order, refinement of a well ordered household radiate all around light and blessing; the abode of ignorance, strife, vice, is a moral curse to the neighborhood. Each member helps to form the character, and shape the experience and life of the whole. Each member has a sense of shame in the moral discredit of the family and a satisfaction in its moral thrift. Indeed this unity of the moral life in the family is such that each member feels this shame or satisfaction in the moral failure or success of every other member.

The family life is thus a true moral life, specifically differing, indeed, from the personal moral life, as the social differs from the individual, but possessing like that the great determining attributes of a proper moral life, being under a divine constitution, engaging largely man's free moral activity, and charged throughout with a true moral responsibility which reaches both to the joint and individual character and action of the members. This is further witnessed in the sense of pride or of shame that is felt by them as the family life moves in the line of a pure morality or otherwise, and in the ready praise or censure bestowed by other men, and also in the ordinary retributions visited in the course of Providence on the family life as moral or vicious.

§ 142. The seat of authority in the family, while it is primarily and predominantly in the will of God, is secondarily and subordinately in the parental head.

Seat of authority.

As a derived and subordinate seat of authority, parental rule is never legitimate when it violates the law of God, that is, when it contravenes the settled principles of morality. The parent is yet presumptively the rightful interpreter of the law; and no disregard of that authority can be justified unless such authority is in its exercise clearly subversive of morality.

§ 143. The classes of duties in the family are determined from the consti-

Classes of duties.

tuent relationships of the members. They are three in number: 1. *Marital* duties between the parents; 2. *Parental* duties between parents and children; and 3. *Fraternal* duties between the children.

We will consider these classes in their order, and in connection with their correlative rights.

CHAPTER II.

MARITAL RIGHTS AND DUTIES.

§ 144. MARITAL RIGHTS AND DUTIES subsist between the husband and the wife as the joint head of the family community. These rights and duties have their foundation in the covenant of marriage.

Nature and ground.

The marital life has its proper origin in this covenant in which one man and one woman unite themselves in reciprocal affection and helpfulnefs for life.

Origin.

§ 145. Polygamy is forbidden most clearly in the divine ordering of the equality in number of males and females in the human race.

Monogamy.

There could be no more authoritative ordinance than this which is written in the very constitution of the race—that there be in the family institution one man and one woman as its constituents.

That polygamy is morally wrong, is also inferrible from the consideration that it necessarily degrades woman and is incompatible with a true family life.

§ 146. The marriage covenant as a reciprocation of affection and interest, must be freely entered into by the parties in the exercise of their best intelligence and heartiest determination.

Marriage covenant.

They must hence be of suitable age to act with discretion and a full understanding of the engagements by which they bind themselves. They should be guided by parental counsel rather than coerced by parental authority and constraint, that their perfect freedom be not overborne. It imports a moral imperfection in the customs of society that children should be betrothed in their mental immaturity or be contracted to strangers for whom there has been given no opportunity for the rise of a free affection, or be urged into matrimonial alliances in any way or for any object which do not admit the exercise of a free intelligent affection.

§ 147. The marriage covenant is morally indissoluble but by death.

Indissoluble.

The marriage union is the closest and most inviolable that can be formed between human beings. Even the filial relation, we are emphatically taught in the Scriptures, must be held in subordination to it. The parties in it must leave father and mother, if need be, to perfect the union which is to be as that of "one flesh," in the thorough blending of interest, of affection, of ministry. Importing, as it does, a full reciprocal devotion of each to the other, it utterly forbids the thought of the union being other than for life. Its obligations hence continue upon each party as long as fulfilment is practicable, that is, till either the death of the other party or his annulling of the covenant by actual marital alliance with another party. Hence the allowance of divorce by civil tribunals on grounds less conclusive than those of death or marital alliance with another person is to be deprecated as hostile to a pure and sound morality. Absence, estrangement of affection, cruelty, may justify separate living; the old common law divorce from board and bed—*a mensa et thoro*—may be admissible, while yet the sanctity of the marriage vow be maintained by withholding a full divorce from the bonds of marriage—*a vinculo matrimonii*—during the life of the parties, except for the one cause mentioned—marital alliance with another. The covenant, it should be remembered, like all covenants, may be dissolved by reason of essential fraud in the making or by reason of its being made between parties within the forbidden lines of consanguinity. The fraud which shall be allowed to annul the formal covenant must pertain to the essential nature or end of the covenant—to the natural competency of the parties to the marital union. Parties within the lines of consanguinity are incompetent to make the covenant. Such covenants, although in a true sense null and void, yet leave the parties not altogether free from obligations. They are of the nature of unlawful vows. See § 280.

§ 148. The marriage covenant, as being *Civil and religious ratification* vitally related to the highest interests of civil society, as also of morality and religion, is worthily solemnized by established formalities which evidence its ratification and the open public entrance upon the new life which it begins.

These formalities are very properly both of a civil and religious character. They are imposed in part by the state, for its protection, and in part by the church, that the new life may be pursued under the sanctities and benedictions of religion. This solemnization is, however, but the outer indication or evidencing; the true life of the marriage compact is in the free covenanting of the parties. It is in close analogy to the entrance upon civil office, which is evidenced under established formalities, including religious sanctions in the oath that is administered and in the proper religious rites that often accompany it, the true authority of the official life, nevertheless, being derived, not from the formal inauguration, but from the election or appointment that has gone before.

§ 149. The rights and duties of hus-
Parity of rights. band and wife in relation to each other rest upon a basis of perfect moral equality and reciprocity.

As equally endowed with full moral attributes and having a like origin and destiny under the same moral rule, they are bound to render each to the other the same sympathy and affection, the same courtesy, truthfulness, beneficence, and justice, which their equal personality requires.

§ 150. As the united head of the family
Joint parental authority. community, their authority is joint and indivisible.

In the guidance and control of the family interests their participation is equal and common. The obedience which is exacted is due, not to either party, as separate, but to the united head. If the specific command be given by either, it is given only as the utterance of the concurring authority of both. Disobedience to one must be held to be disobedience to both. It is in this light and in this spirit, that parental authority is ever to be administered and to be obeyed. The parent offends if he seeks to enforce his rule by his own right, independently of the other parent; and the child offends if he seeks to please one of his parents in opposition to the known will of the other. It is one of the puzzling questions in casuistry how to act morally when the conditions of moral action in the case are immorally determined, as when the commands of the parents are in opposite directions. The general principle of morality here is, however, indisputable; parental authority is a joint authority; the administration of it by one parent must be accepted as having the sanction and support of both; disobedience to one is disobedience to both. It is too often the bane of family discipline and rule that it is exercised and submitted to as the several rule of one of the parents, and not as legitimately but the joint authority of both.

Rights complementary. § 151. While the basis of marital rights and duties, as between the husband and the wife, is that of equality and reciprocity, these rights and duties are yet, as they may in perfect consistency with this idea of their equality be held to be, truly complementary of each other.

The rights and duties of the husband towards the wife are not the same, although of like rank and reciprocal obligation, as those of the wife towards the husband. The antithesis of sex, which runs through the physical and spiritual constitution, and which is the occasion and condition of the marriage covenant, gives rise to separate functions and duties and rights under that covenant. The physical superiority of man in respect to muscular force and endurance, and the masculine characteristics of spirit corresponding to them, clearly indicate his to be the sphere of the sterner, the severer, the bolder virtues; while the gentler, tenderer, more sympathetic nature of woman indicates for her the sphere predominantly of the graces of trust, tranquil acquiescence in the orderings of Providence, and cheering hopefulness. It is rather his part to lead, her's to follow; his to provide, her's to economize and encourage; his to attend to the outer duties of the family, her's to minister in the offices of indoor life; his to protect, her's to sustain and soothe and cherish. Summarily, these relative offices of husband and wife are to be regarded as properly complementary, one to the other; each party ministering to the needs of the other and to the common wants of the household, according to the respective capability, convenience, and general suitableness of each.

CHAPTER III.

PARENTAL AND FILIAL RIGHTS AND DUTIES.

Origin.
§ 152. The duties of parents and of children, as also their correlative rights, have their origin in the family. These duties and these rights are, consequently, to be measured and determined in the light of the family relation. They rank as secondary and subordinate to the general rights and duties subsisting between the family as a whole and the individual members. The true interest of the family must not, therefore, be sacrificed for the supposed good of individual parent or child. On the other hand, the general good may require the sacrifice of the individual interest. It is a worthy spectacle when a father or a child intelligently and freely resigns plans, hopes, interests, dear to himself, for the good of the other members of the household.

Parental authority and direction are, accordingly, to be administered in the general interest of the family; and the good of the individual is to be secured through the well-being of the family. All the duties of children to parents and to one another, also, are to be discharged under the felt obligations coming upon them from the family as a whole. The individual interests should be harmonized as parts of a whole comprehensive interest. When doubt arises as to which should be preferred, the family welfare, rather than that of the individual member, should have the benefit of the doubt. The family rights and interests are the paramount rights and interests, and must measure and shape those of the individual members.

§ 153. The duties of parents to their children are the correlatives of the rights of children in respect to their parents. In the same way filial duties are correlatives of parental rights.

Parental and filial rights correlative.

What the parent owes to the child, the child has a right to receive from the parent. The parental duty of protection, for instance, is the filial right of protection. Even in earliest infancy, the child has rights; for it is a person, not a thing, no mere animal. It has a right to protection in itself, and not merely because the parent owes it to his own self-respect or to the interests of society to protect his own offspring.

§ 154. While the comprehensive duty, alike of parent and of child, towards each other is sympathetic affection and good will, to be expressed in all appropriate ways, the specialty of the relation marks out some special duties arising from it, in which this love is to be chiefly shown. This relation, as the basis of rights

Parental duties.

and duties, is characteristically the relation of dependence. The duties on the part of the parent, founded on this relation of dependence in the child, are the following:

First, Protection from all physical and moral harm;

Secondly, Provision of whatever is needful for the well-being in body or in mind of the child within the resources of the parent;

Thirdly, Counsel in all cases of perplexity or doubt;

Fourthly, A training and education, physical and mental, suited to the condition of the family and the prospective relations of the child to society and to life here and hereafter;

Fifthly, A wise, loving, yet authoritative rule, to which obedience shall be enforced by suitable sanctions—by rewards or by penalties—in physical good or evil, or by some proper retributions through the conscience of self-approval or of remorse and shame.

The rights of the child correlative to these parental duties are those of protection, support, counsel, education, and rule, on all occasions when needful.

§ 155. The filial duties, springing out *Filial duties.* of the relation of dependence, to a certain extent correspond to these duties of the parent. They are:

First, Grateful affection in return for parental kindness;

Secondly, Cheerful trust in parental maintenance and care;

Thirdly, Willing obedience to parental authority;

Fourthly, Faithful service in the interest of the family;

Fifthly, Reverence to parents as superiors.

The rights of parents correlative to these filial duties, are those of gratitude, trust, obedience, service, and reverence.

§ 156. The obligations subsisting reciprocally between parents and children are far from being absolute. They are limited by the finite nature of the relation; by the incapacities and the delinquencies of the parties, who, at best, are but imperfect men; and by other relations which the parties sustain to society and to God.

Obligations limited.

First, the relation itself is finite; it morally ceases with the maturity of the child, elevating him above the condition of dependence. The duties themselves, on both sides, change, and gradually modify themselves with the advance to this stage of maturity. Less assiduous protection and supply of wants and instruction and authority, are required, as the child grows in physical and intellectual and moral strength. But the child, if life is continued, ultimately becomes a man, and is invested with the rights and responsibilities of a man. Infirmities, too, creep along with years, and ultimately change the relations of dependence; the aged parent comes to depend on the vigor of the child. The child is then called to care for the parent. Grateful love and reverence still bind, but bind to other duties

1. By finiteness of relation.

than those incident to dependent childhood; they are the duties of affectionate and respectful care and solace and help.

The line which bounds this relation of filial dependence cannot be drawn in moral strictness. It varies with the peculiarities of families and of individual members of them. The usages of society and the necessities of civil order, have fixed upon a certain age, which shall be generally accepted as determining when the child enters upon his majority —his freedom and right to act for himself. This age in this country is twenty-one years, at which time the child becomes free and is liberated from the control of the parents. Persons under this age —minors—have no legal rights of property or of covenant, except in cases specified by statute, or through the medium of parents or guardians or trustees.

<small>2. By imperfection of parties.</small>
Secondly. The incapacity, or the culpable remissness or violation of duty, in either party in this relation, so far impairs the rights, and relieves from the duties imposed by it. The father who neglects to maintain and educate his son, cannot rightfully claim his son's full service; and the undutiful child so far impairs his rights to support. Love withheld by the one party so far hinders the responsive affection of the other. Immoral authority on the part of the parent is not obligatory on the child. When, however, there is doubt as to the morality of an act that is required, the dependent child may rightfully presume that the parent is right, and so be held to

obedience, on the ground of the positive authority of the parent, although not on the perceived morality of the act itself.

Thirdly. The rights and interests in the family are all circumscribed by the higher and broader relationships of man to society and to God. The state may take the child from the care of its parents for training, or for service, in cases of exigency; and all parental rule must be subordinate and subservient to the divine rule. There are rights of conscience belonging to minors which override parental control.

<small>3. By relations to society and to God.</small>

CHAPTER IV.

FRATERNAL RIGHTS AND DUTIES.

Origin and measure.
§ 157. The rights and duties between brothers and sisters, as they have their root and origin in the family, are to be measured and determined in the light of the family relation.

The children are but a part of the household; their relations to each other are the relations of parts. Their rights and interests are subordinate to those of the family, and cannot morally be exalted above them, but must ever be kept in harmony and subservience. As a class, fraternal rights and duties rank lower than the parental and filial. When collision arises, if there is no other ground of decision, parental right must override the right of a brother or sister; and the duties of children to their parents outrank those which they owe to one another.

Parity.
§ 158. Fraternal rights and duties rest upon a general basis of moral equality and reciprocity.

Age and sex, individual capacity to serve on the one hand and need of service on the other, only modify these general claims of duty based on natural equality, as in all human associations the functions of the respective members should aim to be complementary of one another.

§ 159. *Special duties.* The special duties of this class are sympathetic affection and kindness in all the forms of courtesy, truthfulness, trustfulness, equity, and beneficence.

The obligations here are closer and faster and more enduring, than those between neighbors. The grounds for this are in the natural instincts in the subject of duty predisposing to sympathy and affection; in the readier and larger receptivity on the part of the object of duty for fraternal kindness; and in the more abundant occasions for acts of goodwill and service, supplied in the ordinary condition of brothers and sisters of the same household.

PART III.

DUTIES IN THE STATE.

CHAPTER I.

THE STATE—ITS END AND MORAL NATURE.

Defined. § 160. A STATE may be defined to be a natural society, organized among men occupying a defined territory, for the furtherance of their common secular interests.

The definition embraces some leading attributes of a state, which require separate consideration.

I. THE ORIGIN OF THE STATE.

A natural society. § 161. The state is a natural society. It comes to be under the orderings of Divine Providence, in exact analogy with the unfolding of the flower from the bud, or of the branches from the trunk. The first glance over human history and condition discloses to us the great fact that men were made to live in a morally organized society. The moral order which his nature demands is attained for the smaller circle of the family under the parental authority. But as men increase in numbers, the parental home becomes too scanty; the crowded members swarm into new homes, families multiply, and the moral relationship, that human nature requires ever to be recognized and that at first directly bound only individuals in the same family group, now extends to the different family groups themselves. The tribal condition generally has followed the first stage of expansion from the family; but the tendency is strong and constant in the continued increase of numbers—the multiplication of tribes, it may be, as well as of families—to the full mature condition of a morally organized state—to the national condition. This is a law of the human race. It is established in his nature as social. Political society—the nation—the state—is thus truly and fully an ordinance of God, who so constituted men, and determined the conditions of their existence. "The powers that be are ordained of God."

II. THE STATE AN ORGANIZED COMMUNITY.

An organized society. § 162. The state is not a merely aggregated mass of individuals or of families, without any common bond holding them fast together in the pursuit of a common interest.

It involves a unity of aim, in reference to which the collected mass is ever acting; a relationship between the members, which binds them together and which originates certain rights and imposes certain corresponding duties; a common participation in hopes and fears and in a common destiny, prompting a reciprocal sympathy and enforcing reciprocal ministries. It involves a diversity of functions, corresponding to the diversity and magnitude of the particular interests which are combined into the single whole, with successive gradations from higher to lower, but each ministering in its place and in its way, to the realization of the one common aim.

As is true of living things generally, the beginnings of the state-life are germinant, nascent, from rudiments hardly recognized. Yet a number of men can not be brought together into permanent relations without being sensible that a kind of moral order enfolds them, and constrains and regulates and animates them. The fully developed political organism appears as the social life of the community advances, and the state proper—the nation—at last comes to be, with its manifold offices and ministries, forming a single body with many members, all under a more or less perfect subordination, and performing their several functions in reciprocal helpfulness and sympathy. In a true and most important sense, the state has a proper life; it is truly called a body politic, being organized with appropriate official appointments, in their several ways co-operating for the common good.

3.—THE SPHERE OF THE STATE.

Locality of sphere.
§ 163. The state is a community of persons living in contiguous territory. Its proper boundaries are territorial. All persons living within its proper territory are parts of it. Generally, indeed, they have had a common origin; the family has expanded into the tribe, and the tribe into the nation. But community of blood only helps to the state; it is not the principle of its proper unity and being. Nations have arisen from the union of peoples of different races. They readily receive into their common life strangers of other lineage. All residents in the recognized territory are subject to the national rule that is established; they are made to contribute their support to it; they share in its protection and care; their social activity is ever going out into the common life around them; their interests and hopes and destinies are bound up in the common experience. The bond of the family is identity of blood; that of the nation is identity of residence.

4.—THE STATE A POWER.

A power.
§ 164. As the essential nature of the individual man distinguishing him from a thing is, that he is the source of action—a power—, so the state, as the collective man, is pre-eminently and essentially a power. It is, indeed, the aggregated power of its people, organized into singleness of movement and action. All our conceptions

of the state thus regard it as a power. It is so absolutely in its essence, as being but the collective power of individual men, and also relatively to that of individuals. It is accordingly a common thing to speak of states as powers—as the powers of Europe,—states being so preëminently powers, as compared with individuals, that they are assumed to be the only powers. State and power are used synonymously.

The state exists simply because it is needful as a power. It is not mere condition; not mere relation; it is a substantial power, for it is power which is needed to protect, sustain, and effectively further the interests of beings like men. As a power, its being is to act; and as aggregated power, its action is to be commensurate with the community of men whose power is collected into it.

§ 165. Political power—state-power—like all rational power, has its seat and source in the free-will. States thus act, as individual men act, by willing. The strength of the state is measured by the strength of the collective will. Its particular actions are expressed in the terms of will: they are resolutions, determinations, orders, statutes, and laws, which are expressions of purpose, and are addressed to other wills who are to obey and execute.

Seat of its power.

State-power, as the aggregation of the social secular power of the community, is consequently the predominant power; as the predominant will-power, it is the ruling, governing power in the community. Its power should accordingly be the prevailing power, mightier than that of any one man in the political community, or of any portion of the community.

Political power, like that of the individual man, works itself out necessarily and legitimately through material instrumentalities. It avails itself of their ministry. It hoards up its accumulated power in them. It acquires and holds, that it may use, all kinds of material possessions needful for the purposes of its existence.

§ 166. As collective power, political power can express itself only through individual organs—its officials. Even if this power be devolved in part on collective bodies, as legislatures, these bodies are yet composed of individuals that speak though the lips of individual men. All such officials represent, it is true, the state; they bear its name, are invested with its insignia, wield its authority, and act solely for its interest; the world sees the state only in their persons and acts. But they are more than mere representatives; they are proper organs through which the state acts and lives, receives and imparts, assimilates and gives forth all that ministers to the secular social life or nourishes and expresses that life. Officials may be imperfect, unfaithful, corrupt, as bodily organs may be more or less paralyzed or diseased. But as organs are necessary to the physical body, and through their right discharge of their respective functions the body maintains its proper life, so these officials, representing the state, are real and necessary organs of the body politic. Unfaithful-

Its organs.

ness and corruption no more disprove this organic relation to the one collective life of the state, than do partial paralysis and disease disprove the living connection of the hand or the foot with the physical body.

5.—THE END OF THE STATE-LIFE.

Its end is the furtherance of secular interests common to members.

§ 167. The state exists for the security and furtherance of those secular interests which are common to its members. The immediate end which its legitimate activity respects is the well-being of its members in their collective outward or worldly relations. If we assume the family, the state, and the church as the three coördinate classes of permanent social organisms which naturally come to exist in the progress of the human race, we have, first, the family, distinguished by having its end in the well-being of the immature and dependent among men—the children still in their minority; next the state, by its having its immediate end in the secular well-being of the mature man,—the interests pertaining more properly to the body; and last, the church, by its having its immediate end in the religious well-being of the mature man—the interests that pertain to his nature as immortal.

That the proper end of the state-life is to be found in this furtherance of the secular well-being of men is apparent from the considerations, first, that the state exists only for man while in the body— it has no immortality of its own; secondly, its sphere is bounded by purely geographical boundaries, and its notice and its care can reach directly only outward things; thirdly, its proper activity has in all history been of this secular character, so that, when transcending this, it has been regarded as acting out of its sphere and with injurious results.

The secular interests of men regarded by the state, embrace more than those interests which are purely material; more than those which pertain to outward person—to body or limb or to material possessions. The state, it is true, can act on man only as one man can act upon another, through the medium of outward sense. But its action may indirectly reach other than material goods. A man's reputation, a good name, is a secular interest of exceeding value to him; it is one, in fact, properly guarded by the state; but it cannot be measured nor weighed; it is not material. Intelligence, morality, religion, are immaterial interests; they pertain not to the body but to the immaterial spirit. Moreover, there are interests which pertain to man's immortal being, and shape his condition through his eternal future. Yet so far as secular, so far as they pertain to the present life, they properly come within the regard of the state. The decisive reasons why the state should abstain from the religious supervision and control of its subjects are not at all that religion in itself is absolutely outside of the province of the state, and excluded by the essential character of the state. It is impossible that the state should let religion entirely alone, as will be shown in another more suitable place; the state in manifold ways does and must recognize religion. The legitimate limitation of its action here, as determined by the very idea of the state, is given in the secular bearings of religion on men. Every thing secular, common to the political community, is rightfully within the province of the state. But weighty reasons may be given why the state should have extremely little to do with religion. It can rightfully have to do with religion only so far as it is secular—for this life and its interests—which is the least considerable part of religion, whose main concern is the immortality of man. The entire care of religion is better entrusted to other hands, where even for its secular bearings it will be better cared for than it can be by the state. It is eminently wise, therefore, in the state to abstain from all religious direction and control, except as most demonstratively shown to be necessary for the secular interests of its people.

Morality, much more than religion, demands the attention of the state, inasmuch as all secular interests are more directly affected by it. Public peace, public security, hopeful industry, all secular thrift, depends directly on the morals of the community.

Intelligence, as necessary basis of morality and religion, and as indispensable to a people for the right exercise of its proper sovereignty in the state, bears a still more significant relation to the secular well-being of a political community.—Just so far as this secular well-being requires, education is a legitimate object for the care of the state.

Every thing thus of a proper secular nature affect-

THE STATE—ITS END AND NATURE.

ing the well-being of the people, comes within the purview of political action.

But besides the limitations to state-action even in regard to secular interests already intimated, is the further limitation that this secular interest must be a common interest. The state is for no individual; it is for the community. It is for each individual only as a member of the community. Its action, if ever directed to an individual, as must indeed often be the case, should be not from any private favoritism, but such as would be taken for any other individual or class placed in like relation to the state.

This characteristic of proper political activity indicates the wisdom and propriety of making all legislation as general as possible. To bestow on an individual, or a class, or a section, what in like conditions is denied to others, is in violation of a fundamental principle of political morality.

Relative to spiritual activity. But although the immediate end of the life and activity of the state is thus secular, it by no means follows that this life and activity are in no relation to moral and spiritual interests. In the first place, as the body is for the spirit and the secular for the spiritual, the state, whose immediate concern is the bodily and the secular, must ever act in subordination and in subservience to the moral and spiritual interests of men. Its action does not directly aim at these interests, but its action, to be legitimate, must ever be helpful to them. As with the heart in the natural body, while it beats only in order to propel the blood, its pulsations must yet ever be influenced by the condition of the whole body for whose nourishment the blood which it propels is designed. The circulatory system exists only for the well-being of the whole body; it acts only in sympathy with its condition; it measures its action by it. So the state, whose ministry is directly for the bodily or secular, yet indirectly serves the spirit for which the body exists; it must keep itself ever in true sympathy with the demands of this higher nature and measure its action by it.

Secondly, the state is a community of persons—of moral and spiritual beings—who can never lay aside these higher attributes. The moral nature breathes forth and acts in all the bodily life. The entire free action of the state, even although aimed directly at merely worldly ends, is, therefore, so far morally determined and characterized.

Thirdly, the action of the state, although its end is to be found properly in secular interests, must sometimes seek the furtherance of those interests by the enlistment of the moral and spiritual. Just as the art of medicine, which aims only at the healthy condition of the body, must needs often address itself to the mind, prescribing the measure and mode of its action in order to bodily health, so the state often finds itself under the necessity of legislating in regard to the religious condition of the community while still seeking its highest secular well-being. In this indirect way it is called upon to foster intelligence, the culture of the fine arts, the moral and religious improvement of the people.

Thus the outward social life of man is held like

the personal life of the body, to a strict subordination to the collective moral well-being of the individual members.

6.—THE MORAL ATTRIBUTES OF THE STATE.

§ 168. From what has been said it is clear that the state is in a proper sense within the sphere of morality. Its action is exclusively human action, which is essentially moral; its immediate end and object is in subordination and subservience to the higher moral nature of the individuals composing the national community; it has to do with beings whose natures are moral, and whose outward welfare depends greatly on moral conditions. It is accordingly by no mere figurative use of language that we speak of "a nation's conscience." The collective action of the state is felt to be free as truly as the action of the individual; there is a sense of right and wrong in reference to it which is impelling and constraining; a feeling of shame among the people, also, for national wrong-doing; and an expectation of just retribution for the right or wrong in the life or actions of the body politic. Just as the individual man, in laboring for mere secular interests and in the true secular sphere, must bear his moral nature with him and penetrate his whole outward carriage and conduct with a truly moral shaping and coloring, so the collective man—the state—even in its secular sphere, must evince everywhere the moral nature which characterizes in common all its constituent members.

Its action moral.

The ends and objects which it proposes to itself in its action, the general policy by which it governs itself, as well as the particular measures which it adopts in carrying out this "policy," must all be consistent with a pure and sound morality. Its legislation, its adjudication under the laws of the rights of the citizen, and its administration of the law as thus adjudicated, must in every step be controlled by moral principles and rules. An immoral law, an unjust sentence, a corrupt or wrongful administration, every man disallows and reprobates. Everywhere, thus, in its ends or objects, and in its modes of accomplishing these ends, the state is held to act morally—to recognize itself as subject to moral control, and to yield itself freely to this control. It can never drop from its proper life this moral attribute. There is no difficulty in conceiving how the state may thus be a truly moral organism while its end is purely secular, any more than in conceiving how a carpenter who in his calling aims only at the finished building, must yet appear as a moral man in all he does, building only for uses approved in morality, building honestly in accordance with moral requirements, investing his handiwork with the dignity and beauty of his own moral nature.

Not a merely jural society. § 169. The state has been defined by an able writer—Dr. Francis Lieber, in his Political Ethics—to be a *jural society*, being founded on the relation of right as the family is founded on the relation of consanguinity, having for its principle of action that of right, as the family has that of love for its animating principle, and, moreover, including only jural relations. To this view of the state there are grave objections. In the first place, the relation of right is not the characteristic basis of the political society, for it is not exclusively proper to the state. It exists as truly in the family as in the state; indeed, in every possible association of men, the so-called jural relation—the relation of right—underlies and pervades its whole being and action. In the next place, purely jural relations are not the exclusive relations subsisting in a state in any sense of the statement in which it is not true of the family. The relation of the state to the "great ends of humanity" originates a relation of right, a proper jural relation; but precisely as the relation of the family to the same great ends of humanity originates certain jural relations between it and its parts, which we designate as marital rights, parental and filial rights, and fraternal rights. Strike out this relation of the state or the family to these ends and all jural relation disappears; it has nothing to stand upon, and has no support, no definable limits, no sanctions. In the third place, if the jural relation is the proper relation originating the state, then, inasmuch as that relation exists in respect to religious matters as well as secular, the state must extend its rule and care as well to religious interests as to secular; and thus we find all practical distinction between the spheres of the state and of the church obliterated. Once more, if the state and the family are distinguished from each other simply by this—that right is the animating principle in one and not in the other—then the principle of love is excluded from the sphere of the state, and thus patriotism, loyalty, love of country, are empty names; they designate no virtues. This whole view, plausible as it seems as opposed to certain erroneous doctrines in regard to civil government, is thus logically fallacious and practically most vicious and baneful. Mere legality, mere outward heartless conformity to governmental requisitions, does not fulfil the moral obligations of the citizen to the state, even were it true that the state can in no way directly enforce its claims beyond the outward formal obedience. There is a true allegiance which is broader, deeper, earlier than all mere jural relations which "began before laws, continueth after laws, and is in vigor when laws are suspended and have had their force."

§ 170. As a true moral personality, the state is obliged by the mere force of its moral nature to cherish a sympathetic good-will, towards all the proper objects of its activity, to practice an effective beneficence in respect to them, and to carry out this sympathetic affection in this beneficence in strictest uprightness.

Bound as a moral person.

The moral relationships of the state are of a threefold division:—to itself; to its citizens: to other states. Its relationship to God properly comes into consideration in the division of duties pertaining to God, and is accordingly omitted here.

CHAPTER II.

THE RIGHTS AND DUTIES OF A STATE IN RELATION TO ITSELF.—I. EXISTENCE.

Rights of the state.
§ 171. As in the case of the individual man, so in the case of the state we may properly speak of certain rights and duties as pertaining to it individually—to itself.

The several comprehensive rights and corresponding duties of a state are those of: 1, *Existence;* 2. *Self-rule* or *autonomy;* and 3. *Growth.*

1. Of existence.
§ 172. I. It is the right of a state to be: it is its corresponding duty to maintain its existence.

It is not within the proper province of an existing state to raise the question whether its birth was legitimate. The fact of its existing has settled that point.

Threefold origin.
§ 173. States come to be in fact in three ways: First by regular *growth* of the family into the tribe and then of the tribe into the state. Such was the rise of the earlier nations.

Secondly, By *separation* from existing states. As to the question: what can legitimate a rebellion or secession, it may be answered that the law of the state from which the separation is proposed, must necessarily prohibit and resist it. No state can for light cause legalize self-disintegration. Further, nothing but extreme necessity can justify a part of a nation in dismembering itself from the political body to which it belongs. Such disruption naturally is in violence and brings inevitable distress. Intolerable oppression or hindrance of sound political life, with sufficient magnitude and strength to maintain healthy existence, alone can warrant disruption.

Thirdly, By *aggregation* of existing communities. Bodies of people conveniently situated for a proper state organization, whether tribal communities or dependencies of some one state, or of different states, may be drawn together into a legitimate state-union under the natural instinct of man craving a social order for the nurture of common secular interests.

§ 174. But a state having under providential orderings come into being, it then has a right, as it is its highest duty to maintain its existence. Subordinate only to the supreme law of God and of universal morality, its maxim is to preserve itself— *Salus populi, suprema lex.* Its right and duty, here are threefold: 1, of *support;* 2, of *defense;* 3, of *enforcing its rightful rule.*

<small>Threefold duty of self-maintenance.</small>

§ 176. THE SUPPORT required for the state

2. Of support. comes from the public resources or from the citizens. Of its right and duty to employ its own resources in self-support there can be no question. Equally beyond question is its duty, as the general rule, to use these resources of its own before having recourse to the individual citizen. Of the necessity or the expediency of requiring the help of the citizen, the state is sole and supreme judge. It has the right, and if it judge it to be necessary for its own existence it is its duty, to appropriate the property and the service of its citizens.

Of the extent and the mode of bringing into its use individual property and service, the state is sovereign arbiter. It is bound, however, by the principles of political morality to make no exactions beyond the public necessity; to distribute the burden as nearly as possible equally and fairly, according to ability; to proceed with all practicable tenderness for the individual interest; and to have a steady regard to the general interest of the community.

§ 177. The state has a right to take, if necessary and in proper ways, any of the property belonging to the citizen. (1). It has thus the right, so called, of *eminent domain*—of superior right above the individual to appropriate any of the lands or other estate of its citizens, giving, of course, reasonable compensation. (2). It has the right to tax its citizens for its support. (3). It has still further the right to the personal service of its citizens for war, for the suppression of insurrection or other crimes against the peace and order of the community, and for civil office. Its right is founded in the very nature of civil society which is but the organized social secular life of men and enfolds all public secular interests and rights. The property which it legitimates and protects, and the personal service which it upholds and fosters, are in moral reciprocity bound to minister to its necessities, as the members of the physical body must minister, even to the extent of entire self-sacrifice if necessary, to the common life from which they spring and thrive.

Kinds of taxation. § 178. Generally the chief reliance of the state for its support is on taxation, which may be *direct—taxes* proper,—or *indirect—duties*. Direct taxation is upon the person—*capitation* or *poll*-tax,—or on the property of the subject—*property* tax. Indirect taxation is either upon property produced within the state —*excise duty*,— or upon property imported from abroad—*imposts* or *customs;* or upon business—as by *stamps;*—or upon income.

Of the relative amounts to be levied by the state from these several sources of revenue, as has been already stated, the state is sole arbiter. Its judgment must vary in different communities and under different conditions. Some general considerations may be stated which will influence the selection and distribution.

1. Direct taxation. § 179. 1. *Direct taxation* is more sensibly felt than indirect. It therefore gives rise to friction between the state and the subject, and also to temptation of concealment and false valuation, and consequent unfairness in the listing of property. On the other hand it keeps alive and active the sense of the state-life in the subject, and a feeling of responsibility in the legislator, restraining him from excessive levies. Where, as in the United States, the nation and the more local communities—the several states and territories—collect their revenues separately, it is a wise distinction, as far as may be, to allot to the nation all indirect duties—customs—and to the local community—the state—all direct taxes. A twofold system of appraisal and assessment in the same territory must necessarily give rise to much chafing as well as occasion a twofold expenditure. Moreover, a fundamental provision in the constitution of the United States requiring that all direct taxes shall be distributed according to the census, such taxes would work unequally between the states by reason of the unequal distribution of wealth.

Indirect taxes are less felt by the payer; they are more fairly laid and more fully collected; and consequently give less occasion for chafing and fraud. False valuation of merchandise and smuggling are the two chief temptations to be guarded against. Impost duties, however, hamper foreign commerce, and are therefore held in disfavor by some advocates of free trade.

2. Capitation taxes.

§ 180. 2. *Capitation taxes* are legitimate, inasmuch as persons, alike with property, enter as constituents into the body politic, sharing in its protection and care. It is well, moreover, that every citizen be reminded in some sensible way of his personal relationship to the state. Only a moderate portion of the necessary revenue of a state, however, can be realized in this way; and the great burden must rest on the property of the subjects.

§ 181. 3. *Excise duties*, being levied on the products of home industry, are objectionable as burdensome to production, which it is a leading duty of the state to foster. But articles of which there is danger of excessive or injurious or wasteful use, such as distilled liquors and tobacco, are not liable to this objection, and are therefore wisely taken to bear the burden of taxation to the full extent which they will bear.

<small>3. Excise duties.</small>

§ 182. 4. *Imposts* or *customs*, levied on imported commodities, constitute a leading source of revenue in the general administration of governments. The considerations that favor this selection, especially for national as opposed to municipal revenues, are manifold. The collection of it is more in the immediate control of the government. In maritime countries it incidentally furnishes a nursery for a naval force, and also a ready instrumentality for furthering commerce, as by affording aid to vessels in need, furnishing protection to the coast, and a watchful supervision over the needful provisions for safe navigation, such as lights, beacons, removal of obstructions, and the like. It necessarily brings the whole influx of foreign goods under the inspection of the government, so that, the kinds and quantities all being made known, profitable suggestions may be derived for any needed governmental regulation—for repression

<small>4. Imposts.</small>

of injurious or increase of desirable products, and also for the encouragement and direction of the productive industry of the country.

This kind of taxation is less sensibly felt by the tax-payer. He pays at his own pleasure and convenience, just as and when he chooses to buy, and pays no more than he chooses. He does not come into direct conflict with the government or its generally unwelcome instrument — the tax-collector. This kind of taxation is therefore generally borne more quietly.

Where the revenues for national and for state or municipal support are separately levied and collected, the collection of imposts for national revenue is less expensive and less annoying to the tax-payer.

Further, a revenue from customs—by a tariff, as it is familiarly called—enables a government indirectly to foster more judiciously and effectively certain interests of more or less vital concern to the community. Every wise tariff system must be more or less discriminative. An exactly horizontal tariff, that is, a tariff of equal duties on all imports, is hardly practicable, and certainly would be most unreasonable.

There may possibly, and probably will, be discrimination required in reference to the country from which the imports come—according to treaty-regulations with the different nations, reciprocating free or dutiable admission of products.

Discrimination may be necessary in reference to the interests of revenue itself; some desirable commodities may not bear the full measure of a horizontal tariff. Indeed it must ever be a leading problem in adjusting a tariff, what amount of duty will afford the largest revenue. A tariff may be so high as to be prohibitory; or it may so enhance the price to the purchaser that the sale, and consequently the importation, will be so far lessened that a higher duty will produce less revenue than a lower. Moreover, some commodities will yield too small a revenue for the cost of collection. A wise principle in adjusting a tariff system is to make those commodities pay most that pay best.

Discrimination may be required in the interests of public morals. Hurtful commodities may be kept out of the country by prohibitory duties; and the introduction of dangerous or useless articles may be hindered or repressed by relatively high duties, as, for instance, distilled liquors and tobacco.

Discrimination may be wise in reference to luxuries, which will bear and justify a heavier duty than mere necessaries or comforts. Silks and wines are thus properly discriminated against by the imposition of higher than average duties.

Discrimination should be made in the interest of classes in the community less able to contribute to the support of the state. A leading objection to a revenue by tariff is that no difference can be made directly between the rich and the poor. Wealth is not taxed as wealth; but only purchase. If all the citizens purchased the same things, under a horizontal tariff the poor would contribute equally with the rich for the support of the state. There is weight in this consideration, although the burden of this kind of taxation is more effectually proportioned to the ability of the payers than other kinds, inasmuch as it is regulated by what a man freely buys. Hence, as in equity property should be burdened according to its amount, it is requisite in an equitable tariff system that luxuries be taxed heaviest, conveniences and comforts less, and the necessaries of life which all must have, least of all.

Once more, discrimination may be needful in the interest of domestic production. As the augmentation of its resources is one leading duty of a state, and as the resources lie mainly in the possessions or wealth of its citizens, resulting from productive labor, the fostering of all the legitimate modes of augmenting the wealth of the country should be a leading object with a government. It is its duty, therefore, in every department of its administration, and especially in the matter of its tariff system to see to it that in all its parts, and in its legitimate effects, it shall not only not hinder but positively promote all the productive and distributing industries of the country whereby its resources may be augmented. The relative condition of these different industries may reasonably require intelligent discrimination in favor of one rather than another.

The objections to imposts as a source of revenue are: 1. That they are a tax on the productions of foreign countries. But they are so only as for the profit of the producer they are consumed in the country. If the duty was prohibitory, he would have no right to complain: for every purchaser, whether nation or individual, has a right in the freedom of trade to refuse to purchase.

2. It hampers trade and intercourse between different countries. This is true and it is a valid objection, so far as it goes; but it suggests rather carefully considered modes of collection than repeals of tariffs. It is the frauds, the lawless exactions, and the discourtesies of collectors, rather than the duties themselves, that so exasperate commercial men and travelers. The outcries against a revenue by tariff are mostly from these classes and those immediately connected with them and those whose special industries happen in the unavoidable imperfections of any system of revenue to be more closely touched, and not from the great mass of the people, at least when free from political partisan bias and pressure.

3. The collection of duties gives large occasion for corruption. This is true; but the evil is an unavoidable one in any system of revenue collection.

4. It is a ground of international alienation and animosity. This is true, but only to a very limited and really inconsiderable extent.

§ 183. 5. *Stamps* and all taxes upon business, while they may be justified in the extremities of a nation's need, are objectionable, not only because the national welfare imperatively requires that the ways of business should be as unobstructed as possible, but because they are generally inconvenient for the payer, and are relatively small so as to be unworthy of a great nation.

5. Stamps.

§ 184. 6. *Income taxes* are, perhaps, the most

6. Income taxes. odious to the payers. Incomes are not a fair measure of ability to pay; they are not easily ascertained; they are apt to be disguised and understated; they are matters of privacy into which it is very offensive that the public eye should penetrate; they hinder the accumulation of capital. Income taxes thus lead to fraudulent returns; disturb the free tendencies of investment by capitalists and of productive enterprise; and occasion perpetual friction between the tax-payer and state. They are the last modes of revenue to be resorted to by a state in its necessities. They are most tolerable in old and wealthy states where there is a large surplus of capital for investment.

II. Right of self-defense. § 185. SELF-DEFENSE is a natural right and duty of the state, while it may not trespass on the rights of other states or of its own subjects so as to provoke aggression or rebellion. When assailed it is one of the fundamental laws of living being that it should defend itself. As, against the violences of natural forces—storms and earthquakes and conflagrations,—against the maraudings of animal and insect life, against all physical and animal force and harm, it is bound to protect its citizens, so equally against the force of men, against assault upon their liberties and good order and possessions, whether from foreign force or from insurgents at home. There should be patience, forbearance, as in the case of assault upon persons; but there is a limit beyond which unresisting sufferance is an immorality. War should be the last resort—*ultima ratio;*—but it may be righteous as such resort. As the spirit of philanthropy—good will among men—advances in the world, peace will more and more prevail; the occasions and the justifications of war will lessen. But while imperfection remains, the liability to lawless oppression and to wars will continue.

For its own defense, the state rightfully holds the entire community of resources within its domain, subject to its use and control. Property and personal service being the very constituents of the united social interest, the ruling power in it must dispose of it according to its own sovereign determination. The usages of peace and the rights which have grown up under these usages, even statutes themselves, may be compelled to give way. Laws are dormant in war—*inter arma leges silent*. The state in war appropriates, or even destroys, the possessions of individuals; it conscripts their persons. This great power it is, however, bound to exercise only so far as the good of the whole shall require on the clearest occasions of necessity, with the utmost forbearance and consideration, and with full compensation out of the public resources.

§ 186. 3. THE MAINTENANCE OF AUTHORITY—the right and duty of enforcing its rightful rule—appertains to the state by virtue of its very being. The state exists as a ruling power; it ceases when its rule ends. Its will in its sphere is rightfully supreme: it is its right and duty to exert that will and make it effectual, otherwise it would be preposterous to will or to claim the right of willing. The means and methods by

III. Of rule.

which it may rightfully enforce its will are precisely determined by the nature of its province, which is the secular interest of the community. As all secular interests are incorporated into it, they are its to use in the fulfilment of its end. All secular power within its control to its utmost limit it may thus lawfully employ. The enforcement of its laws by penal sanctions to the extent of taking property, personal liberty, life itself,—all secular coercion by secular means—belongs to it by right of its very being. Only a perfect community can dispense with the use of physical constraint. To the good the constraints of civil authority will be no terror; in the sense of harm to their persons or property, the law is not for them; but so long as there are lawless and disobedient members of civil society, there will be need and rightful use for the sword. It is a grand fallacy to reason from the immortality and the higher spiritual nature of men that none but proper spiritual and eternal motives should be addressed to them. This would be no more logical than to infer from man's being in civil society governed by secular influences that there should be no family rule. The grand fact that man exists in a physical body, in time and in place on earth, places him in the secular sphere where he must in truth to his condition act in secular relations and be correspondingly acted upon by secular forces. Secular ends are legitimately attained by secular means. As a secular power, the state rightfully employs secular constraint—outward, physical coercion—in the enforcement of its rightful rule.

§ 187. The legitimate and principal means of maintaining political authority are found in the sanctions of law.

Sanctions of law.

It should never be forgotten, however, that the very manner and spirit in which the government frames and executes the sanctions of its laws, are vitally concerned in the maintenance of its authority. Unjust, immoral, barbarous, partial, or capricious, arbitrary, reckless legislation and administration are fatal to authority, which must rest mainly on the respect and confidence of the body of the political community. Wise and righteous laws are their own support with an orderly and intelligent people.

The sanctions of law are either *rewards* for loyalty and obedience, or *penalties* for disobedience.

§ 188. REWARDS express the lawgiver's approval of loyalty and obedience. They are in the form of public recognition of patriotic service and acts, military and civil distinctions, monuments, bounties, abatements of dues, and the like. They constitute but an inconsiderable part of the sanctions found necessary for the enforcement of authority. They are yet a needful help in encouraging the spirit of order and loyalty. Wisely distributed they win the sympathy and affectionate confidence of the people towards the government.

Rewards.

§ 189. PENALTIES express the lawgiver's disapproval of disobedience and his corresponding determination to prevent it.

Penalties.

They are a necessary part of law; for, as it has been forcibly asked: "What can be called law, which does not express supreme abhorrence of transgression?" Penal laws which are characterized by a spirit of indifference to loyal obedience or to the great ends of society for which laws are ordained, are a mockery of proper authority. If the lawgiver is indifferent, why should not the subject be so? The moral sense of the community—its love of right, its abhorrence of wrong—must pervade all its legislation, and, most of all, its penal legislation. The one great end of penal laws is to discourage or prevent disobedience.

Secondary ends of penalty—in teaching. § 190. But while the prevention of crime is the primary immediate end of penalty, there are other ends to be sought by it. These ends are in entire harmony with that of prevention and to a large extent helpful to it. A second end in penalty is thus, *the moral teaching of the community*. All penal laws, as has been already observed, express the moral sense of the political community. Such expression should have its full legitimate effect on the minds of the people. It is an end to be had distinctly in view in framing penal laws. As legislation should be the expression of the highest wisdom of the state, penal laws may properly be somewhat in advance of the average morality of the community, while yet not so far as to be beyond their sympathy and respect. They should aim expressly at inculcating respect for rightful authority and for the majesty of law, love of order, hatred of wrong.

§ 191. A third legitimate end of penalty, to be applied in subordination to the two ends already named, is the reformation of the offender.

In reforming.

§ 192. The modes of punishment by states are by pecuniary fines, by imprisonment, by personal suffering. They must vary with the state of society and with the character of the people. In early stages of history, retaliation of the wrong done in mode as well as degree—wound for wound, tooth for tooth, life for life—was well nigh a necessity; as it is an immediate suggestion of natural instinct, moreover, punishments were inflicted wholly or in part by the party wronged. Fines are collected even now in civilized states sometimes by the party suffering from the offense; even prosecutions for crimes against public order are left to individual complaints. But in the progress of civilization, the law of exact retaliation—*lex talionis*—gives way and the prosecution of criminals and the infliction of penalties on the guilty are wisely taken from the hands of the individual and committed to the public official.

Modes.

The second end of punishment named—the moral teaching of the community—forbids all such modes of punishment as unnecessarily shock humane sentiments or offend against public decency. More and more, with the progress of society, public inflictions of penalty on the person of the offender become offensive, and are wisely replaced by more private execution of the law.

§ 193. The degrees of penalties vary, first, with the nature of the offense. The principle of natural justice enjoins this;—that, aside from all other considerations, the degree of the penalty should in some way measure the heinousness of the offense.

<small>Degrees vary, 1, with heinousness of the offense.</small>

§ 194. Secondly, the degrees of penalty vary with the difficulty of detection and conviction of offenders. Those offenses which it is more difficult to detect, such for instance, as those committed in the night; must receive heavier penalties.

<small>2. With difficulty of detection.</small>

§ 195. Thirdly, the degrees of penalty vary with the number and strength of the offenders. Conspirators in the perpetration of a wrong are thus more severely punished than individual offenders.

<small>3. With prevalence of wrong.</small>

§ 196. Fourthly, the degrees of penalty vary with the moral sentiment of the community. As that becomes more pure, more firm, more pervasive, less severe inflictions are necessary.

<small>4. With public sentiment.</small>

CHAPTER III.

POLITICAL AUTONOMY.

Defined.
§ 197. It is the right of a state to rule itself;—to shape its own organic law, to enact its own statutes, to interpret and administer its own laws;—generally to manage its own affairs without the interference of other powers. This is the right of self-rule—autonomy.

Ground.
§ 198. The right of self-rule is involved in the right to be. The very idea of a state is that it is the embodiment in a single organic whole of the power to rule all the secular interests of the community. Interference from without with the free exercise of this ruling authority must either reduce to provincial subordination or infringe on the integrity of a state.

The right of autonomy is not necessarily impaired by a distribution of political authority into the more strictly national and the local or municipal rule. But in order to the unity of the organic life of the state, the municipal must be held ever subordinate and subservient to the national. With this subordination, it is wise policy to subdivide political rule so as to give to districts or provinces—States—the immediate rule over what of secular concern lies within the State or province; to allot, moreover, to smaller districts, like subordinate rule over the political and civil concerns within such district, till the smallest convenient local community is reached. Indeed, it is in the same line of wise policy to leave ever to the individual citizen all of freedom to rule and manage his own concerns consistent with the good of the whole, § 208. 3.

§ 199. It is equally the duty as it is the right of a state to maintain its own autonomy, The state owes it to its own prosperity and vigor, to the independence of its action and consequently to its proper relations and degree of responsibility, and to its own self-respect, with unyielding firmness and at any sacrifice to resist all dictation and all constraint from other powers. A subject sovereignty is a contradiction in terms and a monstrosity in being.

Autonomy as duty.

§ 200. The autonomy of a state is exerted chiefly in the distinct spheres of its organic law; its legislation; its judiciary; and its executive administration.

Spheres.

As all finite rule, while in freedom, is yet under responsibility, in these several spheres of autonomy there are respectively in part distinct modes of responsibility in each. The people themselves who constitute the state are for their collective action responsible to God, and, in a certain degree, to the fraternity of states. The departments of political administration are responsible to the people and so far as courtesy and reciprocal respect are concerned, also to the co-ordinate departments; as also more or less to the particular political power which creates or appoints the officials in them. The measure and kind of responsibility vary with the relationship. There is no absolute autonomy among men. Accountability, in its ten thousand forms and degrees, enters, as an element not to be got rid of, into all modes of human activity—personal or social. The only questions that can arise are: to whom, to what extent, and in what way, is this accountability to be recognized and enforced.

§ 201. THE ORGANIC LAW of a state is the expressed will of the political community in reference to the principles and forms of its government. It is the fundamental law by which the entire action of the political community is to be ruled, and which is ever to be recognized as supreme. From it there is no appeal but to the original seat of all political authority— the community itself.

<small>Organic law defined.</small>

This organic law may appear in full and proper form as in written constitutions, or only in parts and fragments, as the advancing history of the people has developed them. In communities, properly free, it is drawn up under the direction of the people, or at least is formally ratified by them in such way as the circumstances may admit, so as to be recognized as the expressed will of the people. In older historic nations, brought together and constituted into a single political body, perhaps, by outward force and by degrees, it appears in the form of subsequent concessions, as in the case of the *Magna Charta* of King John of England, and the fuller charter of Louis XVIII. of France; or in the form of compacts entered into by existing powers in the state between themselves or with the governed. Established usage, moreover, may stamp additional features on the fundamental law of the state, as implying the consent and will of the sovereign community.

Its purport. It is the purpose and object of the organic law of a state (1) to confer the power of political rule possessed by the community on designated individuals or bodies of men; (2) to define the limits within which, and also the modes and forms in which, this conferred power is to be exercised.

All power not thus conferred, directly or by fair implication, is reserved to the community itself. The right to revoke, or alter, or amend its organic law or constitution is also reserved, although the mode by which such revocation or change is to be brought about may be properly or wisely prescribed in the instrument itself.

The organic law thus creates and shapes the outward organism through which the social life of the community is so far to be expressed.

Threefold political function. There is a threefold division of the functions of the political organism adopted generally by the most mature and most highly perfected states. They constitute the other spheres mentioned of state autonomy—the legislative, the judicial, and the executive.

§ 202. The function of the *state legisla-*
ture is to ordain law for the government
of its own action and that of its citizens.
It is the seat of authority for the nation. Its
enactments are binding on the conscience of the
subject, unless contravening the higher authority
of right morals or the fundamental law of the state
—its organic law or constitution.

1. Legislative function.

In nations most advanced in civilization, the legislative power is commonly entrusted to the joint action with the executive of two distinct bodies of representatives—one more popular, elected immediately by the people, and having a briefer tenure of office--the House of Representatives, the House of Deputies, the House of Commons ; and the other designed to be the more conservative body, having a longer tenure of office and appointed by other functionaries or organisms in the state. The union of the executive with these representative bodies is wisely required for a more perfect adaptation of law to the practical needs of administrative power, and to existing relations with foreign powers.

The ordinances of the legislature, at least so far as pertaining more directly to the general welfare and for general observance, are called *statutes*. They constitute the great body of the written law of a nation—its *lex scripta*.

§ 203. It is the proper function of the
Judiciary to interpret in their application to particular cases the laws of the
state—its organic law, its statute law, and its unwritten law—*lex non scripta*. This unwritten law

2. Judicial.

—the common law as it is sometimes designated in distinction from the statute law—it interprets and declares out of the principles of natural justice as recognized and accepted in the usages of society.

The only allowed occasion for the action of the judiciary is a case of question among citizens, officials, or political communities. Its authority reaches no further than the points controverted in some actual litigation; its function being solely to interpret the law in its specific applications to existing occasions. Its decisions rank as precedents which are binding until set aside by higher authority. They are regarded with peculiar deference, not merely because civil judges are expected to be both competent and upright, but because the controversy between interested litigants is supposed to bring out the full light of truth in the case so as to afford the best possible opportunity for a just determination.

The sphere of the judiciary reaches to all kinds of civil and political law—organic, statute, and common. It interprets all, harmonizing them with the higher principles of morality or the established usages or unwritten law of the community. If it finds statute enactments irreconcilable with the organic law or with common morality, it declares it not to be law applicable to the government of the citizens. It is competent to enact no law; its province is simply to declare what is law.

§ 204. The judiciary recognizes a distinction between *legal rights*—rights existing under statute law or judicially declared common law—and *equities*

—rights not covered by known law, which perhaps no general law could be framed to meet, but yet real and needing to be protected. Sometimes, the state creates separate tribunals for these two provinces of judicial action—courts of law and courts of equity or chancery. Sometimes the same tribunal is authorized to adjudicate cases both of law and of equity. A court thus may have its law side and its equity side. In either case it is governed by fixed principles of practice and of adjudication, so that no collision may arise.

§ 205. It is the proper function of the *Executive* of a state to execute the statutes and ordinances of the legislature and the decisions of the judiciary, so far at least as is not otherwise expressly provided As the political head of the state, it is the function of the executive officer to represent the state in all its intercourse with other states. He is properly charged with such general supervision of the condition of the community as will enable him to recommend suitable measures to the legislature or to the people for their adoption.

3. Executive.

CHAPTER IV.

POLITICAL GROWTH.

§ 206. It is the right of a state to grow; to carry on its proper political life to its maturity and highest perfection. The great comprehensive end of the state being the furtherance of the common secular welfare of a contiguous people, it is at once the right and the duty of the state to promote to the highest degree this secular well-being of the community in all its departments.
{Right of growth.}

Growth is an essential attribute of life. The predominant instincts of a community are towards the extension of the common good, which the fundamental laws of being require to be obeyed and gratified in suitable ways and within proper limits. No moral interest is necessarily harmed by such growth; all moral interests, as perfectly harmonized and organized into a whole of universal good, under the divine direction and rule, demand this growth of every existing state. Its very existence imports increase, improvement, perfection.

§ 207. This growth of the state is to reach all

<small>Sevenfold departments.</small> departments of its being. There is no good ground to be found in the essence of a state for excepting any. As finite, it is subject to manifold limitations; but these limitations do not lie in the proper being of the state. The several departments in which this growth is to be sought and furthered are the following:

1, Territorially; 2, in population; 3, in strength of political union; 4, in wealth and material resources; 5, in the sanitary condition of the people; 6, in public intelligence; 7, in public morals.

<small>Maxims.</small> § 208. Especially applicable to this mode of political activity—the furtherance of the proper growth of the state— are certain maxims of political action which, while indeed of universal pertinence, may properly be expressly stated here.

1. All furtherance of political prosperity must be directed steadily towards the one end for which the state exists—the common secular well-being of the people. Only as requisite to this common good can personal or class or sectional action be justified.

2. All political action must be within the lines of fundamental morality, as for instance of courtesy, justice, and beneficence.

3. What can be, should be left to individual care and enterprise, to associations, or to local communities. This maxim is founded on the principle that the highest perfection of the state lies in the richest right activity of its subjects. This activity should be therefore stimulated and encouraged in all practicable ways. There are in support of this maxim

the further considerations that individuals and local communities are better able to discern what the common good requires ; and that they are better qualified to devise the modes of execution, and generally to act more efficiently, more wisely, more economically than mere official representatives of the state. § 221. The maxim *laissez faire*—let the subject do what the public interest demands—is a sound maxim ; but it must ever be applied so as not to set aside the right and duty of the state to see to it that the public good is ever protected and furthered. It is a directive, not a supplanting maxim.

SECTION I. TERRITORIAL EXTENSION.

§ 209. The state has the right to grow territorially.

Modes of Territorial growth. The modes of territorial extension are threefold : by annexation ; by acquisition ; by conquest.

By annexation. 1. ANNEXATION is of territory not belonging to any other states. Unoccupied lands adjacent to its borders, a state may rightfully incorporate into its own domain. There may arise a question whether lands are occupied or not. It is generally accepted that nomadic, wandering tribes acquire no permanent right of domain. As they begin a settled life and give indications of intention to hold and improve for permanent uses, they acquire rights which more powerful nations are bound to respect. Only on the clear ground of the peremptory demands of universal humanity, as in a spreading conflagration the destruction of a dwelling may be justified to save a city, can such deprivation by a powerful state of a weaker community be sanctioned. The earth was to be populated; it is in violation of the natural law of increase, that a few scattered barbarians should hold a relatively large territory, keeping it from occupancy and from improvement. But the case should be a clear one, a strong one, to justify the dispossession of the weak few in the interest of the mighty many; and the gentlest means and the fullest recompense are enjoined, when such dispossession is deemed necessary in the interests of the race.

By acquisition. 2. ACQUISITION is by purchase from bordering states. Dismemberment, we have seen, § 173, is not, except for the welfare of the whole, allowable in morals, but such exceptional cases occur. Even an independent state may incorporate itself on stipulated conditions with another state.

By conquest. 3. CONQUEST of territory is justifiable only in case of war otherwise justifiable and in the way of compensation for losses suffered in rightful defense.

SECTION II. INCREASE OF POPULATION.

§ 210. The State has a right to grow in population. It may rightfully thus further in all suitable ways the natural increase of its people, by promoting the public health, and the conditions of comfortable subsistence, with distinct reference to this remote end. It may also encourage immigration from other countries. The restrictions on its action in this direction are, that it should not harm by weakening other nations, and that it should not jeopard its own unity and strength by admitting elements that cannot be properly assimilated to its own life. Especially in free governments, where the participation in political rule by suffrage or otherwise is widely extended, the state owes it to itself not to incorporate into the body of its citizens strangers, perhaps ignorant and indigent, unless with great caution.

SECTION III. PUBLIC IMPROVEMENTS.—WEIGHTS AND MEASURES—MONEY—MAILS.

§ 211. The state has a right to grow in internal strength, to promote the fullest union and harmony and inter-communication between its own members.

Threefold modes. The leading specific modes of thus strengthening the union and organic interaction of its members are by the provision of (1) thoroughfares of travel and traffic ; (2), of needful means of commercial exchange ; and (3), of methods for the intercommunication of intelligence among its citizens.

§ 212. *Public Improvements.* It is indispensable to the full life of a community that the members be brought into the best

Public Improvements.

10*

possible communication with one another in respect both to person and property. While it is most true that the opening and maintaining of public roads, of canals, of railways, may generally be left to private or local enterprise, § 208, 3, it is still the right and the duty of the state in its relation to the highest good of the entire community to see to it that such thoroughfares are provided and maintained; to extend in clear cases of necessity its aid more or less directly; and especially to see that the use of these public thorougfares be not hindered or molested.

2. Means of exchange—Weights and Measures.

§ 213. *Weights and Measures.* As needful for the interchanges of property as are roads for persons, are standards and instruments of commercial exchange. Manifestly indispensable thus are national standards of weight and measurement, and a national currency. The determination of both is properly held as the prerogative of political sovereignty.

Of the first mentioned means, it need only be said that the great requisites in regard to all state regulation are that the system of prescribed weights and measures be stable; be uniform for the whole country; be simple and easy of use; and, so far as may be, in accordance with the systems in use among other nations. The parts or denominations, as in the money system, have generally been determined by the convenience of the individual community, and have been gradually introduced in the progress of the people. The tendency in commercial states at present is to a general adoption of the decimal ratio, as one most familiar, most likely to be universal, and most convenient. The standard—the respective unit in a system of weights and measurements—in order to stability and universality, it has been wisely sought to fix in reference to some dimension, obtained in physical or astronomical science, as that of an arc of a meridian circle of the earth, or the force of gravity on the equator.

§ 214. *Money.* The right and duty of a
Money state in reference to money grow out of its duty to promote the prosperity of the community to the utmost of its power. As the increase of wealth depends almost entirely on the facility for making exchanges of commodities, a convenient instrument for this purpose becomes a necessity. The term *money,* while having other associated meanings, in its stricter sense denotes just this instrument.

MONEY may accordingly be defined to be
Defined. a representative medium for facilitating exchanges of commercial values.

Money is a representative of value; it is not a value itself, except as merely representative. A piece of money may have an intrinsic value of its own; the mere material of which it is made may have such a value before it was made into money—before it was coined; it may retain this intrinsic value, which may be equal to the value represented or less than that, after the stamp—the coinage mark—upon it has been effaced, and so it has ceased to be money. Gold may be coined, may receive a stamp, and be thus made into money; the inconsiderable value which it has, irrespectively of this intrinsic and previous value, is its value as representative; this is all the value which a gold coin has as mere money. This truth is fundamental to a clear and accurate notion of money, of its proper nature and use. Its sole value as money lies in its being representative. Hence the increase of money, the issue of more money, does not add to the wealth of a community, as simply stamping a piece of gold weighing 232 grains fine, or 258 grains with one-tenth alloy, and so certifying it to be an eagle of commercial value, makes no considerable addition of value to it.

The sole function of money is as a medium—an instrument for facilitating exchanges of commercial values. The necessity for such a medium is easily shown. The farmer produces grain; he does not produce clothes, sugar and tea, furniture, dwellings. He does not need all the grain he produces, and he does need these and manifold other things which he does not produce. He must needs exchange the one for the other. But to take to the tailor just so much grain as will be a fair equivalent for the clothes he needs, and to the grocer so much for the sugar and tea he needs, and so on, would be well nigh impracticable. If he can take his surplus grain to the flouring mill, or to the mercantile house, and get from the miller or the merchant what will enable him to use just what he needs of the price to take respectively to the tailor, the grocer, etc., his task is incalculably facilitated in getting just what he wants of clothing, groceries, etc., for his grain. Money does precisely this for him. This is its one function—an instrument of exchange.

The exchange which money facilitates pertains to commercial values. By this is meant that money facilitates the exchange of anything having a value in the market for any other thing in the market having an equivalent value.

<small>Standard of value.</small> § 215. But money as an instrument of exchange presupposes a standard of value and a unit of value adopted by the state. A piece of money represents so much purchasing value; that is, it represents what will be received in the market as equivalent to so much value in any other commodity in the market. It is clearly necessary that there should be some standard by which things that are bought and sold or exchanged in the market should be valued. For this purpose something is taken in reference to which all other marketable things shall be valued. Different nations in different ages of the world have adopted different things to be standards. Gold and silver, called by reason of this use the precious metals, have more generally been selected. The value of a commodity depends ultimately on the cost of producing it. The relative value of gold and silver to each other has changed perhaps less than that of any other two things produced by men; and the cost of producing either in reference to the average cost of producing other things generally has changed but inconsiderably for ages. Gold and silver are accordingly preferable as standards to any other product or products. It is the duty of the state in prescribing

the money standard to fix the value of the material selected, and obvious considerations require that this value should fairly represent the cost of its production relatively to that of other products generally.

It will equally be its duty to determine precisely what quantity of this material shall constitute the unit of value; to determine, for example, that, when that is the current coin, 258 grains of gold of nine-tenths purity, shall be rated as one eagle. If the relative cost of production should change, then it will easily change this quantity chosen to constitute the unit. The parts or multiples of this unit will form the several denominations of money, which convenience in use will require. Such a measure and unit of value are presupposed in every monetary system; but obviously money is not properly in itself such a measure of value. It is the quantity of gold taken in the 258 grains with one-tenth alloy, which constitutes the standard, the unit, the measure of value; and the money, the coin—the eagle—is conformed to that.

As money is properly representative of value, it would seem at a first glance to be a matter of indifference whether the material for money be of more or less value—whether it be equivalent to the value to be represented as gold, or comparatively of merely nominal value as paper. As a matter of fact, the most commercial nations have adopted both kinds—a gold currency and in connection with it a paper currency under various forms and regulations. This has been the case in spite of the recognized and obvious desirableness in itself of a single kind of money. The objections to a currency having an intrinsic value, quite, or nearly, equal to the value it represents as money are: 1, that the only material in nature having the requisite qualities for money—gold—is not furnished in quantities sufficient for the uses of the commercial world; 2, it is costly; and 3, it is for many commercial uses inconvenient, not easily or safely transmissible in large amounts, and liable to be stolen or lost.

The objections to a material for money of a merely nominal value—to a paper currency—are: 1, that being confined to the state that issues it, the circulation is necessarily more local; 2, that it is not so easily convertible into values for use in other states; and 3, that it requires, for obvious considerations of security, precautionary regulations for its conversion into international equivalents which a state or its officers are strongly tempted to overlook or omit.

§ 216. From this brief exposition of the nature of money it will be easy to determine what elements and attributes a wise and sound political economy prescribes to a state to incorporate into its monetary system.

Its needful qualities.

1. As a basis for its money or currency it must fix upon a proper standard and unit of value, which shall be characterized by stability, uniformity, and accordance with the usage of other nations, and be carefully estimated from its relative cost of production as to its relative

1. Fixed standard.

value, as compared with other commodities generally.

2. The parts or multiples of this unit should be determined by convenience in use, preferably in decimal denominations.

2. Convenient denominations.

3. In respect to the material to be selected, when the intrinsic value is to equal the value it represents, the qualities to be sought are these: it should be stable in relative value; durable; receptive and retentive of distinct impression; difficult to counterfeit: convenient for use; and neat and attractive.

3. Material.

The precious metals contain these qualities in a greater degree than any other material. But as no one material can equally well answer for all amounts of value, gold has been wisely selected for all larger values, silver for smaller, and some baser metal for the lowest denominations.

4. If the two kinds of currency be adopted, then divers provisions are needful; as (1), the paper currency must always be readily convertible into the metallic money, or some international commercial equivalent, since otherwise it does not represent truly the value—it is false money. (2.) It accordingly must always sacredly be sustained by a considerate provision of means for conversion at the will of the owner into gold or some other commercial equivalent. (3.) Security from being counterfeited, durability, and neatness through frequent redemptions and re-issues, are especially requisite.

4. Mixed currency.

5. The money system of a country must be

5. Legal tender. authoritative in all matters of dispute as to equivalents in commercial exchanges. All legal money should be *legal tender* in adjustment of all commercial claims.

6. Stable. 6. The money system should be subject to as little change as is possible. It would be manifestly unjust so to change the value of the circulation as to oblige one party to an obligation to receive from the other party a less value, or to pay a greater value, than that contemplated at the time of creating the obligation.

7. Adequate supply. 7. The amount of currency should be adequate to the needs of commerce.

This amount of course varies greatly. It varies with the varying prosperity of a country; it varies with the population; it varies with the seasons of trade.

There is, however, no absolute necessity for determining upon a certain fixed amount. For if the currency of a country be in excess for the commercial wants, it must necessarily obey the law of all commodities and find its equilibrium. If gold coin be in excess, it will be melted up for use in the arts, or exchanged for foreign valuables. If the paper currency be in excess, it will be returned for conversion into its commercial equivalent. There is little danger of over-issue in the case of a true money. If it be of gold undebased, the coinage will not exceed the quantity of bullion which is furnished to be stamped. If it be of paper, there is an analogous necessity of providing equivalent means of redemption or conversion. An unrighteous nation may debase coin or may issue paper money with no means of redemption, in each case for corrupt or profligate uses. The unrighteousness deserves a like reprobation in each case. The necessities of a state, as in time of war, may compel a resort to forced loans and a subsidizing of commerce and trade, just as they may compel to the appropriation of the property and the conscription of the person of the subject. *Necessity has no law*, is the loose maxim applicable to all these practices. When no necessity compels, simple justice requires that the money of a country be ever true money—a representative of a real value corresponding to its face or stamp. Of such true money there is no real danger of excess of issue; all the principles of trade forbid any fear of it.

Nor is the evil of an under-issue so very formidable. Commercial exchanges may still be effected by simple barter—commodity for commodity; or through credits on accounts; or through checks and bills of exchange. In the large emporiums of trade, commercial exchanges and adjustments are mainly in these ways, even when there is an ample currency, nine-tenths and more of the aggregate settlements of dues being effected without the use of any money other than checks and bills of credit. The exact determination of the amount of money to be provided is accordingly not imposed by any necessity. The usages of trade easily suit themselves to the monetary conditions under which they exist. The great requisites are security, uniformity, stability, with a medium of exchange in some reasonable approximation of amount to estimated wants.

§ 217. *Inter-communication of Intelligence.*—Indispensable to the highest social life of a people is the free communication of mind with mind, thought with thought. The sympathetic interest between the parts of a community depends on these exchanges of information; and the means of mutual helpfulness are equally dependent on them. Sound political wisdom at once dictates accordingly the provision and effective maintenance of all postal conveniences. If needful for the social well-being, the state may properly take the telegraph as well as the mail-service into its own care and control. How far it should assume the expenses of maintenance is a question of political expediency.

<small>Postal Facilities.</small>

SECTION IV.—DEVELOPMENT OF RESOURCES.

§ 218. The state has a right to grow in *external power.*

<small>4. Material power.</small>

The power of a state is necessarily purely secular; it is such only as can be exerted in the interests of the present world.

This secular power is of two kinds: moral and material. It lies in the state itself as one political body or is distributed among the citizens. It is the right of a state to seek, and equally its duty to secure, in all righteous ways, the steady increase of this secular moral and material strength, both as it properly pertains to itself and also as it may be possessed by its subjects. It will be convenient to consider this growth in external strength without exact discrimination, in all the particulars to be named, between these two repositories of power. The increase of moral power will be more readily presented under succeeding heads; and our view will here be confined to the increase of proper material power—the increase of the material resources and wealth of the state.

Productive industries to be fostered. The natural resources of a state, whether lying beneath in the deposits of mineral wealth,—of coal and iron, the precious metals, and the like—or on the surface of the earth in forests or fertile lands under genial skies, are made available and are increased only on the condition of human labor. Political economy accordingly very justly assumes as a fundamental principle that material wealth is the product of industry and that the exchangeable value of particular articles depends ultimately on the labor expended in producing them. The principle is of course general and subject to divers modifications. It is safe to assume, however, that productive industry is the condition and means of increasing material wealth. It necessarily follows that the state in effecting its growth in material power must foster the industries of the nation by which wealth is increased.

§ 219. These industries are of three leading classes:—(1) developing; (2) productive proper; and (3) distributive.

THE DEVELOPING INDUSTRIES are those which

1. Developing industries. simply extract from nature what is valuable for man's use. They are chiefly applied to the extraction of mineral wealth; and the principles of political morality are sufficiently illustrated in their application to this particular species of developing industry—to mining and metallurgic industry.

2. Proper productive. THE PRODUCTIVE INDUSTRIES proper embrace as the two leading species, the *agricultural* and the *manufacturing*.

3. Distributive. THE DISTRIBUTIVE INDUSTRIES are those which effect the needful exchanges of products and are sufficiently represented in the commercial life of the nation; although here evidently belong all the activities of a people enlisted in the carrying business, in any way, on land or on water.

We have then as the great representatives of the productive industry of a country, its mining, agricultural, manufacturing, and commercial industries.

Duty of the State in respect to productive industries. § 220. The ethical position of the state in relation to all these departments of productive industry is easily determined from the nature of a proper state organic life viewed in itself and as illustrated in actual history. The state exists, as we have seen, for the common secular well-being of the community. All righteous endeavors to secure this common secular welfare in the highest degree, are, therefore, politically right and obligatory on the state. There are no limits within its proper boundaries territorial and teleological—within its geographical sphere and that determined by the end for which it exists—to be prescribed to this increase, so long as no principles of morality are violated in effecting it. Nothing in the essential nature of a state, nothing in a constituted political organism, which makes it ethically wrong for a state to carry on any one or all of these productive industries itself—in its collective and organic capacity—or through its individual citizens—or the smaller local communities embraced within it. History reveals to us instances of a government prosecuting mining industries in its own name and by its own direction; superintending and cultivating its forest lands and indeed its pastures and its grain lands; producing fabrics needed for its own use in defense or for the necessities of the people; and even effecting the distribution of commodities by providing thoroughfares and conveyances, and directing the use of them for its own needs or for the benefit of the people. Nothing is more contradictory to reason or to the teachings of history than the proposition that the function of a political government is limited to a mere negative, a mere protective sphere. On the contrary, the right and duty of every state is positively to promote and encourage and foster the entire productive industry of the political community.

This positive fostering care must of necessity be directed, as occasion may require, to this or to that particular department of productive industry. The state is an organic whole whose welfare depends on the healthful condition and ministry of every member.

If a particular member is diseased or weak, is suffering in any respect, it is the obvious duty of the state, as an active organism, to remedy its ills, to provide for the recruiting of its strength and the stimulating of its ministry. This is a plain principle of reason and of common sense, and equally the dictate of analogy and of experience.

There are, however, two grand limita-
Its limitations. tions of this duty of the state to promote the productive industry of the country. First, its aim and end in this must be solely the common welfare. Not for the sake of the particular productive industry itself, but only for the health and vigor of the entire political body, may a state engage directly itself in mining, or agriculture, or manufacturing, or commerce; nor may it extend special aid or stimulus to individuals, or associations, or local communities in behalf of such particular interest, but only in the interest of the general welfare.

Secondly, such special exertion or aid should be extended only in case of well ascertained inability or negligence on the part of individuals or local communities. The grand principle here, already stated in another application, § 208, 3, is: leave to individual or local enterprise all that safely can be. The sufficient reasons for this limitation, even under the full admission of the ethical right of a state to engage directly in the productive industries of a country, are:

1. It is for the highest vigor and soundness of the whole political body that all the particular

members be enlisted in the active ministry to the common weal to the highest degree. It is better for the physical body that the blood vessels themselves throughout exert their propulsive power than that the whole force in propelling the blood through the system be left to the pulsations of the central organ alone.

2. Individual enterprise is more wakeful, more sagacious, more economical, more efficient than collective, especially than governmental, enterprise.

3. The temptations to abuse, corruption, mismanagement in the prosecution of public enterprises by a government are many and formidable, and difficult to prevent or remedy. So great are these temptations that the common weal may require of a government that it forego many enterprises unquestionably of promise and utility rather than expose its officials to them.

4. Governmental competition in productive industry is discouraging and hurtful to individual enterprise. The mere fear of it, which would generally exist if governments were to engage in these pursuits except in prescribed limits and in special cases of necessity, would be repressive to individual undertakings.

It is accordingly a sound maxim of political morality that a state should not embark in any productive enterprise unless it be clearly settled first, that individual or local enterprise cannot or will not assume it; and secondly, that the public good requires the undertaking, even after full allowance shall have been made for the probable evils from official corruption or incompetency, and from the embarrassments to individual enterprise arising from governmental competition. Generally the presumption is against the government's undertaking any productive work; a clear case of necessity should be made out to justify it. For the most part all proper productive industries may most wisely be left to individual or local enterprise. To this the progress of civilization has steadily tended to conform the practice among the nations.

§ 221. The modes by which the state may foster its productive industries through its citizens or local communities, are twofold—direct and indirect.

<small>Modes.</small>

The direct modes are in the form of *bounties*, as for the encouragement of certain desirable agricultural products, the preservation and increase of forests, the destruction of predatory animals, or removal of obstacles to production, or of discoveries and inventions of useful processes and products.

<small>1. Direct bounties.</small>

The indirect modes are by furnishing the conditions of safe and successful enterprise to its citizens, as by imposts on foreign competitive production.

<small>2. Indirect.</small>

The state, thus, in the first of these ways, fosters individual enterprise by such legislation as shall afford adequate security to honest industry in its rights to its products. This is the fundamental condition for healthful individual enterprise in a country. The legislation of every prosperous government is large-

<small>By legislation to this end.</small>

ly in the form of general laws securing the rights of productive industry. Special legislation also is common in the form of laws regulating patents for inventions, copyrights for books, etc. It may also with the same result open and maintain safe avenues for the exchange of products. Governments thus stimulate and foster commercial industry by opening harbors, improving navigation, maintaining light-houses, providing help for vessels in distress, sending its navy to foreign waters for the protection and promotion of commercial enterprise. Probably no industry receives so much of the distinctive protection of governments as the commercial, and none in a wiser economy.

§ 222. In the second place, it may be well for a state to encourage special productive industries by impost duties on foreign productions. The general principles of political morality applicable here are the following: First, we have the fundamental maxim of political wisdom, that the choice of productions should be left to the individual, without interference on the part of the government. Generally, the generous policy dictated by the consideration that what is best for the world is best for each of the particular nations that make up the world, is the wise policy. The individuals composing the respective political communities, left to their own choice, will, in the long run, fall into the production of those articles which they can produce best and at least cost. Freedom of commercial intercourse between the nations moreover is eminently desirable for the

By imposts.

world's advantage in divers ways, and should be assiduously encouraged and promoted. Free trade, thus, is the wise policy of a state as the general rule. To this general principle, however, there are, as would naturally and reasonably be anticipated, exceptions in its practical application.

Secondly, the principle of free trade should not be applied so as to work with relative disadvantage to home industries. If home products, thus, are for any necessity of the state, subjected to taxation in any form, the same products, when imported from abroad, should be subjected to at least an equal burden.

Thirdly, special state necessities may require that certain articles should be produced at home, independently of foreign supply. Those things, thus, which are of indispensable necessity in war, it is a clear dictate of wisdom that a state seek to have produced within its own limits. Otherwise its very existence might be suspended on the pleasure of a foreign power. It may obviously be the clear duty of a state to secure the production of such necessaries for self-defense by its own subjects; and the best, perhaps the only effectual way of doing this, may be by extending to them in this undertaking all needful protection from envious competition from abroad. The principle of free trade should sometimes give way in regard to the production of military supplies. So, also, in the same interest of self-defense, the maintenance of a vigorous commercial marine being the condition of an effective naval force, the state may wisely sacrifice the inconsiderable advantage from free trade for the encouragement of those industries which are concerned in the building of ships. It may be wise, thus, to encourage the production of timber, or of iron, or other material required in naval architecture, or the building of ships at home, by proper discrimination in a system of impost duties against importation from abroad. Dependence on a foreign power for its ships may be incompatible with self-security in these days of universal commerce between the nations of the world. A clear case of state necessity, thus, may justify and require a departure from the policy of absolute free trade.

Fourthly, it is clearly supposable that exceptional cases may arise in which it may be the duty of a state seeking the complete development of its resources to encourage special productive industries. A new country, thus, with large undeveloped natural resources, but in the conditions of insufficient capital, high wages, imperfect machinery, distant markets, and other hindrances to cheap production, may, in obvious duty of self interest, provide that private enterprise may move in reasonable security against being overwhelmed in its incipient struggles with stronger, more advanced, and better advantaged producers abroad. Competition is, indeed, the life of trade—its needful stimulus, regulator, and check; but competition among men is often overbearing, hostile, oppressive, and even destructive. The earliest productions of a new industry are invariably costly; and even with vastly greater advantage in natural resources, infant enterprise may yet be unable, if unsupported, to stand against jealous and unscrupulous rivals in trade. Wherever, therefore, there is good reason for the belief that temporary support may insure in the end development of resources that otherwise must be unimproved, or may permanently cheapen production of commodities, the intervention of a state may be justifiable for the help of private enterprise; and, certainly, it cannot be assumed that the particular mode of protection, by preventing, through a judicious tariff of imposts, a ruinous foreign competition, is forbidden by any just principle of political morality. A prohibitory duty may seldom be necessary; a properly regulative duty, which shall simply secure against an excessive reduction of price, may be imposed in consistency with a wise political economy, applied under the dictates of common sense.

SECTION V.—PUBLIC HEALTH.

§ 223. It is the right and the duty of the state to care for the health of the community.

5. Public health.

Health of body is a fundamental blessing of the secular class. Care for it finds a place at once in the sphere of secularity occupied by the state. This care cannot always safely be left to individuals or to local communities. In divers ways the positive interposition of the state may be indispensable to the highest common welfare. Sanitary laws may not have been always judicious; and they may have been badly administered. To a certain extent, nevertheless, they seem necessary. Quarantine regulations, to prevent the introduction of contagious diseases, as well as sanitary laws for the cleansing of streets, the ventilation of buildings, the removal of garbage, the establishment and maintenance of pest houses, hospitals, and dispensaries, the provision of trustworthy medical experts, the enforcement of universal vaccination, and the like, come clearly into that class of public necessities which cannot be trusted entirely to individuals.

SECTION VI.—EDUCATION.

6. Education. § 224. It is the right and the duty of a state to secure intelligence in its citizens.

Intelligence is a crowning blessing in the present life of man. While it is a condition that must follow him into his immortal future, it is yet a true secularity within the proper sphere of the state. As such, a true secular good, so far as it is a common interest, it belongs to the state to care for it and foster it.

This right and duty belong to it in its care for its own security and the safe and prosperous administration of the government. In free commonwealths the proper exercise of the elective franchise involves as its condition general intelligence; and under all governments the needful check on power and authority under a sense of responsibility to the governed also involves general intelligence as its condition. General intelligence is necessary to the prosperity of the state in material resources. Skilled labor has been proved by ample experience to be immensely more valuable than unskilled in all departments of productive industry. In any occupation a man is worth more than a mere animal. Intelligence is a means and condition of happiness to men; and it is within the province of a state to promote the present happiness of its subjects. Intelligence, moreover, is a prime element of man's immortal condition; and inasmuch as the state is for man, not for itself, and as its sphere and function is to care for his secular condition in society so that the highest end of his being as a being of immortality shall be furthered, intelligence, it must be admitted, is to be one of those secular interests which fall within the sphere of the state.

It may be that in certain conditions the interests of education may be better left to individual care. It is still the duty of the state to see to it, that these great interests are thus adequately sustained. If in any respect such individual care be inadequate, the state is bound to supplement it as well as always to supervise and regulate and encourage it. It is a fact of experience that these interests have not been fostered to excess by states hitherto.

§225. The degree to which the state should
Extent. seek to carry the general education of its subjects will vary on the one hand with the wealth and ability of the state, and on the other with the condition of the people. In an impover-

ished community there may be inability to spare even the time and labor of children for an advanced education, or to support them while receiving it. There are few, if any, communities desiring to be recognized as states which are not able to educate the people generally to a degree of intelligence sufficient for the ordinary duties of a citizen—for voting safely and for laboring productively. But, in truth, no good reason can be given why the state should not seek, in wise consideration of its own strength and the competency of its subjects, to carry up the education of its people to the highest degree attainable; to make this its ideal in its educational administration. Circumstances will sufficiently moderate all tendencies to excess. The mass will only reach the lowest stages of educational training; fewer than could be desired will rise to the stage reached by what is known as skilled labor; fewer still, and still less than could be desired, will find the time or the means to reach the highest attainments even with the most municifent educational establishment. The state maxim in regard to education is: Supplement private provisions for furnishing the highest and best and most universal education which the means of the state and the condition of the people admit.

§ 226. In regard to the modes of action proper for the state in its care for education, it may be said, first, that it should enforce, as far as practicable, attendance on educational means on its entire people. Compulsory education is within the legitimate province of polit-

Methods.

ical action, as embracing the entire secular well-being of the community. It is as fitting that a state see to it that the children be decently educated, as that they be decently clothed, decently housed, decently fed.

Secondly, The state should encourage and foster, in all suitable ways, all endeavors on the part of individuals and of local communities, in the interest of a sound general education; as well as, in the manifold ways open to it, further the ends of general intelligence and sound learning. It should encourage science and learning, literature and the arts, as its proper right and function.

Thirdly, The state should endow and adequately sustain institutions for the training of men for its own needs, as for its army and its navy. An advanced stage of national progress may render equally necessary schools for training in its civil and diplomatic service.

Fourthly, The state should provide either directly by its own agency, or indirectly through the local communities, schools for the education of all the children in the commonest branches of training, and, as rapidly as circumstances shall allow, higher schools for training in the productive arts. Even proper professional training comes within its legitimate care and may call for its direct support.

SECTION VII.—PUBLIC MORALS.

7. Morality.

§ 227. It is the right and the duty of a state to promote sound morals in the community.

The state we have found to be a true moral power. It is not less a power because a collective power. Its action has all the moral attributes that belong to individual action. It is free, above the constraint of physical necessity. It may be in sympathy with the welfare of others—of its own members and of other states; it may be beneficent; it may be upright; or it may be the reverse of this according to its own free election. It is under responsibility; men judge it, and approve or condemn; retribution is visited upon it in the established orderings of providence. This retribution is not less retribution because it is limited to this world. Retribution to a nation is necessarily secular, inasmuch as the state is a secularity.

As properly moral in its being, the state should be true to itself—should act out its own nature—should act morally. Its action, also, should be in harmony and sympathy with all that is properly of a moral nature like itself. It should, therefore, in obedience to the dictates of its own proper nature, promote morality everywhere and in all ways.

Moreover, as the moral interest is the highest in man, and as the state exists for the furtherance of the highest interests of men so far as common, its action should ever regard this high ulterior end of its being.

The interests of sound morals cannot safely be left to the sole care of individuals, or of the family, or of the local community. Even if this were the case it would still be within the legitimate province of the state, and therefore its proper duty, to see to it that this care be in fact exercised. But the world is far from having reached that state of perfection in which the state may safely be exonerated from the duty of supplementing the action of individuals and local communities in the interest of morality.

<small>Methods.</small> § 228. There are manifold ways in which the state may legitimately and efficiently act in the promotion of sound morals.

<small>1. By example.</small> 1. Its own action should be a safe and influential example. Its legislation, its administration of justice, its execution of the laws, should be characterized as courteous, just, beneficent; as forbearing, lenient, and merciful; as unselfish, impartial, upright; as kind, gentle, and helpful. Its selection of officials, — rejecting the base, the corrupt, the dissolute, and exalting the worthy, the honest, the pure in life ;—its control over places,—banishing all the incitements and instruments of vice, and maintaining an atmosphere of purity in its legislative halls and surroundings, its halls of justice, its prisons and other state institutions of whatever kind, the streets and public places under its control ;—its action in respect to persons and places under its control ; should exemplify the principles of morality before its citizens and before

the world. In truth, the entire life of a state is of moral significance, and operates with incalculable power in the way of example on the lives of men and on the character and actions of other nations.

2. *2. By prohibition.* The state should promote sound morals by the exclusion from the community of whatever tends to debase or corrupt the morals of the people. It may prohibit the publication of immoral writings and pictures; it may disallow corrupting exhibitions; it may suppress gambling-houses, dram-shops, and brothels; it may forbid open indecencies, brawls, and vicious amusements. It may discourage, by discriminating taxes and impost duties, even when it may not be wise to prohibit, the production at home and the importation from abroad of articles tempting to abuses or excesses, and hurtful to public sobriety, purity, and virtue, as well as the traffic in such articles. The regulation of the traffic in liquor, by requiring the formal permission of public authorities and payment of stated fees—the licensing system, so called—may be in the interest of true morality, implying no sanction or approval of intemperance or of temptations to it, as the design of the legislator may be wholly for its restriction or removal.

3. *3. By positive encouragement.* The state may more directly and positively promote the interests of sound morals in the community by lending encouragement to all that is pure and virtuous in tendency or in fact in the manners, usages, and pursuits of its citizens. It may reward acts of self-sacrifice or heroism in the interest of the state or of

humanity; it may commemorate in monuments the lives of patriots and public benefactors; it may second in manifold ways all efforts in the cause of virtue and philanthropy; it may incorporate into its whole outgoing life a true sympathy and concern for whatever will make its people upright, pure, and virtuous. Limited to the secular sphere and to the use of secular means and instrumentalities, it cannot, indeed, look directly upon the heart and the conscience—the proper seat of morality; it cannot take cognizance of the inner workings and intents of the spirit; its action necessarily confines itself to the outward, the tangible. But all the outer manifestations of the spirit, all that goes out of the heart into the external life,—all this is under its inspection and for its cognizance and regulation. Control here reacts upon the heart itself, inciting or depressing. Indifference here, unconcern for these highest interests of men, is disloyal to God, its providential master and judge, dangerous for its citizens, suicidal to itself. The state must be moral, act morally, enforce morality in its community, or it must decline and die. History is predominantly the record of the retributions visited upon nations for its disregard of the public morals.

CHAPTER V.

THE STATE AND THE CITIZEN.

§ 229. The second grand department of moral relationships pertaining to the state is that which exists between it and its members. It embraces the rights and duties of citizens in respect to the state.

Citizen defined. The term *citizen*, in a larger but looser sense, extends to every resident, even every transient sojourner within the geographical limits of a state. In a stricter sense, it is limited to persons either born in the country, or naturalized—accepted as citizens—by legal authority. The language of the constitution of the United States, as amended, is:—"All persons born or naturalized in the United States, and subject to the jurisdiction thereof, are citizens of the United States and of the States wherein they reside." Women and children are included in this definition. In a still narrower sense, the term is limited to a person having the right to participate in the government of the country—the right to vote and to be eligible to office. The rights of citizens generally are denoted by the phrase *civil rights*. But sometimes the distinction is drawn between the general rights of citizens and the special rights of voting and of being voted for; the latter being designated as *political* rights and the former as *civil* rights in a narrower sense. Foreigners, and native women and children, thus, under the law of the United States, have civil rights, but not political rights.

It is important to recognize here, as elsewhere, the double correlativeness between rights and duties, and between the subject and the object of duty. Every right implies a duty; and every right or duty of the subject of duty implies a corresponding duty or right in the object of duty.

The entire field of the moral relationships between the state and its citizens will therefore come under review in a full survey of the rights and duties of persons in the state.

SECTION I. — THE RIGHTS OF INDIVIDUALS IN THE STATE.

1. To pursue the ends of his immortal being unmolested. § 230. The first right of the individual person in the state is the right to exist and to pursue unmolested the great end of his being.

Man was designed by his creator to exist within some state, inasmuch as states were designed to fill up the geographical limits of the earth. He was designed to live as organic member of the political community within whose bounds his lot is cast.

He can rightfully demand that this right be recognized and be held inviolable.

Farther, man was designed to outlive the state whose existence is purely secular—one of time and of earth,—to live into an eternal future. His highest and truest interests, indeed, lie beyond all secular confines in that endless hereafter. As social and as secular in a certain part and relation of his nature, his grand destiny must be wrought out in social and secular conditions, which in fact are in divine wisdom and goodness established simply for the purpose of furthering those immortal interests. The state is for man; not man for the state. The state cannot therefore rightfully in any way obstruct or hamper the individual man in his paramount duty to secure his immortal well-being. He has the right to be exempt from all molestation by the state in his endeavor towards this high end of his being. It is clear that the state owes it to itself as well as to the individual not to interfere with this endeavor. The personality of the state is constituted exclusively of immortal natures, whose instinctive drift and tendency in the direction of their eternal well-being, it is unwise for the state to resist, as thereby it opposes its own proper aim, as well as hinders the highest common good of its members, and wastes its strength as well as moves counter to its proper aim.

More than this is to be maintained. Man has a right not only to pursue unmolested this high end of his immortal nature, unmolested by the state, but he has the right to claim from the state that it sympathize with all his just endeavors in this pursuit, and while not transgressing the limits of its secular and social nature, second and aid, as it may, those endeavors. This sympathy and aid are not necessarily to be extended in direct action designed to affect purely spiritual interests; it is enough if the state keep its action ever in harmony with the aspirations of its citizens towards this higher life.

<small>2 To pursue certain secular ends unmolested.</small> § 231. Secondly, the citizen has secular interests which lie outside of the proper sphere of the state, which, therefore, he should be allowed to care for unmolested by the state.

All those interests which pertain to him as an individual, in which there can be no community with others, even though of a secular nature, are thus outside the province of the state. It is his right to regulate and foster those interests in his own way, provided always, that he does not in his care of them, break over into the common secular field which belongs to the state, and in which he only shares with others in his degree and in his relation to them. Here are the strictly private, personal, rights of free thought, free opinion, free conscience; here are the innumerable private acts of life in choosing avocations, companions, dwelling-places; in determining food, dress, and physical regimen as well as the culture of the spiritual nature; in ordering the particular steps of daily occupation. If he do not offend in these things against public decency, public morality, public interest, he has a right to move on without molestation from the state. Indeed, more than this: it is practicable to a certain extent, and to this extent it is obligatory on the state, to maintain itself in sympathy and indirect helpfulness to the citizen in all these properly individual interests. The principle is all-pervading, that true state-life is in perfect harmony with all true personal life; their true interests are not colliding interests; although their aims and ends may be diverse, their allotted paths run ever parallel.

§ 232. Thirdly, more directly and positively, the citizen has a right to claim from the state its protection of all his lawful interests from injury, whether by fellow-citizens, by state officials, or by foreign power.

3. To protection.

The citizen may claim this protection at home or in foreign lands. His rights of person—of life and limb and free movement; his rights of property in acquiring, holding, and using; his rights of reputation and character, the state is bound to recognize, and to protect against all unlawful aggression. He may claim both protection against threatened injury and also redress for inflicted wrong. It is a paramount duty of the state to bring within the reach of all its members this protection and redress to the fullest extent practicable.

§ 233. Fourthly, in case of absolute need he has a right to help and succor from the state.

4. To succor.

It is thus the duty of the state to provide for its poor and helpless, its deaf and its blind, its maimed and diseased. Its help and succor must, indeed, be secular, by outward means and instrumentalities, and for secular wants; yet its ministry in this direction may and should be in sympathy and indirect relief and solace in regard to the needs of man's whole nature. The bleeding spirit may be best healed in the sympathetic treatment directed immediately on the lacerated body. It would be inhuman to withhold this higher cure when possible to bestow it; it were most impolitic, contrary to the very design of a state to administer to the relief of physical necessities, in heartless indifference to mental distresses which attend on these outer troubles.

SECTION II. THE DUTIES OF INDIVIDUALS TO THE STATE.

1. Of loyalty. § 234. The fundamental duty of the citizen to the state is genuine *loyalty*.

Love of country is native to the human heart. Man is not a true and full man without this sentiment in full and vigorous exercise. One's country, so far as its action is worthy of itself, is deserving of his true and warm affection; its best support and thrift have their roots in the generous love of its citizens. Reciprocal sympathy and affection is a prime law of nature for state and subject.

This fundamental affection on the part of the citizen, shows itself, in the first place, in the form of respect or reverence towards the state as superior, in all its organs or representatives, its acts and its rights. He is therefore forbidden to " speak evil of dignities;" he is required to "honor the King" as the representative and organ of the political community. In free governments the liabilities to offenses against this principle of morality are many and great. It is the more necessary in them therefore to inculcate the principle, and to insist that partisan zeal shall abstain from all abuse and disrespect towards those who represent the authority of the state. Measures of policy, acts of administration may be freely criticised, while due courtesy and respect are expressed to official persons, and due deference to all civil procedures.

§ 235. A second specific duty of the citizen to the state, involved in the fundamental duty of loyalty, is *obedience*.

II. Of obedience.

The state is the rightful seat and source of authority. Its ordinances, so far as consistent with general morality, are to be obeyed with unhesitating obedience. In cases of doubtful morality, it should be remembered that the state is the higher judge and presumably is right. The case should be a clear one in which the civil law may be resisted because supposed to be opposed to the higher laws of morality. Unless the conscience of the individual is positively offended, obedience is due even to a law that may be deemed to be immoral and unjust. A war may be declared on supposedly unjust grounds; the citizen may not therefore resist taxation or conscription for its prosecution. While he does all that as a citizen he may lawfully do in the interest of peace, inasmuch as the moral responsibilities do not rest on him, his individual conscience is not necessarily wounded in doing the duty of a subject. He cannot, where it is not his province to choose, interpose his private conscience as an excuse for declining patriotic service Were this permissible, the individual judgment would be exalted above that of the community. All social order would be undermined, if every man were left to do just what was right in his own eyes. It is not permissible ethically, further, to find satisfaction of the public justice in paying the penalty affixed to disobedience. The authority of the state is violated if the will of the state be resisted, no matter what may be true of the sanction, unless it be clear that the state intends a free choice between compliance and the pecuniary contribution. Suffering penalty is not meritorious obedience. "To obey is better than sacrifice."

§ 236. A third duty of a loyal subject is personal support to the state.

III. Of support.

The state lives and acts and accomplishes its end only as this support is yielded it from its members. They must pay the taxes and render the service necessary for its life and action. They must help along its policy and its measures. He is disloyal who opposes or obstructs the administration of the government for the furtherance of personal or partisan aims. It is the duty of the citizen to aid in the detection and punishment of crime. His sympathy for the suffering culprit must be kept subordinate to the interests of political justice. There is indeed a liability to err in this very matter of patriotic zeal. Partisan support of an administration may be excessive, to the detriment of other interests, and in violation of other rights. It should never be rendered in immoral ways. Lying in politics is as wrong and as disgraceful to the offender as lying in the market, or in the neighborhood, or the family. True loyalty will yield a ready, cordial, efficient support in all righteous ways to all the lawful actions of the government, subordinating all personal and partisan aims and interests. He is a poor patriot, a disloyal citizen, who sinks his country into a means of private emolument, or of factious advantage.

Expatriation. § 237. It has been a disputed question between nations whether a subject may rightfully transfer his allegiance from his native country to another. The maxim "once a subject, always a subject"—*nemo potest exuere patriam*—formerly was generally received. But in the advance of civilization involving progress in personal rights and personal freedom, the maxim has been less favorably regarded; and the right of self-expatriation is receiving recognition. A freer intercourse between the nations, a more settled international law, a larger allowance of personal freedom, and, moreover, an expansion of national strength in increase of territory and of population, are removing the necessity of this restriction on individual choice. Inasmuch as it is simply living in certain geographical limits which originates the relation of subject and state, nothing in the nature of the relation forbids a change of citizenship with removal of person.

There are, however, certain ethical restrictions to which the exercise of this right of self-expatriation should be held subject. It would be wrong to desert one's country in the time of its necessity or distress, when the support and help of every citizen must be counted upon. Much more base would it be to transfer one's domicile and allegiance in betrayal of a trust, or in rupture of contracted obligations. Moreover, citizenship is too high and sacred a relation to allow of fickleness and caprice in the change of allegiance. Considerable lapse of time is requisite in order to indicate that the residence in the new state is to be permanent, as also in order to fit for a right discharge of civil duties in a new community. It is also to be borne in mind that every state must be allowed the right to prescribe the conditions of naturalization. If the great rights and interests of humanity forbid a state, except in extraordinary emergencies, to shut its doors against immigration, the principle of self-preservation may require of a state to refuse admission to the full rights and privileges of citizenship. It has been a mooted point in international law, whether a man who has left his native land and been naturalized—admitted to citizenship—in another nation, may, on a temporary return to his native country, be held to his civil responsibilities just as if he had remained at home. The progress of international law in this respect is in favor of the freedom of the subject.

It is worthy of remark, in this connection, that Cicero ranked among the strongest principles of Roman freedom, that every man should be allowed to retain or relinquish his jural relations at his own pleasure:—*Hæc sunt enim fundamenta firmissima nostræ libertatis sui quemque juris et retinendi et demittendi esse dominum.* Pro Balbo.

CHAPTER VI.

INTERNATIONAL MORALITY.

<small>International Law.</small> § 238. The third grand department of moral relationships pertaining to the state, is that which exists between it and other states.

The rights and duties between nations compose the subject-matter of what is called International Law—*Jus gentium,* or more exactly *Jus inter gentes.*

<small>Divisions.</small> International Law has been distributed into two divisions: *Public,* which respects the relations of states to one another; and *Private,* which respects the relations between subjects and other states or subjects of other states.

<small>Sources.</small> § 239. As there is no secular authority above that of the individual state sovereignty, there can be no proper legislation over nations prescribing law to them in common and enforcing obligations upon them. The principles and rules which make up the body of International Law are founded on reason and practice

—on the essential nature of state organizations, and the usages and special acts of states. The more direct and specific sources are: (1) Text writers of authority; (2) Treaties; (3) State Ordinances, particularly marine ordinances in respect to cruisers and prizes; (4) Judicial precedents; (5) Professional opinions; (6) History.

From the nature of the case, international law must, in the advance of civilization, ever be subject to growth. As morality advances among men, particular rules of morality must be modified to meet the relations arising under a more perfect practice. States have ever been growing into closer, more fraternal relations towards one another. The interchanges of peace have been multiplied; the atrocities of war have been mitigated. Reason has gained upon brute force in the arbitrament of national disputes. The principles of international morality, too, have been brought into clearer light; precedents have been multiplied; and the aggregation of international rules has become more organized, growing ever into the form of a full, systematic body of law.

§ 240. As a true moral personality, the state is the subject of rights and duties exactly analogous to those pertaining to individuals. The important points of difference are: (1) that the immediate ends and means of political life are secular, while the ends of personal life reach directly through time into the eternal future; (2) political life is collective, while personal morality is of the individual; and (3) the

Analogies of national and personal morality.

state is sovereign, while the individual is to a certain extent subject to social rule.

Subject to these modifications, the rights and duties of states may be systematically comprehended under the same specific heads as those of persons, already stated as given by the threefold constituents of all duty—love, beneficence, rectitude,—and distinguished as one or the other of these elements is more predominant and characteristic.

SECTION I.—INTERNATIONAL GOOD-WILL.

I. Good-Will. § 241. States are subjects of those rights and correlative duties which have their seat more predominantly in the subject of duty—sympathetic interest and good-will.

No nation lives or can rightfully live for itself just as no man can live for himself; it must in duty seek the good of other nations.

It must not look on other communities with indifference. Laying aside jealousy and envy, it should rejoice in their true prosperity—in their successful prosecution of the great ends of national life as in perfect harmony with the ends of humanity and conducive to them. Equally should they sympathize in their misfortunes and distresses. Pestilences, famines, conflagrations, in whatever lands, demand for the sufferers the commiseration of the world. To such observed and commiserated sufferings, states are under moral obligation to cherish a disposition to afford all practicable and reasonable relief.

This sympathy and good-will is the rational ground and condition of all proper co-operation for the promotion of the interests of humanity. It is the ground also of such special alliances for each other's welfare as the exigencies of their changing condition may dictate.

Resentments. In this disposition of sympathetic affection and good-will are embraced the responsive sentiments—the resentments of gratitude for kindness received, and of retaliation and forgiveness for wrongs suffered.

Ingratitude is as truly base in a nation as in an individual; and forbearance and forgiveness as noble. Retaliation—redress of wrong or return of evil for evil—has a somewhat broader ground than in personal morality; for states have no secular superior to redress their grievances. States, moreover, have no eternal future to which the individual man may safely defer retribution for present wrongs.

Retaliation. § 242. The principle of retaliation for wrongs—*jus talionis*—can have no application in a perfect race. It is only because men are in a state of moral imperfection that relations come to be which can find no entrance into a perfect condition, and which impose different obligations from those which exist in such a condition.

Grounds. The following considerations seem to justify retaliation by states: 1. The offender cannot complain if his offenses are visited back upon him in equal justice. 2. It is due to the interests of morality, as also of humanity itself, that some fitting protest be made against wrong-doing. 3. The instincts of the race prompt it and lend their sanction to it. 4. The divinely authorized antediluvian and Mosaic precepts enjoined it; in itself, therefore, retaliation cannot be wrong; vengeance cannot be exclusively the divine prerogative. 5. The evangelical principle of forgiveness, while admitted to be governing, cannot yet be proved to be without possible exception. 6. The safety of states seems to necessitate recourse to retaliation in certain exigencies.

Retaliation, then, may be justified; but the case should be a clear one and a strong one to authorize it.

§ 243. Political retaliation—*retorsio*—is (1) properly *vindictive* or (2) *amicable*.

I. Amicable retaliation.

AMICABLE RETALIATION is without violence, and consists in applying to a nation the rule of conduct which it has practiced towards others.

In manifold ways may such retaliation be made for practices affecting unfavorably the interests of other nations. Restrictions on free intercourse in trade or travel, as by passports, by port charges, impost duties, closing of ports of entry at home or in colonies, and the like, as well as hampering communication between state authorities themselves, and also partialities towards certain states or persons, may justifiably be protested against in exactly answering restrictions. So also the gathering of a military force which may be dangerous to a nation at peace—the mobilization of armies and the aggregation of fleets—may warrant, or even in the interest of public security necessitate a like proceeding on the part of other nations. Such are examples of amicable retaliation.

II. Vindictive Retaliation.
Proper VINDICTIVE RETALIATION is resorted to as a forcible means of redress of national wrongs instead of regular warfare. It may be exercised in reprisals upon the persons or the possessions belonging to the offending nation. The tendency of recent international law is to the exemption of innocent persons from such reprisals, and to the abandonment of the practice of granting letters of reprisal to private citizens—to the restriction to the state of making reprisals, and to the allowance to it of reprisals upon the property only of foreign subjects, and not upon their persons.

SECTION II.—INTERNATIONAL COURTESY, TRUTHFULNESS, JUSTICE, BENEFICENCE.

§ 244. States are subjects of the rights and duties which have their seat more characteristically in the object of duty—*Courtesy, Truthfulness, Justice, Beneficence.*

Courtesy.
I. COURTESY, as a moral principle, respects more directly the outward deportment of nations in their intercourse and communication with one another. The conduct of nations may, like that of individuals, be characterized as respectful or insolent, as cordial or repelling, as complaisant or cross and testy, as courtly or rude.

There are manifold ways in which this principle may be acted out in the intercourse of nations. In fact, many forms of it have been recognized in international law so as to make up a body of rules under the general designation of the *comity of nations*.

<small>Comity of nations.</small>

In respect to superiors, in the form of respect, the general principle appears in certain distinctions accorded to the representatives of nations as superior or inferior. The equality of sovereign states is indeed a fundamental principle of international law; but this principle is not violated in according a certain deference to greater age, or power, or some other like attribute. Certain states in Europe are recognized, for example, as entitled to what are called *royal honors*, which accord to such states a precedence over all other states, with the right of sending public ministers of the first rank, as ambassadors, and also certain distinctive titles and ceremonial distinctions. European states have been ranked in their order of relative precedence, and serious contests have arisen between the sovereigns in reference to it.

§ 245. In the proper comity of nations, resting directly on their equality or moral personalities, divers usages and practices have been established which are recognized as law, the violation of which might be a just cause of war. Of these rules of comity the following are leading specifications:

<small>Rules of comity.</small>

1. It is a rule of comity that the existence of every nation be recognized

<small>1. Of recognition.</small>

as such in all appropriate ways. In the case of a new nation coming to be, as when a portion of a state or a colony rebels and succeeds in establishing its independence, other nations are bound in comity to recognize such independence. They are each, however, to judge for themselves whether independence is fairly established and the permanence and stability of the new nation assured. The same courtesy is required, when a change of government or of ruler has been effected, in formally recognizing the new government or the new ruler. This right and duty of *national recognition* is a first principle of international comity.

2. A second principle of international comity embraces the rights of *legation*.

2. Of legation.

Every state has a right to send public ministers to any other state, and to receive ministers from it, and to this right pertains the correlative obligation. To suspend or to refuse diplomatic intercourse without good reason, is a rank discourtesy that may rightfully be resented. The persons of all such accredited ministers, are, by comity, exempt from the ordinary local jurisdiction.

The Congresses of Vienna (1815) and Aix-la Chapelle (1818), established the four following classes of public ministers: 1. Ambassadors and papal legates or nuncios; 2. Envoys, accredited to sovereigns; 3. Ministers resident, accredited to sovereigns; and 4. Chargés d' affaires, accredited to the minister of foreign affairs.

3. A third rule of international comity requires that the national flag be prop-

3. Of salute.

erly saluted whenever met at sea or in port. The flag is the symbol of the state; and honors to it or insults to it are justly regarded as rendered to the state itself.

4. *Exemption from jurisdiction.* A fourth principle of comity accords to the persons of sovereigns, and also to their armies or navies, exemption from local jurisdiction, both civil and criminal, when within the territorial limits of another state.

5. *Respect for executed laws.* A fifth principle of international comity accords to the executed laws of another country, their legitimate effect everywhere, so far as not prejudicial to the rights of other states and of their citizens. Wills made under the laws of the state where the testator is domiciled, are carried into their effect in regard to the disposition of personal or movable property in all the states of Europe, and in regard to real property everywhere on the European continent. So also, personal qualities, such as citizenship, majority, bankruptcy, marriage and divorce, which have been judicially determined under the laws of one country, follow the person into other lands where they may come to reside.

§ 246. II. TRUTHFULNESS in all communications between nations rests on the same moral foundation as between individuals.

Truthfulness.

It has been the practice of nations to allow, to a certain extent, modes of deception towards enemies which would not be allowed to others. Ambuscades, wooden cannon, false flags, are justified in war, on the ground that the enemies have no right to know the truth in such cases; it is part of the very act of warfare which both parties expect and practice without complaint or protest. It seems clear, however, that if such acts of deception may be not blameworthy simply because there is no person concerned who has a right to know the truth, no practice can be justified which sullies the worthiness of man himself, and which cannot be allowed by his Creator. It is a nice distinction which moralists seek to draw between justifiable practices in deceiving an enemy, as by laying ambush, displaying men so as to mislead as to the numbers engaged, and the like, on the one hand, and such practices, on the other, as decoying a foe into danger by false signs of distress, by white flags, and the like. It is difficult to apply perfect morals to a condition of moral imperfection; to enforce the precepts of love and good will in a state of murderous warfare.

§ 247. III. JUSTICE, the practical recognition of the rights of other nations and of the individual subjects of other nations, is equally enjoined on nations as on individuals.

Justice.

The prominent rights which international justice requires to be accorded, are the following:

1. In respect to possessions.

First, each nation has the right to claim that its ownership of its territory and other property acquired by original occupancy, by conquest, or by cession, be recognized by all other nations. As with individuals, lapse of time in the quiet use or occupancy — prescription — gives to nations a valid title to property. All the property within a state belongs by right of eminent domain to the state, § 177. Vessels at sea are construed as within the limits of the nation to which they belong; and the same rights of property attach to them and the property on board of them as to property in the proper territory of the state.

2. Allegiance of subjects. Secondly, each state has a right to the allegiance of its own subjects. It is in violation of this right that the subjects of one state are forced to fight against their own country. This right to allegiance may be terminated by self-expatriation; but till this be the case, the right remains.

3. At sea. Thirdly, each state has the right to unmolested travel and traffic over the high seas. The territorial jurisdiction of a state over adjacent waters is generally recognized in international law as extending to a line three marine miles from the land, and as embracing also waters lying within lines drawn from headlands to headlands. The right of visitation and search of vessels at sea is a recognized right of a belligerent in time of war; but otherwise it is disallowed, except under express treaty.

Beneficence. § 248. IV. The duty of BENEFICENCE is a principle of international as of personal morality. It is indeed but the effect and result of expressed good-will. More and more in the progress of civilization have the expressions of international good will, in sympathetic and courteous helpfulness, appeared in history.

SECTION III.—INTERNATIONAL INTEGRITY.

§ 249. The class of rights and duties vested more directly in the act of duty, comprehended under the general designations of uprightness, honesty, rectitude, pertain as truly to nations as to individuals. States owe it to themselves as well as to the world that their transactions with one another, and all their actions affecting one another, should be in the line of perfect rectitude, never transgressing the rights of any, and ever tending directly to their professed aim and end.

SECTION IV.—WAR.

§ 250. A state of war introduces a peculiar class of rights and obligations between nations, called *rights of war—jura belli.*

War defined. War has been defined to be a contest by force between independent sovereign states.

The question has been mooted: is war ever justifiable? In a condition of perfect morality, where good will towards men and among men universally prevails, certainly war could hardly be supposed to be possible. A war, therefore, implies a defect in practical morality somewhere. But the same may be said of most civil litigation, even in cases where no special immorality could be fairly charged upon either of the litigants. There may be, in a true sense, just wars, as there may be just civil litigation. All wars are wrong in the sense of being incompatible with a condition of perfect universal morality; and yet some wars may arise in which no special blame can be charged on either party. Offensive wars may be as justifiable as defensive; as aggressions may be made on the rights of a state which are not properly acts of war, but which, nevertheless, are as offensive as declared warfare. Generally the same grounds may be alleged in the justification of war as have been stated in the case of retaliation, § 242.

But if war may be defensible on the basis of the moral imperfections of the race, they are occasions of such stupendous evils that they are never to be resorted to except in the extremest necessity. Only on sore provocation or urgent need of self-defense, and not until all milder methods of obtaining justice have failed, can a nation justify itself in exposing itself and its subjects to the incalculable losses and sufferings of war, or in inflicting these evils on other communities. War should ever be, as it has been said it is, the last argument of sovereigns— *ultima ratio regum.*

War is a fact; the rights of war arise as soon as the fact exists. They do not depend on the sufficiency of the causes of the war, or on its righteousness. Certain things must indeed characterize a contest between nations, to make it properly a war to which the rights of war pertain. Thus it has been said with some authority: war must be characterized as a contest public, with arms, and just. "*Bellum est contentio publica, armata, justa.*"

§ 251. War, accordingly, must, in the first place, be public. It cannot exist between individuals; only sovereign states can be parties to proper war. Hostilities may indeed exist, in which only parts of states are engaged, and when they are of sufficient proportions, in the interests of humanity, certain belligerent rights may be recognized and enforced in these contests, such as the exchange of prisoners, the commissioning of cruisers by letters of marque which remove from the vessels and the crews the character and liabilities attaching to piracy. In modern warfare, partisan and guerrilla bands are beyond the protection of the laws of regular warfare, and are regarded as outlaws and punishable as robbers and murderers. The individual subjects, indeed, of a country in war, are construed to be in a state of hostility to all the subjects of the hostile country; but they do not engage in the contest with force except under the regulations of the state. Private property on land, therefore, is exempt from the ravages of war. The use of arms against a declared public enemy by individuals acting of themselves, without the authority of the state, on land is outlawry, and on sea is piracy, which invalidates all rights of protection. The sole parties in regular war are sovereign states.

1. Must be public.

§ 252. War, in the second place, must be with force of arms. The use of poison, of destructive chemical agents in missiles which are designed to torture the person, the employment of savages, and generally the use

2. With force of arms.

of other than usual agents or instruments, are entirely disallowed or regarded with disfavor in the adjustment of rights in war. The very object of war is so to distress and disable the enemy as to force him to yield what is demanded; but restrictions on the means and instrumentalities to be employed have been constantly growing up into the authorized customs and usages of regular warfare. The grounds of distinction between the lawful and the unlawful it is not always easy to perceive. Poisons and certain torturing chemical compounds are forbidden, while hot shot, explosive shells, torpedoes, are permitted.

3. Just.

§ 253. Thirdly,—war must have, at least, an ostensible ground of being prosecuted for some just claim. It must, in this sense, be just. A war for merely frivolous pretexts, a war for mere conquest, a war for mere entertainment, modern morality would reprobate. There must be some claim of right as the ground of war, which shall serve to limit its range and effect; and it must be prosecuted in fair and just methods. Certain arts of deception, as we have noticed, § 246, may not be condemned, such as stratagems, ambuscades, wooden cannon, and the like; but proper fraud is prohibited. Flags of truce, demand of parley, offer of surrender, must be respected in good faith, as also all agreements for temporary suspension of hostilities, passports, safe conducts, licenses, and the like, are to be kept. Spies are recognized as permissible agents in war; but, if captured, they are, from the necessities of war, punishable with death, not, it is said, because they are morally unlawful agencies, but because they are dangerous.

§ 254. Besides the parties immediately engaged in war, there are others affected by it. There is thus the distinction between the rights of combatants—belligerents—and the rights of non-combatants.

Belligerents and non-combatants.

Non-combatants are either individual subjects of a belligerent state, or neutral states and their subjects.

The effect of war on the individual subjects of a belligerent is the immediate interdiction of commercial intercourse with the hostile nation and its subjects and allies. Private contracts with the enemy's subjects are accordingly unlawful. The property of the citizens of the hostile state is liable to be confiscated; but the debts of the nation itself to an enemy's subjects are held inviolable. The lives of non-resistants and of captured prisoners are held to be inviolable, as well as the property of individuals on land. Buildings devoted to civil purposes, monuments of art, repositories of science and learning, are exempted from the general ravages of war. The ravaging of a country is permissible only as necessary to effect the general object of the war.

§ 255. The existence of war of necessity affects the interests of neighboring nations, to whom accordingly pertain certain rights and obligations. Generally the interests of a neutral power are, so far as practicable,

Neutrals.

to be protected. Its ships on the high seas are not to be molested, even although conveying the enemy's property, or even his ministers and munitions of war. But in case of a blockade, the right of visitation and search belongs to the belligerent. On the other hand, neutrals are bound to observe a strict impartiality between the contending parties. They must not allow the crossing of their territory by either belligerent; nor the arming and equipping of vessels or enlistment of men in their territory; nor vessels of war to lie in wait in their ports; nor cruisers to take prizes into their harbors except under stress of weather or like necessity. All captures, moreover, on neutral territory, are unlawful. Such are the leading applications of international law to neutrals in time of war.

BOOK II.

DIVISION III.

DUTIES TO GOD.

CHAPTER I.

NATURE AND CLASSIFICATION.

Nature. § 256. DUTIES TO GOD or Religious Duties are at once indicated in the light of the moral relationship of man to God.

It is assumed that God exists ; that he is clothed with all the attributes of rational excellence in their highest degree, in infinite perfection—with omnipresence, omniscience, omnipotence, with perfect goodness, righteousness, and holiness ; that, moreover, he is the creator and the sovereign disposer and ruler of men.

God thus exists in closer relations to man than is possible for any other being ; ever with him, ever upholding him, ever caring for him, ever loving him, ever ruling him. Emphatically in God man lives and moves and has his being. The infinitude of

God's being, and the perfection of his character exalt this unrivaled intimacy of relationship to the highest degree conceivable. The duties which man owes to God are beyond all comparison first in rank and sacredness, deepest in obligation, and most constant in their claims. Such, indeed, is the relation of God to the entire universe as creator and governor that, in a true sense, duty to God comprehends immediately or remotely all possible duty. His moral nature, which we find expressed through his creative and providential will, is the foundation of all morality — of all rectitude and goodness. As all the capacities of man and all the relations of his being are established by God and controlled by him in his universal rule, all human duty must be embraced within his authoritative will ;—the divine law is the all-comprehensive law for man. Even the ordinances of civil authority are through his appointment and so receive from him their highest sanction. Love to man is deepest and strongest when rendered in the spirit of the brotherhood of all men under God as the common Father of all.

God is not only the original source of all morality by reason of his being the creator of all moral beings and of his endowing them all with their moral natures, but he is also the life and soul of all true morality. The consciousness of God as ruler, as sovereign and judge, is the best and highest inducement to a moral life, the most effective restraint from all immoral practice. A godless morality is shallowness and stagnancy ; it has little endurance against the heats of temptation, little vigor for heroic virtue. Hoping in the favor of a personal God and fearing his displeasure, while resting firmly in his authoritative will, man is strong to bear and strong to do. Only as the will of God is regarded in it can there be full satisfaction to the conscience in the fulfilment of any duty. A consciousness of his presence and of his authority, must pervade all sound moral practice.

§ 257. The authoritative will of God is *How enjoined.* promulgated in the moral relations which are discoverable in his works of creation, the dispositions of his providence, and his express revelations to man.

The moral nature of man answers with exactness to these utterances of divine authority. Every requirement has its answering capacity; the duty claimed is exactly commensurate with the ability in man to discharge. The divinely imposed sanctions of obedience are re-echoed in the consciences of men.

§ 258. The particular duties which man *Classification.* owes to God show here, as before, their readiest distribution and classification when viewed from the threefold element in all duty—the subject of duty, the object of duty, and the act of duty. We will follow this order, considering, first, those religious duties which are more characterized by their being seated in the subject of duty in man as morally related to God; secondly, those seated in the object of duty—the character and acts of God in relation to man; and thirdly, those characterizing the act of duty itself. It may not be entirely superfluous to repeat that each of these enumerated duties implies the presence of all of the elements mentioned; as we have before found that goodwill, rectitude, and goodness, necessarily imply each the others. § 21.

We find here, moreover, the distinction of duties into personal and social. These two classes it will be convenient to consider separately.

CHAPTER II.

PERSONAL RELIGION—PIETY TOWARDS GOD.

Piety defined. § 259. PIETY denotes the right act or state of the subject of duty towards God.

It is love to God viewed rather from the side of the subject of duty than from the object or act of duty.

It imports a loving sympathy with all the manifestations of God; a loving disposition towards him —a true godliness of spirit; and a loving purpose —a true devotion to God.

It imports 1, sympathy. 1. Made in the image of God, man is constituted by his very nature to be in heartiest *sympathy* with all that is truly divine. It is only proof that his nature has become fearfully vitiated, if the spirit of man turns away in indifference or coldness from any manifestation of Divine power, or wisdom, or goodness; much more if it is positively averse to recognition and contemplation of these manifestations of God. As everything that is, especially everything that moves or breathes, is of God and is a revelation of him, there is ground for perpetual sympathy and communion with him. For this was man made; and to this he is called in duty.

<small>2. A godly disposition.</small> 2. The sympathy which is awakened by every successive display of God to the heart of man should pass into habitual disposition, so that the soul shall be the seat of a true godliness. The allowance of sympathetic pleasure in the works and ways of God on the several successive occasions of their entering into the experience, bends the spirit God-ward and determines its growth under the laws of habit into this shape and character.

<small>3. Love.</small> 3. The embrace of this godly sympathy and disposition with the free-will is love to God in its essential completeness—is true devotion to him. It is religion in the subject of duty. It is proper piety.

All duty to God, all religious duty implies piety —implies a living agent in hearty sympathy, in loving disposition, and loving purpose in respect to God. All other denominations of religious duty are but the outworkings of this pious sentiment and intention towards God. Devoid of true piety, all else is morally worthless. Religious profession, religious worship, religious rites and ceremonies, religious sacrifices, and religious endeavors, are, without piety, but emptiness and vanity, or worse, hypocrisy and mockery.

<small>Gratitude.</small> § 260. The responsive affection in religion is *gratitude*:—it is the *re-sentiment* of the divine goodness. The other re-

sentiment, that which has by its predominating sway among men crowded out its sister affection from its proper recognition in common modern speech—retaliation for evil experienced—has no place in reference to God, since his work is all in perfect goodness. Evil comes, indeed, to man, and it comes from divine appointment. Yet is all physical evil from him essential love. Punitive justice is in the interest of a true universal benevolence; and trials are disciplinary, tending to bring about the perfection of character in man which is the condition of highest blessedness to him. If God's gracious design in the visitations of sorrow is allowed to make its full and true impression on the heart, there will be such a sense of the divine goodness in the experience of trial as will kindle a complacent gratitude that shall be full of joy and satisfaction.

CHAPTER III.

PERSONAL RELIGION.—REVERENCE—PRAYER.

Reverence. § 261. Of the duties to God, which are more distinctly characterized by their reference to the object of duty, that class which are seated in the sensibility—the capacity and faculty of form—are comprehended under the general duty of *reverence*.

As in the intercourse of man with his equals this class of duties take the general form of courtesy which towards his recognised superiors among men passes into respect, so in the intercourse of man, the finite creature with God, the infinite creator, they take this form of reverence. Every manifestation of God in his word, his works, his ways, should be responded to by man, the whole answering attitude towards him should be, in this reverence. The higher stage of this emotion is reverential awe—an emotion not necessarily painful or repulsive, but one, it may be, of the deepest joy and satisfaction, as the form in which the most loving and confiding affection may express itself. It is naturally inspired by the greater and sublimer demonstrations of the Divine character.

<small>Humility.</small> The counterpart on the human side of this reverence is, on the divine side in the inter-communication between man and God, *humility*. The one ever implies the other; the spirit that is reverent towards God is ever humble in view of itself.

<small>Prayer defined.</small> § 262. The reverential carriage and deportment which should characterize all the responses of the human soul to the manifestations of the divine preserver finds in prayer its more prevalent and familiar exemplification. Prayer is the address of the human spirit to God.

Prayer embraces all the proper expressions of the soul to God. As the respective character of God and of men is regarded, reverence takes the form of adoration on the one side, of self-humiliation on the other. As farther, the relation of man to God is fundamentally and comprehensively that of dependence, the sense of this dependence expresses itself naturally in praise on the one side, and of supplication on the other. The natural <small>Constituents.</small> constituents of prayer as the form of address to God by man, are accordingly adoration, self-humiliation taking the form of confession under a consciousness of sin, praise, and supplication.

<small>Properties.
1. Unceasing.</small> § 263. As God is omnipresent, to be recognized in every place and at all times, and as man is ever dependent on him, prayer becomes the *unceasing* duty of man.

2. Reverential.

The fundamental and most essential quality of prayer is that it be *reverential*. Prayer might very well be defined as the outgoing of a reverential spirit in a sense of dependence and so of want. So far as this quality is in defect, prayer is imperfect or fails. All lightness and flippancy are incompatible with true prayer.

3. Trustful.

Another requisite of prayer is that it be *confiding and expectant.* "He that cometh to God must believe that he is, and that he is a rewarder of them that diligently seek him." There is, of course, no prayer in any proper sense where there is no sincerity—a form of words does not constitute prayer. Only where there is true expression, actual address, of soul to God, is there prayer. The belief in God as he is, as real, as infinite, as good, is involved in all sincere address to him. Adoration and self-humiliation can spring only from a conscious sense of his greatness in compassion with human littleness; praise and supplication can go forth only from a soul conscious of the divine goodness and of its own needs. This apprehension of God as infinitely good—compassionate, forgiving, loving—and of the soul's entire dependence on him and of its urgent necessities, must make prayer, not only earnest, but believing—trustful and expectant.

Duty enforced.

§ 264. The duty of prayer is enforced by manifold considerations.

First, it is natural and meet that man, being made in the image of God, should be in communion with him, as a son with his father.

Secondly, the addresses of God in his works and his ways to man continually call forth suitable response taking the form of prayer.

Thirdly, such prayerful communion with God as the all-perfect one, is the necessary condition of growth into the highest perfection attainable by man.

Fourthly, as dependent, as ever needy, supplication to the only being who can supply the needs of man's spirit is a natural duty. To withhold prayer is to resist the most sacred instincts of man's dependent nature. If these instincts may be stifled for a time, occasions of distress and danger call them forth and give them their proper power over the human spirit. The habitual sense of dependence, equally with the habitual sense of the divine greatness ever encompassing them, should keep alive in the hearts of men a true spirit of prayer that shall break forth in full and formal expression whenever the occasion shall allow.

§ 265. The objections to supplicating

Objections. prayer founded ostensibly on the divine omniscience and goodness, or on the uniformity of his providence, are not valid. That God must know all our wants, and that therefore it is needless for us to tell them to him, and that as infinitely good, he will supply them so far as can consist with wisdom without our asking, is an argument that would by necessary implication forbid all communion with God and all expression of our sense of absolute dependence on him for all good. It runs counter to the strongest instincts of the human spirit. The loving parent knows the wants of his child better than itself; it would be most unwise to hinder the communion that must consist in great degree of the expressions of felt wants, because of this knowledge. Supplication is the natural expression of the sense of dependence; certainly that must be a most mistaken conception of the relations of God to man which would exclude the propriety of expressing this sense of dependence. Indeed, the good to man which may come through the communion with God as the proper expression of this sense of dependence may supposably exceed the good that could come from the granting of the prayer.

The argument against prayer in the form of supplication for blessings, particularly for blessings of a temporal and outward character, which is grounded on the alleged inviolable uniformity in nature, is equally invalid. It assumes, what cannot be proved, that the element of prayer cannot be incorporated by infinite wisdom into uniformity with natural sequences. It assumes without warrant that the sequences in nature cannot be changed from what they would have been but for prayer, by an interposition of God through natural causes and means without any violation of natural law. If the hand of a man may, without disturbing the uniformity of nature, prevent the withering of a plant simply by conveying to its roots the needed supply of water, who shall dare to say that the hand of omnipotence is incompetent to turn the cloud in answer to prayer from wasting itself on desert or ocean to a field threatened with drought, without disturbing the uniformity of nature. The argument limits omnipotence, denies to divine power what is allowed to human. Answers to prayer, involving the greatest changes conceivable in physical sequence that real human needs can demand, may be without miraculous power. Yet, who can presume to say that miracles may not be wrought—works in nature that are beyond all known natural agency—by Him who created and gave laws to all that exists.

But objections to prayer for temporal blessings overlook the fact that from the very nature of the case all true prayer is submissive to the higher wisdom of God. "Not my will, but thine be done," is the essential characteristic of all true prayer. The real want that prompts the prayer may underlie the specific desire and not be expressed in it but by implication. At least, the felt want may often be best relieved by the supply to the soul of a more fundamental good. Not infrequently, doubtless, is the specific desire gratified in some such larger supply to a deeper and broader want. The feverish child asks for water; the wise and loving parent withholding the specific desire, bestows what cures the fever which occasioned the thirst.

§ 266. The sin opposed to reverence is *irreverence*. Like its opposite, irreverence rather indicates a habit, a disposition than a specific act. The more common outbreaking form of it is profanity. It is a vicious indulgence to excess of the natural instinct, to em-

Irreverence.

phasize certain of our utterances. Like all excesses in habitual character, what at first seemed strong and forcible, soon comes to seem but moderation ; and blasphemy becomes the ordinary utterance of the lips. It is an easily entrapping vice ; but its effect on the spirit is as hardening and debasing as the sin is offensive to God.

A milder form of this vice is that of the indulgence of ridicule ; and a still less heinous form is that of levity in respect to religious objects or themes. When not positively irreverent, these habits indicate at least a lamentable deficiency in the spirit of reverence.

CHAPTER IV.

PERSONAL RELIGION.—GODLY SINCERITY.

Defined.
§ 267. By SINCERITY towards God, is meant truth in our cherished and uttered thought of him. It has two sides, inward and outward; truth in our views of God, and truth in our utterances to him, corresponding to the two forms of truthfulness, before indicated among the duties to persons; candor and veracity. § 119.

1. Involves a true thought.
§ 268. In the first place this duty involves a true thought of God. It implies a candid unbiased apprehension of his character, and of his works and ways.

God manifests himself to man in such way that it is practicable to form a true notion of him. His eternal power and godhead are clearly seen from the creation of the world, and may be truly known by the things that he has made. His righteousness and his mercy are revealed in history and in his dealings with every human soul. The conscience testifies of him; the native sense of dependence alike witnesses to him; the experiences of his care and kindness and the cravings of his favor for the present life, but especially for the life to come, teach truly of him. It is man's duty to receive into his thought these impressions concerning God just as they are made. Not only are there these manifestations of God in nature and providence, and through the personal experience; more fully and impressively are they given in his express revelations through the written word. He is in these manifold ways set forth as not only the creator of men, but as their moral governor and judge; as, moreover, their gracious redeemer and sanctifier. Nature, history, personal experience, written revelation, harmoniously testify thus of God. This testimony it is the duty of men freely to receive; and to allow it its lawful impression on the mind.

But "truth in the inward parts" involves more than this—a candid reception of the testimony given respecting God; it involves, besides, a candid conforming of the whole thought to these impressions. What is suggested in these revelations is to be carried out in reverent contemplation into all its lawful results and conclusions and applications.

Such is religious candor, embracing a free, hearty, unbiased reception of all the revelations of the divine greatness and glory, of his moral rule, of his gracious work, also, in the redemption of men, and a reverent thoughtfulness in respect to them, conforming the whole spirit to them, and applying them to all the specific phases of personal experience.

<small>2. A truthful expression.</small> § 269. In the second place, godly sincerity imports a truthful expression of our thought to God.

It requires that in all communion with him the

addresses to him be more than empty sound or form; be positively significant, and be expressive of the real thought and intent of the heart. All religious forms, all religious acts and words, thus, are to mean something; and this meaning must be the true meaning of the heart.

§ 270. The vices opposed to inward sincerity are *idolatry* and *superstition*.

<small>Idolatry.</small>

IDOLATRY substitutes a false, an unreal, for the true God.

In its grosser form, idolatry elevates creatures to the rank of the divine. Even to the creations of man's own hand, in its lowest form, it attributes a kind of divinity and acknowledges a kind of religious dependence on them. In a less debasing form the idolatrous spirit, turning from God, who is the only satisfying portion for the human soul, seeks its supplies from lower springs; from fellow men, or from its own resources; from condition or circumstance, or attainment other than in the line of virtue and religion. In a somewhat mixed form, it mingles the recognition of Jehovah with the service of other gods; it pays its devotions to the instruments or helps of worship; or depends on the abundance or excellence of its own prayers or services. Idolatry substitutes something, as object of worship or ground of dependence, in the place of the true God.

§ 271. SUPERSTITION exaggerates the real; it fancies something specially divine in what is only the ordinary form of the divine operation.

<small>Superstition.</small>

It misinterprets what is revealed of God in his common providence by imparting to it a higher significance and import than what belongs to it. Dreams that are but the vagaries of unregulated thought, are erroneously interpreted as of supernatural significance; certain events, trivial as the thousand experiences of every-day life, are selected out of the great current and interpreted to be the channels of special divine warning or promise. All superstition is opposed to the truth concerning God and his ways.

§ 272. The vices opposed to outward sincerity are *hypocrisy* and *formality*.

Hypocrisy.

HYPOCRISY is false expression; it proposes to utter what it does not mean. It assumes the garb of religion; it appears in the place of religion; it takes the attitude of religion; it uses the ends of religion; while it knowingly simulates, and aims to deceive man if not God; it utters religion while irreligion is consciously in the heart.

§ 273. FORMALITY is the mere negative opposite of outward religious sincerity.

Formality.

It is form without indwelling substance. It is empty sound. If hypocrisy is more the sin of the ungodly and the irreligious, formality is more the fault to which a really religious spirit is liable. Devotion must needs be habitual; and what is habitual is liable to become merely formal. Repentance is the only cure of hypocrisy; God-fearing watchfulness is the great safeguard against formality.

CHAPTER V.

PERSONAL RELIGION.—RELIGIOUS TRUST, OBEDIENCE, AND SERVICE.

Threefold duty from attributes. § 274. There are other cardinal religious duties which respect more immediately the moral attributes of God, and which are analogous to that class of duties to persons which are characterized by having reference to the moral nature of men. They are *Trust, Obedience,* and *Service.*

These religious virtues severally respect the attributes of God declared in the three successive stages of the divine revelation of himself to men. To Abraham, God revealed himself as the Almighty: "I am the Almighty God." As possessed of all power, he holds the destiny of all his creatures in his own hands, and dispenses good or evil at his pleasure. He is, therefore, the one comprehensive source of all that can move the hopes and fears of men. As hope and fear are the fundamental instincts of man's moral nature, and as the good and evil which they respect are entirely at the disposal of God, reliance on him for the fulfilment of hopes and removal of fears, is a fundamental religious duty. Trust in Him is the primal virtue in religion. It is presupposed in all riper graces; it manifests itself earliest in the religious experience of man. It is the soil in which obedience and love fasten and nourish their roots.

§ 275. The requisite qualities of religious TRUST are that it be, 1, *entire*, since no good or evil is beyond the control of God ; 2, *perfect*, since God's disposition to bless with all good and to save from all evil is infinite ; 3, *directed upon God himself*, as the giver of all good, not on the gifts themselves, since otherwise there is no religion in trust, and it sinks to selfishness or to idolatrous reliance on false gods or on creatures ; 4, *loving*, since all that is moral and religious must be from a loving heart. God, as good, as loving, beneficent power, is the immediate object of religious trust, which penetrates through the good it craves or the evil it fears and fastens on him who holds both in his power.

1. Trust.

Religious trust regards God as the beneficent, all-wise, and all-powerful providential disposer of the interests of all created beings—it respects God as providential ruler.

§ 276. To Moses, God, in the second stage of his special revelations to man, declared himself as the God of authority, "I am Jehovah"—the appellation significant of sovereignty and rule. To this attribute in God the duty of obedience in man is the proper correlative. As God commands, it is the part of man to obey.

2. Obedience.

Obedience is a duty of natural religion. The conscience of man testifies of a law imposed on him from without. Not without some just ground in reason has the first proof of God's existence been found by some philosophers in this imperative which is felt in the conscience; so early and so commanding is this witnessing voice. The awe-inspiring words: "Thou shalt," or perhaps in the still earlier prohibitory form, "Thou shalt not," break upon the ear in early childhood. The voice of command stirs the heart through a presupposed trust—through the hopes and fears. Obedience, as already intimated, roots itself in trust. An indifference to one's destiny, recklessness in regard to the future, is as fatal to true obedience as it is foreign to man's true nature. Obedience is fed up and made strong by trust contemplating the possible evil to be averted and the possible good to be realized. The deeper and richer the trust, the more perfect will be the obedience.

Religious obedience regards God as the sovereign of men, who has made known his will in a law that is perfect, wise, and good, reaching to every power and affection and condition of man, and that is supported and enforced by infinite sanctions of good and evil—promises of good to the obedient and threatenings of evil to the disobedient. God is administering this law over men, in perfect justice and righteousness and truth. Obedience respects this moral rule of God.

§ 277. The requisite qualities of religious obedience are that it be 1, *universal*, since he that offends in one command offends in all, transgresses the authority of the whole law; 2, *whole-souled*, with all the mind and soul and heart and strength; 3, *directed upon God* the law-giver himself, since to have a sole regard to the sanction of the law—the good of the promised reward or the evil of the threatened penalty—is not obedience but self-seeking; 4, *loving*, since the law is good, and the law-giver is good in giving and administering it, and as thus good is worthy of a loving obedience. A constrained, a servile obedience contradicts both the free nature of man and also his filial relation to God. Only a free, filial, in other words, a loving obedience can be accepted of God or satisfy man's conscience.

3. Service.
§ 278. In the third stage of God's special revelations of himself to men, he declares himself as the God of grace and mercy, forgiving iniquity, transgression, and sin—"the Lord, the Lord God, gracious and merciful." As having thus a gracious purpose in the accomplishment of which he enlists his boundless resources and the infinity of his loving heart, in whose final and complete success lies his whole pleasure and the very glory which is the end of his whole rule and work, God presents to men the possibility and at once the privilege and the duty of a most acceptable service and ministry.

There is a service of God that does not so prominently reveal itself as an act of obedience. All service is, indeed, commanded; the authority of Jehovah is beneath it; and all service must be in obedience as done with the authority of Jehovah and in deference to it. But, as religious duty may be characterized sometimes as obedience rather than trust, although all obedience must be in trust, so religious service is sometimes characterized not so prominently as rendered directly and exclusively in reference to the divine commands. God has an end which he seeks; to this end man may directly minister. In so doing he may in truth be said to be ministering to the pleasure of God and to the glory of his name. God is building up a kingdom of grace among men. In the progress and ultimate triumph of this kingdom his pleasure and his glory are alike concerned. To this revelation of God as a God of grace, religious service is the proper correlative on the part of man.

Religious service thus regards God as in his gracious economy seeking the salvation of men with an infinite mercy and compassion, with the enlistment of all the resources of heaven and earth, in the exercise of infinite wisdom and boundless power, as also of infinite goodness and love. Religious service respects God as such a gracious ruler.

§ 279. The requisite qualities of true religious service are that it be (1.) *whole-hearted*—that with all earnestness of zeal and full consecration in spirit in all the regulation of the life, in the choice of pursuits, the framing of plans, and in the performance of particular acts, the interests of God's kingdom be held in paramount regard; (2.) *unquestioning*—that it minister to those interests in whatsoever field they may require and in whatever way service may be effective; (3) *personal to God*—that it be rendered to God personally in the particular interest to be advanced, not to the interest itself; (4) *loving*— that it be in hearty sympathy with the will of God, and as securing his highest favor and thus placing the soul in that condition which brings to it its highest joy and satisfaction.

§ 280. The formal engagement of one's self to this service to God constitutes the proper religious *vow*. But in the wider sense the vow includes all engagements to service whether to be rendered to God, or to one's fellow men, or to one's self. It is thus an engagement under religious sanctions.

<small>Religious vow.</small>

The special principles respecting vows are: 1. They should not be made rashly or inconsiderately nor on trivial occasions. 2. They should be sacredly fulfilled. 3. If the fulfilment should be unlawful or impossible, the obligation is not of course to be regarded as satisfied, but is to be discharged in some other way that shall in its effect be equivalent.

CHAPTER VI.

PERSONAL RELIGION—RELIGIOUS INTEGRITY.

Division. § 281. The last class of personal religious duties to be considered are those which have more characteristic reference to the act of duty. Here are to be noticed those distinctions in duty which are marked more prominently by one or another of the leading elements or constituent attributes of moral rectitude. They are of two species according as these attributes are essential or relative.

The first species, embracing those duties which are marked by an essential attribute of religious rectitude or integrity, includes, first, *singleness of heart* towards God; and, secondly, *unswerving directness* in duty.

Singleness of heart. All moral rectitude implies an aim which is single and true. In religious duty this aim is directed towards God singly. There are two mistakes here to which men are liable. One is in aiming only at the particular interest concerned in the duty, without a governing recognition of God in it. The aim, thus, may rest solely in the service rendered, the act of worship done. This aim may be a worthy one; for its accomplishment there may be worthy and successful endeavor; but unless God be recognized in it, the act is religiously defective. The aim in all acceptable religious duty must reach ever to him. On the other hand, the aim may reach beyond him to the good that may reward the fulfilment of the duty. This may be truly worthy and desirable; but it is to be sought only as the result and consequence to follow the fulfilment of the duty. To regard this following good as the immediate aim, vitiates the act. The aim in all religious duty must, thus, reach on the one hand beyond the immediate object to be accomplished to God, and on the other must rest in him as the one end in all religion.

§ 282. Further, religious integrity implies unswerving directness in the performance of duty. It is opposed to all crookedness, indirectness, obliquity. True religious activity must, to be perfect, be straight forward in its movement.

2. Unswerving directness.

§ 283. The second species of religious duties, marked by a relative attribute of rectitude, embraces those of *direction* and those of *degree*.

Harmony with other duties in direction.

In direction, all duty must be in harmony and parallelism with all other duty. The lines of duty are all laid in perfect wisdom, and can never cross. It is a sign of moral error when duties clash. When we clearly discern the boundaries of another's field of duty, we are admonished that if the path we are pursuing trespasses upon it, we are in the wrong, and need to retrace our steps or bend our course. In the same way, when different specific duties pertaining to ourselves collide, we may be sure there is moral defect somewhere. Religious rectitude implies that all duty is harmonious and consistent;—" her paths are peace."

§ 284. Again, all specific duty has its own just measure and degree; to be perfect it must neither exceed nor fall short of its due limit. Religious zeal may be true and single, while it may be imperfect either through excess or through lack of fervor.

Moderation in degree.

CHAPTER VII.

SOCIAL RELIGION—FAMILY RELIGION.

Division. § 285. Inasmuch as man is a religious being, religion may legitimately find a place in all associations of men, even such as are temporary or accidental. But it is in the several spheres of the three great permanent societies existing among men—the Family, the State, and the Church—that social religion is best seen in its native and special obligations. We will consider it in the duties which it enjoins in these several spheres in order.

Religion in the family. § 286. We must begin with a full and distinct recognition of the close relation which religion bears to all the great interests of man, and of its special influence on these interests through the family organization and life. The great interests of man lie in the eternal hereafter; and to this future life his temporal life is to be made subservient. It is, moreover, in his relation to God that the highest interests of man are centred. The family trains for this life and for the future. This training must be radically deficient if religion does not enter into it as the guiding and sustaining element. Indeed, an irreligious household, that is, a household where the relation of man to God is excluded from view, must lack a chief requisite for its own peace and well-being, as well as for its efficiency in effecting the training which is entrusted to it. It is in childhood that character is shaped; it is in the family that the germs of piety for the most part are started; it is there that religious culture should be begun and carried so far as permanently to determine the habits and the conduct. In the religious home, all unconsciously to itself, the spirit of the child breathes the atmosphere and receives the shaping influences which form character. The impressions of the earliest years are the deepest and the most ineffaceable. As the family is the great nursery for the state, and the character, and consequently the destiny, of the nation hang on the character of the families which compose it, the religious household is a necessity of national as well as of individual well-being; while, in regard to the individual man, so long as it remains true that "Godliness has the promise of the life that now is, as well as of the life to come," religion in the family affords the most hopeful condition to him of success here and hereafter.

§ 287. The family life has its initiation in marriage. Inasmuch as the family sphere is inclusive of both secular and immortal interests, marriage must have both a religious and a secular side. Whether the state and the church are united in one organization, and

In marriage.

whether the head, in that case, is properly civil or ecclesiastical, or whether they are separate and distinct in organization and rule and duty, in every case, marriage must be both civil and religious. It is a civil contract which reaches to secular interests that properly lie within the domain of the state. It very properly, therefore, invites civil regulation and civil formalities. It is the ground of most important civil rights—those of protection, support, inheritance. But marriage not less vitally concerns spiritual and immortal interests. It is fitting, therefore, that it take place under religious as well as civil sanctions. It is, indeed, in a true sense, a sacrament, in so far as it involves a covenant before God, under the order which he has imposed, directly reaching to the highest spiritual, as well as to temporal and secular interests. The family life should begin in religion.

§ 288. Farther, the plan and ordering of the on-going family life should be religious. The dwelling in its arrangements, its furniture, its library, may fitly show that the home-life contemplated in it is not to be wholly godless. The ordering of this life from day to day may fitly give a place for religious observances. The collective life of the family circle may recognize God, and yet not infringe at all upon proper freedom of conscience. Even the mere outward and formal observance is better than none; as we expect the outward deportment to be civil and decorous from even the boorish and base in spirit. The form of virtue may invite the inward life.

In the household life.

§ 289. Moreover, the family life should, in its actual progress, exemplify religious duty. The training of children imperatively demands this of the parental head. Just as the habitually profane will set a guard upon his lips when his children are by him, so may the outward respect for religion be evinced even when its spirit does not rule in the heart. A reverence for all things sacred, a candid and honest treatment of religious matters, a deference to religious claims, may be shown where the tremendous responsibilities of a parent's charge may not have inspired a true and full personal consecration to a godly life.

Positive religious training.

Still further, family religion involves a faithful inculcation of piety on the subordinate members of the family. Religious instruction is a leading household duty. Parents are expressly enjoined in sacred scripture to bring up their children "in the nurture and admonition of the Lord."

§ 290. The true religious life ever seeks to express itself in outward rites. Family religion demands its observances. It is sufficient to say here that in the family, religious rites should have a place in the regular order of the household; they should be stated and regular; they should be simple and familiar and attractive. They may well enlist all the proper elements of worship, the service of song as well as of prayer and meditation of religious truth. As the table is at the centre of the family life, bringing all the members together at stated and frequently recurring intervals, it seems to

Family worship.

present the best occasions for the common religious services of the household. It suggests dependence and calls to gratitude for realized blessings, as well as awakens the spirit of trustful expectation for future good. The regular recurrence of sleep also brings along with it suggestions to devotion and affords convenient occasions for united service of religious worship in every well regulated household.

CHAPTER VIII.

SOCIAL RELIGION, THE STATE

The State a religious as well as a moral personality. § 291. The sphere of the state life, as we have found, is purely secular. The one immediate end of its action is the promotion of the common secular interest of its citizens. But we have also found that the state is a truly moral personality; it must in its secular sphere act morally. Precisely on the same grounds must the state be admitted to be a religious personality. Man, as already noted, is a religious being; and this religiousness of essential character, like his moral nature, follows him every where into his social as well as his proper personal life. The being and the sovereignty of God are truths which concern man every where; it would be worse than stolid in the state to ignore them. The state is subject to the providential rule of God; and his righteous retributions wait on all political as truly as upon all personal action. The religious interests of men are their paramount interests; the state, which is but a community of men acting in a political sphere, cannot wisely be indifferent to these highest common interests of all its members. Even the best secular ends common to them cannot all be attained except through religion. The sanctity of the marriage relation, the veraciousness of witnesses, the fidelity of officials, for example, invoke the sanctions of religion. The rights of religious freedom and of religious practice, which reach in all directions into the pursuits and the possessions of men, demand the protection of the state, equally with other rights. The state is capable of religious action ; it may recognize its dependence on God in manifold ways ; it may administer the sanctions of religion in oaths ; it may suspend civil administration on days hallowed by religion. In divers ways, thus, it is under the necessity of acting in reference to religion.

The argument for the entire exclusion of all reference to religion by the state which rests on the ground that all such action must of necessity infringe on the rights of conscience of some of its citizens, is one of inconsiderable weight. In so far as the religion of the state only recognizes the being of God, his attributes, and his relations to men, as accepted by all who believe in a God, and these make up the great mass of the members of every civilized nation, there is no possibility of infringement upon conscience. For those who believe in God certainly have no grounds of complaint on this ground, and it is difficult to comprehend how any others can have any conscience at all to be troubled. History abundantly shows the practicability of a true religious freedom even under a national church ;

certainly, it may exist where there is no ecclesiastic establishment.

It is not necessary, it may be observed, however desirable it may be held to be, that the formal recognition of the being and rule of God, be incorporated into the constitution and organic law of a people, any more than a like formal recognition of the existence of neighboring nations. It is enough that the rights and duties in each case be faithfully observed in the actual working of the state.

§ 292. The particular rights and duties pertaining to the state in reference to religion, are substantially embraced in the following enumeration:

Special duties.

First, The state must in no case act irreligiously—in direct and positive violation of religious duty. Such practice must ever be needless, since all the lines of duty in all the spheres of human activity are parallel. It must, at least, ever be unwise and impolitic.

1. Not to violate religious obligations.

§ 293. Secondly, the state is bound to protect, so far as lies in its power, all the secular rights of its members in the enjoyment of their religion. It must lend its courts to adjudicate and enforce all the secular obligations arising in their religious associations. It should hold itself in favoring sympathy with all the sincere endeavors and aims of religious men, not antagonistic to the well-being of the state. As, while men remain imperfect, it may be reasonably expected that, with the best intentions, collisions of state interests and individual convictions may arise, the

2. To protect religious rights of subjects.

state should exercise the greatest leniency and considerateness towards the tender conscience. The state does wisely thus to accept pecuniary contribution in lieu of military personal service of those conscientiously opposed to war; as also to allow solemn affirmation in lieu of the formal oath.

§ 294. Thirdly, the state may, with true political wisdom secure, and therefore may be regarded as bound in duty to secure, for the marriage relation, so vital to the best interests of the state, all the sanctions which religion can throw around it. If it have no ministers of religion of its own, it may accept the service of those properly accredited as such as if it were the service of its own officials. It may accept religious formalities in the consummation of marriage to a certain extent, in substitution for such civil procedures as the purity of the family life and the determination of rights in inheritance as well as of other secular rights, may require.

3. To hallow marriage.

§ 295. Fourthly, it may recognize the observance of certain religious seasons by forbearing the usual routine of duty required of its officials, by closing public offices, by refusing to enforce contracts made on such designated occasions, by prohibiting pursuits and practices that may disturb the quiet enjoyment of those seasons on the part of a portion of the community. Civilized nations have thus generally recognized the weekly rest—the Christian Sabbath—as a day on which public offices shall not regularly be opened for business, and civil service by its officials shall

4. Appoint religious seasons.

not be allowed. They have also refused to recognize contracts made on that day as valid, and have forbidden certain kinds of business to be prosecuted which hinder the enjoyment of the season by the mass of the people. The state, moreover, has wisely recognized other great religious days as legal holidays—that is, as days on which the ordinary secular activities are to be intermitted. Indeed, in this case, the observance of a weekly rest from secular care and labor has been found to be so closely connected with the highest secular prosperity of a people as to justify the recognition of it by the state on purely secular grounds.

§ 296. Fifthly, the state wisely recognizes its dependence on God as the supreme arbiter of human affairs, and on occasions of signal successes in national endeavors or of general distress and fear, appoints special days of thanksgiving to God or of humiliation before him to deprecate his displeasure. It wisely recognizes, too, the constancy of this dependence, in stated appointments for general religious service in praise or supplication. There is true political wisdom, also, in recognizing this dependence, on important occasions of administrative service, as the opening of legislative assemblies, of judicial proceedings, the beginning and the ending of important enterprises, as of war, and the like.

5. Recognize its dependence on God.

§ 297. Sixthly, the State may wisely enlist the aid of religious sanctions on various occasions of political service, particularly in the form of religious *oaths*.

6. Avail itself of religious sanctions—Oaths.

THE RELIGIOUS OATH is a solemn appeal to God for the sincerity of a declaration or a promise. Its proper design and effect is to quicken the conscience by a solemn recognition of responsibilities being involved in relation to God, the All-seeing and the All-judging, as well as to men who are unable to read the heart.

Classes.
§ 298. Oaths are of several distinguishable classes. The most common are *judicial oaths*, taken by witnesses upon themselves in giving testimony before judicial tribunals.

Another class of oaths are *oaths of declaration*, as in declaring the amount or value of taxable property, innocence of bribery in elections, and the like.

A third class are *oaths of engagement*, administered to civil officers, binding them more solemnly to a faithful performance of their duties, or to trustees or administrators or guardians, binding them to a right discharge of the trusts confided to them Such oaths may be of general or more special engagement.

A fourth class are *oaths of allegiance*, taken by those who are admitted to the rights of citizenship.

Interpretation.
§ 299. In the interpretation of oaths the general principle is that the oath is to be taken as it is meant by the authority that imposes it—*secundum animum imponentis*—that is, by the state, and not in the understanding of the person to whom it is administered. An oath of allegiance—that is, an oath to maintain

the constitution or organic law of the state—will thus be interpreted by the state as to what is meant by any particular provision of the organic law. It is possible, therefore, that while before the tribunal of his own conscience one may be clear of offense, yet, by the civil tribunal, he may be held to suffer the penalties of perjury.

CHAPTER IX.

SOCIAL RELIGION—THE CHURCH.

Natural.
§ 300. The religious nature of man seeks to express itself in his social life.

A religious society is thus as natural among men as a political society. Their common religious interests require a care and support as truly as their secular interests. To suppress all religious convictions and endeavors in social life would be to cramp and stifle man's highest aspirations, and his best and tenderest sympathies with his fellows. The secular and the religious have in their natures no formidable antagonisms to threaten the peace of the community. If religious controversies have arisen and religious wars have occurred, they are to be attributed not to religion but to depraved passions, working in spite of religion. So ambition and cupidity have occasioned bloody contests; but not, therefore, are fame and property to be exorcised from human experience. All the proper effects and influences of religion are to forbearance, to peace, to order. The community in which true religious convictions sway the lives of its members is that where the highest order and prosperity may be expected to prevail.

§ 301. The forms of the social religious organization will vary with the religious system which is embraced and the general culture and condition of the community. The organization may reach to great detail of creed, of worship, of rules, or extend only to a few and almost inconsiderable common usages and observances. The religious society may be incorporated into the civil organization. Nothing in the nature of the case or in history forbids that the common head in such an event, should be either political or religious. Mohammedanism is primitively and essentially religious, yet is counted a secular as well as religious organization. On the other hand, diverse European states have assumed to themselves the regulation of religion. Or the religious society may exist side by side with the political, in entire harmony, and with reciprocating offices of helpfulness, yet in full independence.

Organization.

The christian church is the best existing type of a religious organization, the leading characteristics of which may be instanced as type-forms of every permanent religious society.

§ 302. Every . fully organized society must have prescribed officials, times, places, usages. The church has in its organization, offices, religious seasons, places, and rites.

The functions of religious officials are, besides

Officials. the general functions of representing and ruling, twofold:—those of teaching and of ministry —*prophetic* and *liturgical*. It belongs to them to preserve, to interpret, to proclaim, and to enforce the body of religious truth which is held by the community, and to apply it and make it effectual in the life and practice of the members. It belongs to them also to minister in the public rites and ceremonies of the community.

§ 303. The religious society must have Social seasons. its social seasons for social religious observances.

These may be prescribed by divine or by merely human authority; they may be traditional or temporary; stated or occasional. The church accepts also from the state, appointments for public religious observances, as has been already intimated.

§ 304. The weekly Sabbath stands The Sabbath. conspicuous among all sacred seasons by reason of its antiquity, its divine origin, its general recognition, its proved necessity to all the interests of men. The principle of the Sabbatic law is that one seventh of the time be withdrawn from secular cares and pursuits and be consecrated to religious uses. The law does not prohibit necessary secular occupations, which indeed, need not hinder the highest religious ends of the Sabbath any more than some religious observances, as at morning and at evening and of taking of food, interfere with secular labor. The nature of the institution does not fix the precise hours to be observed as sacred to religious uses; it does involve a certain proportion of time; and for obvious social necessities the same hours, to be fixed by some common standard, must be taken for the same local community. The Sabbatic law enjoins a consecration of this one day in seven to proper religious uses. It enjoins the duty on every man's conscience so to observe the day as to make it most promotive of these uses. The Sabbatic law is, moreover, a social institution; its very object contemplates a general agreement in respect to the observance.

§ 305. Divers considerations evince the obligatory character of this law for the entire human race.

Grounds of the duty to observe the Sabbath.

First, the religious interests of men demand this appropriation of time; and the institution must fail unless it be observed in the community generally, so as to secure it from all interruption from secular pursuits. To avail to one, it must be observed by all.

Secondly, the secular well-being of man demands it. Careful induction from large observation and experience, has demonstrated the necessity of this weekly religious rest in order to the best condition of worldly interests.

Thirdly, the law was originally given to man as man in the earliest stages of the existence of the race on earth.

Fourthly, it was subsequently incorporated by the express authority of God into the decalogue of Moses

—which is a summary of the rules of moral and religious practice of universal and permanent application to all nations and all generations of men.

Fifthly, the law with a natural and justifiable modification as to the day of the week, yet with no infringement upon its spirit and design was universally recognized and enforced in the Christian church.

Sacred places. § 306. Social religion requires its sacred places as well as its sacred seasons. The tabernacle for the yet wandering life of tribes, the temple for the fixed national life, is a necessity for a religious community in the expression of common religious beliefs. The Church—the Lord's, as the etymology of the name indicates—is the place of meeting between God and his worshiping people. It is worthily consecrated to him, and should be freed from all associations that hinder the highest reverence towards him.

Rites. § 307. Religious rites make up what is meant by religious worship. They are a necessity of social religion.

Worship. WORSHIP may be defined to be an act of communion between God and his people. God meets his people in a peculiar sense; he listens to his people in their praises and their supplications; he communicates his will and his favor to them. This manifestation of himself is made representatively through his recognized minister in the ministration of the divine word. The worshiping people express to God their thanksgivings and their entreaties of his favor, either representatively through the minister or personally in united voice harmonized in song by means of according time and tune.

There may be a ceremonial worship, besides and beyond this proper rational worship, consisting of offerings of incense and the like. Especially are offerings to God, expressive of consecration of service and of possessions to him, legitimate constituents of true religious worship. But in so far as this proper rational worship—merely through heart and voice—is concerned, all that is foreign to this act of rational communion between God and his people effected in the way just specified, is foreign to true worship. God addresses man; man addresses God; this is all. Collective address is possible, however, only on the condition either of a single mouth-piece —a representative head—a minister or celebrant leading the assembly—or of united voices harmonized and brought into unity by means of song and chant—by means of musical time and tune. Religious worship, on the side of man's address to God, reaches its highest elevation in accordant ascriptions by the whole worshiping people of GLORY TO GOD.

THE END.

INDEX.

Act of duty, exemplified in the story of Regulus, 7 ; duties determined from, 159-163 ; two species, 159
Activity, requisite in a moral person, 11
Aim in action, 159
Anger, 140
Asceticism, 99
Attributes of duty, 13
Authority, 77-83, its seat, 77 ; expressed in a two-fold way, 79
Belligerents, 280
Beneficence, 152 ; distinguished from justice, 153 ; correlative of benevolence, 154 ; species, 155 ; modes, 155 ; measure, 155 ; object, 156
Benevolence, 112
Bible, revelation of divine authority, 82
Body, duties in respect to the, 96-106 ; ground, 96 ; of guarding, 98 ; nourishing, 100 ; ruling, 104
Candor, 147
Capitation taxes, 201
Casuistry, 84-87 ; defined, 84 ; leading principles, 86
Character, duties in respect to, 118 ; maxims, 121
Church, nature, 321 ; organization, 322 ; officials, 322 ; seasons, 323 ; places, 325 ; rites, 325.
Citizen, relations to the state, 254-264 ; defined, 234 ; rights, 256 ; duties, 260
Civil Rights, 255
Comity of nations, 271 ; rules of recognition, 271 ; of legation, 272 ; of salute, 272 ; exemption from jurisdiction, 273 ; respect for laws, 273
Condition, duties in respect to, 107-117
Conscience, synonym of moral faculty, 16 ; includes three functions, to feel duty, to oblige to performance, to praise or blame, 16-20 ; pleasure or pain attending, 19
Courtesy to persons, its nature, 143 ; obligation, 144 ; sphere, 144 ; forms, 144
Demerit, 21, 75

Desert, 21, 75
Developing industries, 256
Discourtesy, 144
Duties, classified, 26, 88 ; to self, 92-134 ; to our fellowmen, 134 ; to persons, 135-162 ; to God, 282-326
Duties in the family, 163-181
Duties in the state, 182-281
Duties to God, nature, 282 ; how enjoyed, 284 ; classes, 284 ; personal religion, 286-308 ; family religion, 309-313 ; in the state, 314-320 ; the church, 321-326
Duties to persons, determined from the subject of duty, 137-142 ; from the object of duty, 143-158 ; from act of duty, 159-162
Duties to self, nature and classes, 92-95 ; ground of obligation, 93 ; threefold law, 95 ; in respect to the body, 96-106 ; to condition, 107-117 ; to character, 118-133
Duty, act of, exemplified in the story of Regulus, 7 ; analyzed, 8 ; its three constituent elements, 9
Duty, its attributes, 13
Duty, object of, 22-26 ; a person, 22
Duty, subject of, see *moral person*.
Education in the state, 246-249 ; a duty, 246 ; extent, 247 ; methods, 248
Equities, 219
Ethics, defined, 1 ; different methods of the science, 1 ; founded on psychology, 2 ; one of the three departments of mental science, 3 , method pursued, 4
Evil, opposite of good, 44 ; natural and moral, 42
Excise duties, 202
Executive, in the state, 220
Exercise, 101
Expatriation, 263
Family, defined, 163 ; divinely instituted, 163 ; twofold end, 163 ; rise of duties in, 164 ; moral character, 164 ; seat of authority, 166 ; classes of duties in, 166 ; marital, 168-173 ; parental and filial, 174-179 ; fraternal, 180
Family religion, 309-313 ; the mar-

328 INDEX.

riage covenant, how far a sacrament, 311; in the household life, 311; training, 312; worship, 312
Filial rights and duties, 174-179; correlation of parental, 175; enumerated, 176
Food, 100
Forgiveness, 141
Formality, 299
Fraternal rights and duties, 180
Free will, requisite in a moral person, 14; culture of, 130
Friendship, duties in respect to, 116
Good, essential in duty, 24; the end of all duty, 36; twofold sense, 37; chief good, 39; good in itself, 42; as means, 42; good of condition and of character, 42
Goodness or beneficence, 36
Gratitude, 140; to God, 287
Happiness, 37; gift of Creator alone, 42-44
Hate, opposite of love, 35
Hypocrisy, 299
Idolatry, 298
Ill-desert, 21, 75
Imposts, 202-242
Income taxes, 207
Industries, developing, productive, distributive, 236
Intelligence, requisite in a moral person, 13; culture of, 126
International morality, 265-281; divisions of international law, 265; sources, 265; duties classed, 267; good-will, 267; resentments, 268; retaliation, 273; courtesy, truthfulness, justice, beneficence, 273; integrity, 276; war, 276
Irreverence, 294
Jus gentium, 265
Justice, distinguished from beneficence, 153; defined, 157; sphere, 157
Kindliness, 138
Law, defined, 66; physical and moral, 67; expression of will, 70; harmony, 71; obliging power, 71; imports responsibility, 72; sanctions, 73; natural and positive, 79
Love, as principle of duty, 32-35; defined, 33; stages, 34
Marital rights and duties, 168-173; parity of rights, 171; joint authority, 171; rights complementary, 172
Marriage covenant, basis of marital rights and duties, 168; indissoluble, 169; how ratified, 170
Merit, 21, 73
Money, defined, 227; function, 228; standard of value, 229; material, 230; mixed currency, 232; legal tender, 232; amount, 233
Monogamy, 168
Moral action, 27-31; defined, 21; diversely denominated, 28
Moral faculty, defined, 16
Moral law, 66-76; defined, 68
Moral obligation, 60-65; defined, 60; ground, 61
Moral person, defined, 10; requisites, 10
Moral Science, see *Ethics*.
Moral Sense, synonym of moral faculty, 16
Motives, 51-59; defined, 51; two classes, 53; subdivisions, 53; ultimate and proximate, 56; not moral, 57; wrong selection, 58
Mutilation of body, 78
Natural law, 79
Nature, duties to, 108
Neutrals in war, 280
Oaths, 319; classes, 319; how interpreted, 319
Obedience, religious, 301
Object of duty, 22-26; a person, 22; duties determined from, 143-158; three classes, 143
Organic law of a state, 216
Parental rights and duties, 174-179; origin, 174; correlative of filial, 175; enumerated, 175-179; limited obligations, 177
Penalties, 210; ends, 210-212; modes, 212; degrees, 213
Personal duties, 92-134
Personal religion or piety towards God, 286-308; imports sympathy, 286; godly disposition, 287; love, 287; gratitude, 287; reverence, 289; prayer, 290; godly sincerity, 296; religious trust, obedience, and service, 300; integrity, 306
Political autonomy, 214-220; right and duty, 214; spheres, 215
Political growth, 221-249; sevenfold departments, 222
Political power, its seat, 186
Political retaliation, 269; amicable, 269; vindictive, 270
Political rights, 255
Polygamy, 168
Positive law, 80
Postal facilities, 234
Praise and blame, function of conscience, 19; sanctions of law, 76
Practical morality, 88-326
Practical reason, synonym of moral faculty, 16

INDEX.

Prayer, its nature, 290; qualities, 290; duty, 291; objections to, answered, 292
Productive industries, 237; duty of the state to foster, 237; limitations, 239; modes, 241
Public health, 245
Public improvements, 225
Public morals, 250-253; duty of the state to promote, 250; methods— by example, 251; by prohibition, 252; by positive encouragement, 253
Recreation, 103
Rectitude, 46-50; implies an action, 46; relation of action, 47; fitness, 47; directness, 48; parallelism with all other duty, 49
Regulus, story of, 7
Religious duties, 282-326
Resentments, 139; of gratitude, 139; of anger and forgiveness, 140
Rest to body, 103
Retaliation, 140
Rewards, 210
Right, correlative of duty, 23
Right of eminent domain, 199
Sabbath, weekly, duty to observe, 324
Sanctions of law, 210
Self-love, distinguished from selfishness, 93; its twofold nature, 95
Sensibility, requisite in a moral person, 16; culture of, 123
Service, religious, 303; qualities, 304
Social religion, in the family, 309-313; in the state, 314-320; in the church, 321-326
Stamp duties, 206
State, duties in, 182-281; defined, 182; origin, 182, 197; an organized community, 185; sphere, 185; a power, 185; seat of power, 186; its end, 188; moral attributes, 193; not a mere jural society, 194-196; bound morally, 196; rights and duties, 197; of existence, 197-213; of support, 198; self-defense, 207; maintenance of authority, 208; autonomy, 214-220; organic law, 216; legislature, 218; judiciary, 218; executive, 220; right of growth, 221-242; sevenfold departments, 222; maxims, 222; territorial extension, 223; increase of population, 224; public improvements, 225; weights and measures, 226; money, 227; postal facilities, 234; development of resources, 235; health, 245; education, 246; morals, 250; in relation to the citizen, 254; moral relationship to other states, 265-281; religion in the state, 314; rights and duties of the state in reference to religion, 316
Station, duties in respect to, 114
Straightforwardness, 159
Suicide, 98
Summum bonum, 37
Superstition, 298
Sympathy, 137
Systems of morality threefold, 29
Taxes, 200; direct and indirect, 200; capitation taxes, 201; excise duties, 202; imposts, 202; stamp duties, 206; income taxes, 207
Theoretical morality, 1-87; recapitulated, 88-91
Trust, religious, 301; qualities, 301
Trustfulness, 151
Truthfulness, 145; twofold, 147; inward implies candor and impartiality, 147; outward or veracity, 148
Veracity, 148; sphere, 149; modes, 150
Vow, 305
War, defined, 276; must be public, 278; with force of arms, 278; just, 279; belligerents and non-combatants, 280; neutrals, 280
Weights and measures, 226
Worship, defined, 325; constituents, 326
Wrong, opposite of right, 49

A SELECTION FROM STANDARD PUBLICATIONS

By JOHN BASCOM,
President of the University of Wisconsin.

I. **The Principles of Psychology.**
12mo, Cloth, $1.75.

"To the few who think and investigate, this book will be a rare delight."—*San Francisco Bulletin.*

II. **Science, Philosophy, and Religion.**
12mo, Cloth, $1.75.

"Vigorous, thoughtful, sometimes brilliant, and uncommonly refreshing reading."—*Boston Commonwealth.*

III. **The Philosophy of Religion.** (*May*, 1876.)
Large 12mo, Cloth, $2.00.

IV. **The Philosophy of English Literature.**
12mo, Cloth, 1.75.

"A knowledge of forces as well as of facts is essential to our comprehension of any phenomenon. It is this which the author helps us to gain."—*Chicago Tribune.*

By P. A. CHADBOURNE,
President of Williams College.

I. **Natural Theology; or, Nature and the Bible.**
From the same Author.
12mo, Cloth, $1.50.

"Once taken up cannot be laid down unread."—*Washington Republic.*

II. **Instinct—Its Office in the Animal Kingdom, and Its Relation to the Higher Powers in Man.**
12mo, Cloth, $1.75.

By JOHN J. ELMENDORF,
Professor of Mental Science in Racine College.

The Outlines of the History of Philosophy.
8vo, Cloth, $1.50.

A succinct Chronological Record and Analysis of Systems of Philosophy from the earliest times to the present day, prepared as a guide to the Student and to the general reader.

By JAMES MARTINEAU, D.D., LL.D.

I. **Religion as Affected by Modern Materialism.**
12mo, Cloth, 75 cents.

II. **The Attitude of Materialism Towards Theology.**
12mo, Cloth, $1.00.

"The ablest analyses of Tyndall and his school of thought that have yet appeared."—*London Spectator.*

G. P. PUTNAM'S SONS,
182 FIFTH AVE., NEW YORK.

www.ingramcontent.com/pod-product-compliance
Lightning Source LLC
Chambersburg PA
CBHW031854220426
43663CB00006B/619